JAZZ, BLUES, AND SPIRITUALS

The Origins and Spirituality of Black Music in the United States

HANS ROOKMAAKER

Edited by Marleen Hengelaar-Rookmaaker

P&R
PUBLISHING
P.O. BOX 817 • PHILLIPSBURG • NEW JERSEY 08865-0817

© 2002, 2020 by Marleen Hengelaar-Rookmaaker

Jazz, Blues en Spirituals, copyright ©1960 by H. R. Rookmaaker (Wageningen: Zomer en Keunings); copyright © 2000 by Marleen Hengelaar-Rookmaaker.

"Jazz, Blues and Spirituals" published in *New Orleans Jazz, Mahalia Jackson and the Philosophy of Art: The Complete Works of Hans R. Rookmaaker,* Vol. 2 (Carlisle, UK: Piquant, 2002). Copyright © 2002 by Marleen Hengelaar-Rookmaaker.

P&R Publishing new edition 2020

Printed in the United States of America

Library of Congress Cataloging-in-Publication Data

Names: Rookmaaker, H. R. (Hendrik Roelof), 1922-1977, author. |
  Hengelaar-Rookmaaker, Marleen, editor.
Title: Jazz, blues, and spirituals : the origins and spirituality of Black
  music in the United States / Hans Rookmaaker, Marleen
  Hengelaar-Rookmaaker.
Description: New edition. | Phillipsburg : P&R Publishing, 2020. | Includes
  bibliographical references. | Summary: "Rookmaaker's music history
  explores the development of black music in the United States until the
  1950s-describing the spiritual and cultural origins, rationale, and
  interplay of its diverse new genres"-- Provided by publisher.
Identifiers: LCCN 2019029371 | ISBN 9781629956732 (paperback) | ISBN
  9781629956749 (epub) | ISBN 9781629956756 (mobi)
Subjects: LCSH: African Americans--Music--History and criticism. |
  Jazz--History and criticism. | Blues (Music)--History and criticism. |
  Spirituals (Songs)--History and criticism.
Classification: LCC ML3479 R66 2019 | DDC 780.89/96073--dc23
LC record available at https://lccn.loc.gov/2019029371

Contents

Preface to the First Edition by Hans Rookmaaker   v

Preface to the New Edition by William Edgar   vii

Acknowledgments to the First Edition   ix

A Note on Sources   xi

1. Origins   1

2. Nineteenth Century: Development   21

3. Twentieth Century: Pre–World War I   59

4. The 1920s   79

5. The 1930s   141

6. The 1940s   169

7. The 1950s and Beyond   199

Selected Bibliography to the First Edition   223

Updated Discography and Resources   225

Preface to the First Edition[1]

This book is an attempt to give as complete a picture as possible of developments in black music, past and present, in the USA. I have tried to explain the origin of new genres, the circumstances and reasons behind such developments, and also the comparative development of the different types of music, how they affected each other, degenerated or flourished. Besides the history of jazz music, I have also focused on Negro spirituals and gospel music. Considering recent developments in this area it seems strange that relatively little has been written on this subject so far.

I hope that this book will provide more insight into the spiritual background and qualitative differences of the various genres. Perhaps it will contribute to answering the many questions raised by pseudo-jazz, a poor-quality entertainment music, but also by modern jazz, which often boasts high quality but an existential spirit.

One significant drawback of any writing on the subject of music is that the audience cannot listen to the pieces in question. I have endeavored to overcome that problem by referring as much as possible to records (cassettes, etc.) that are still available [moreover, an updated discography has been included on p. 225]. Musical notation would be of little use since it would not do justice to the style of rendition, to the typical accents and timbres. In many cases the notes would

1. Originally published in Dutch by Zomer en Keunings (Wageningen, the Netherlands, 1960).

be counterfeit anyway, since they would inevitably be the victims of westernization.

H. R. R.
Leiden, 1960

Preface to the New Edition

Jazz music leaves few people indifferent. When it first appeared, in the early twentieth century, some, especially white Americans, published screeds with titles such as "Unspeakable Jazz Must Go" or the racist "Why 'Jazz' Sends Us Back to the Jungle."[1] Others, including notable musicians and composers such as George Gershwin and Igor Stravinsky, embraced it with enthusiasm, finding it fresh and authentic. Maurice Ravel said he liked it better than high opera.

When it first appeared in 1960, Hans Rookmaaker's book, written in Dutch, was a publishing event. It was a defense of this music before a public either hostile, or largely unaware of its beauties. Though his official position was professor of art history at the Free University of Amsterdam, Rookmaaker had already distinguished himself as an expert on the music of African Americans. He was the editor of the European edition of the great Riverside Records. The liner notes on these albums is worth their price in gold.

His work is scholarly and thorough, but it stems from his personal love for the music. He was once in our living room, and we only had a harpsichord, no piano, yet he requested I play "Honky Tonk Train Blues" by the great Meade Lux Lewis. When I was a student we had a jazz band and Hans was our mentor. His beloved wife, Anky, once told me he never studied or did much of anything without jazz

1. Maureen Anderson, "The White Reception of Jazz in America" *African American Review* 38/1 (Spring, 2004), 135.

music being played in the background on 78s or vinyls. He traveled often to the United States and there was able to meet with some of the greats, including Mahalia Jackson. His first meeting with his life's colleague, Francis Schaeffer, was motivated by a hope to learn about jazz from an American.

This love comes across eloquently in these pages. And as we would expect from such a devotee his judgments are also abundant. Rookmaaker constantly reminds the reader not to evaluate the music according the Western standards of "classical" music. He rails against sentimental "pseudo-jazz." He believed there was a kind of "fall" from the purity of New Orleans jazz, as played by King Oliver in the early1920s, to the more individualistic jazz of Chicago style, exemplified by Louis Armstrong. Rookmaaker has little time for modern jazz, as he thought it had been tainted by "Existentialism" and other humanistic philosophies.

The most authentic jazz is inspired by the Christian faith of many of its performers. Jazz originates in the church. It was there that spirituals were generated, inspired by the hymns of Isaac Watts and Charles Wesley. A high point in such music is the quartet styles, such as the Spirit of Memphis Quartet, with its close harmonies and biblical allusions. Duke Ellington wrote three sacred concerts to the glory of God. Even the blues, which are not played in church, carry a message of protest congenial to biblical prophecies. Before dismissing these views as wishful thinking, we need to read these pages respectfully and generously, humbly examining the evidence adduced. Rookmaaker has left few stones unturned. The book is a remarkable piece of ethnomusicology, and an even more remarkable piece of intellectual history.

We may be deeply grateful to the Rookmaaker family for giving us the green light on this republication. And very special thanks are due to the Case Family Properties Foundation for their support of this stand-alone volume. May it be an inspiration to many, in an age when music is so often anything but exquisite.

William Edgar

Acknowledgments to
the First Edition

Here I would like to thank the many friends and acquaintances who have helped me in so many different ways. I will not mention them by all name for fear of forgetting someone, but I have to make an exception for Mrs. M. H. L. Boom-Sybrandi, who made available her late son's study of the blues which was unfortunately never published.

I must also thank the following people and organizations for helping with copyrighting: H. Courlander (copyright of songs by Doc Reed, Richard Amerson and one of the children's verses); W. L. Grossman; Alan Lomax (copyright for extracts from Mr. Jelly Roll [Cassel & Co., 1952, pages 64–109], copyright for "Whoa Black," "Jumpin' Judy," "No More, My Lord," "John Henry," which were collected, edited and published, and who holds exclusive copyright); the songs "Ain't No More Cane," "Here, Rattler, Here," "Do Lord, Remember Me" were published by the Library of Congress and taken from American Ballads and Folk Songs (MacMillan, 1934, copyright John A. and Alan Lomax); the copyright for "Roll 'im on Down" was from David Pryor and Alan Lomax; F. Ramsey Jr. (songs taken from the Folkways Music from the South series); Vogue record company (for copyright of Big Bill Broonzy's "Black, Brown and White"); Philips Phonographische Industrie, Baarn (for helping deal with the question of copyrights, especially Mr. H. van Baaren who has assisted me in all sorts of ways); Decca Record Co., London (permission to quote two of Rosetta Tharpe's songs); Rinehart & Co. Inc. (for permission to quote from N. Shapiro & N. Hentof's Heah Me Talkin' to Ya); Cassell & Co., London (for mediating on the issue of copyright) and A.A. Knopf's Publishing Co. Inc. (for the same). Finally, rights were obtained from Ed Basart (rights for publication of texts from "Out of the Depth" and "I'm Going to Move Up a Little Higher").

H. R. R., 1960

A Note on Sources

The books referred to by shortened titles are listed in the Selected Bibliography at the back of the book. The recordings listed in the footnotes pertain to those mentioned throughout the book. In order to help the reader/listener, I have also given the records ratings according to my opinion of their importance. Records have not primarily been rated according to their quality but according to how interesting they might be to the jazz novice. Four stars mean that the recording makes for essential listening—worth getting hold of; three stars, less so, and so on.

Where a record is hard to obtain, it is indicated with one cross, and, if it is very rare, two crosses. The records are, as far as possible, samplers, i.e., multitrack recordings that feature various good examples of different genres. Two of these are mentioned several times and have been abbreviated and the crosses omitted. They are:

ITJ **** Brunswick 87003 LPBM, *New Orleans, Dixieland, Chicago: An Introduction to Traditional Jazz.*
HCJ ***† *History of Classic Jazz*: a collection of five LPs, bound, with introduction. Riverside SDP 11 (RLP 12-112/116).

Besides the standard abbreviations of the well-known labels, the following abbreviations have been used:

FoW   Folkways

FoW MS   Folkways' *Music from the South* series, nine records,
          also available separately. FP 650/658, indicated here
          as I-IX.

LiC   A Library of Congress recording of US folk music.
          (The Library of Congress is a large scientific institute
          in Washington, DC.) With the exception of a few
          other recordings, it is primarily these albums of black
          folk music that interest us. (There are also recordings
          of Indian music and white folk music.) After "LiC,"
          I have indicated with a roman numeral the number
          of the album that includes that particular track.
          These albums have been released as LPs and are avail-
          able on order.

Note: London records mentioned here are also available on the
Riverside label.

1

Origins

African Music: "Orin Muritali Alhaji"

Africa, the land of rhythm, the land where "the gods speak through the drums" is the creed. You would be hard pressed to find such a diversity and sophistication of rhythm elsewhere. To the uninitiated, African music is an almost indecipherable pattern of rhythmic sound, frequently evolving from a large number of rhythms of different character and nature, played simultaneously on heavier and lighter drums and other percussion and plucked instruments.

Is this music primitive? That depends on the definition of primitive. Performing this music is certainly no mean feat. It requires knowledge and skill. Some would describe it as the voice of primitive humanity—an unrestrained human spirit, unspoiled by civilization. However, it would need to be proved that this art is more direct, more spontaneous, more authentic and purer than that of Western Europe. The Africans have their own culture, which might perhaps in one sense be regarded as primitive, as when referring to a paralysis, a closing of the route to development and progress due to the belief in a hostile spirit world. Here "primitive" refers to little people in an awesome world—frightened mortals amidst the incomprehensible forces of nature, threatened by demons, spirits and mysterious powers, sometimes products of the religious imagination, sometimes real, and certainly evil.

The multifarious and complex rhythmic patterns cannot be said to express joy. Like magic it often evokes hostile gods and demonic forces. It incites a trance to allay fear or to overpower the hostile forces. African rhythms can often be compared with the masks used by the indigenous peoples to disguise themselves during religious ceremonies, to repel, summon or tame powers. They show us how pagans have lost positive touch with creation, paving the way for fear and alienation.

The rhythms are undeniably characteristic of Africa, and also of the Dahomeys and Yorubas who live on the Gold Coast of West Africa, but that does not mean that we have exhausted the subject of their music: indeed, it is more closely related to ours than we may realize. They have developed their rhythms further than Western Europeans have, who since the Middle Ages have paid more attention to harmony, to the sounding together of different notes. Still, African and Western music are undeniably similar in many ways: in the scales used, in the musical approach, in the nature of the melody. We do not know whether this can be attributed to the influence of those blacks who occupied an important place in the court chapel of the Egyptian pharaoh (and which we see portrayed in many murals) or whether there are other factors involved. But those who listen will certainly discover that African music is more closely related to Western European than to Indian, Chinese or Arabian music, for example. Listen to "Orin Muritali Alhaji,"[1] a solemn song of the Yorubas of Nigeria, one of the highest black cultures before the arrival of the Europeans. We hear the polyrhythmic sound of the drums as the foundation, the melody sung by a male-voice choir. If we listen to the royal drums of the Abatusi—possibly the most impressive of pure rhythms—let us not forget that the girls of this tribe from the Congo can sing very melodically whilst clapping their hands in accompaniment.[2]

1. ** FoW P 500 B (together with B, two records, series *Negro Folk Music of Africa and America*).
2. HCJ.

2

WHITE FOLK MUSIC: "BLOW THE MAN DOWN"

Since the Europeans settled in America, they have regarded it as their own, to do with as they please. When its indigenous population did not prove to be as subservient as required, slaves were quickly sought and imported. Murderous battles between African tribes supplied the slaves—prisoners of war—who were sold to the slave-traders, who in turn disposed of them in the New World while pocketing a tidy sum. The Spanish slave owners preferred Yorubas, the French opted for Dahomeys, while the English were partial to Ashantis.

It goes without saying that the slave traders were no gentlemen, and that the quality of their ware was of little concern to them. As long as enough were imported, alive, to secure a decent margin—that was all that mattered. Their victims, spoils of war from the neighboring black tribes, had already been stripped of anything of value before they were sold, so we can be sure that they took nothing with them to their new destination—at least nothing tangible or portable. What lives in a person's mind is less easily displaced. These people took their music, their religion, their views with them—invisible but nonetheless present.

En route and on arrival the slaves were immediately confronted with Western culture. They were certainly subjected to the crudest and least pleasant side, but they were also introduced to its music, shanties and possibly even psalms. One of those shanties was "Blow the man down." Although it originated in England, it was often sung by American sailors. It is actually a work song, sung whilst reeling in the anchor chain. The song has eight beats to a bar and includes a chorus-like stanza:

> Oh, blow the man down, bullies, blow the man down,
> To me way, aye, blow the man down.
> Oh, blow the man down, bullies, blow him right down,
> Give me some time to blow the man down.[3]

3. O. Downes, E. Siegmeister: *A Treasury of American Song* (New York, 1943, second edition), p. 90.

This tune can be traced to the Bahamas where it is sung, in almost identical form, by the black fishermen as they haul their boats up onto the sand for the low season. The recorded version allows us to hear what fantastic singers they are:

> So pull 'im along,
> Well, we pull 'im along,
> Hey, aye, pull 'im along,
> Now we pull 'im along from this old shipyard,
> Give me some time to roll 'im along.[4]

African Music in South America: 'Jesha for Oshun

The blacks who were slaves to the Spanish or French in South or Central America or on the large islands in the Gulf of Mexico seldom saw their own bosses. They lived elsewhere, leaving the supervision to a few overseers. The slaves worked on the plantations, which were often large, and as long as they worked there was no need for their owners to bother about them. Their religion, their music, their lives was of no interest to their masters. If missionaries wanted to evangelize them, that was fine.

Since they had arrived in a Roman Catholic country the blacks became mainly Catholic, but nowhere has the principle of mission, of Christianization by the simple renaming of pagan religious customs, been so avenged. These people did become Christians, but they were often unaware of the basic principles of the gospel. This led to a range of mergers. A Roman Catholic saint might be likened to an African god. The Dahomey god Legba, protector of crossroads, might be likened to St. Antony, for example. Both were portrayed as old men with weathered faces. African religion sometimes existed unashamedly alongside the Roman beliefs.

We can hear pure African sounds in the former Spanish and French colonies; not only work songs, but also cult music, such as the

4. LiC VIII No. 40.

song of the Brazilian, 'Jesha cult followers, which is a call to Oshun, the goddess of Pure Water.[5] This sort of song can also be heard on Haiti. There the god Legba is evoked in pure African style. The drums form a complicated, repetitively rhythmical pattern, whilst the solemn melody is sung by the priestess and all the believers alternately.[6] The alternating solo call and group response is typically African. We call it responsive song because it has the character of a game, of question and answer.

The blacks also became familiar with the music of their Spanish or French owners, depending on which country they ended up in. Some of the European folk songs were adopted in their original form, and some became hybrids. This is apparent on Haiti nowadays where the meringue,[7] French in character and related to the chanson, can be heard. On Cuba the habanera, which is almost purely Spanish, and the guaracha, which is influenced only slightly by African rhythms, are performed alongside the rumba, conga, son, etc. These dances, which are characterized by varying rhythms, have a stronger African definition. The more African the music, the more drums and percussion dominate; the more European the music, the more the percussion is replaced by instruments like the piano or guitar.

AFRICAN-AMERICAN WORK SONGS IN THE USA: "NO MORE, MY LORD"

Things progressed very differently in North America. The plantations were smaller there and slave owners were less indifferent towards their slaves. Because fewer people worked on the plantations and the plantation owners lived there and were in charge, there was a much closer bond between slave owner and slave. This was particularly evident in the case of domestic slaves—servants. The largely Protestant slave owners were of English descent and, in order

5. ** FoW P 500 B.
6. Ibid.
7. Ibid.

to defend their practices, they argued that the heathen slaves must be rescued from the dark realms of idolatry and brought to the true Light of the gospel. Indeed, it seems that efforts were made in that direction and that slavery in North America during the seventeenth and eighteenth centuries, without wishing to idealize it, was not necessarily an unbearable lot. Pagan religion has consequently all but died out in North America. It is still evident in superstition, which stubbornly manifests itself in voodoo, as a kind of degenerated remnant of paganism, just as folklore and superstition live on in old myths in our Western culture. The disappearance of the African religions meant that their rhythm, inextricably linked to the exorcism and invocation of gods and powers, also lost its meaning. Black American music was therefore always based on a simple rhythm, while a number of characteristics of African-style music only survived in a new form.

The nineteenth century saw the import of thousands of blacks and the slave trade assumed a much harder, less compassionate character. And even though slavery was abolished more than a century ago, there are still cases of black convicts carrying out forced labor in penal colonies [in the 1950s] in similar conditions to those of the days of slavery. It was only in the mid-1940s that things began to improve. These colonies have been home to songs of a similar character to the ones heard more than a century ago.

Besides blues and spirituals, which we will come to later, it is work songs that we most often hear in the colonies. The blacks worked there in shifts called chain gangs, supervised by a captain. While they were working they sang songs to help lighten the labor. The chopping of wood, hewing of rock, cutting of sugarcane, harvesting of cotton was accompanied by music strongly reminiscent of Africa. The rhythm was not provided by drums but was much simpler of character—the sound of the axe or the pickaxe. There is always a precentor, a convict like the others, but one who can sing well and has a wide repertoire, while the rest sing the "response" together. This is another example of responsive song. The melodies are sometimes exuberant, frequently solemn, but always musical and interesting, each with its own unmistakable beauty. Here is one such song sung in the Mississippi State Penitentiary during work on the great cotton plantation in the Yazoo Delta:[8]

No more, my Lord, no more, my Lord,
Lord, I'll never turn back no more.

Precentor:

I found in Him a restin' place
And He has made me glad.
No more, my Lord, no more, my Lord,
Lord, I'll never turn back no more.

Precentor:

Jesus, the Man I am looking for,
Can you tell me where He is gone.
No more, my Lord, no more, my Lord,
Lord, I'll never turn back no more.

Another group would sing the next, more exuberant responsive song as a full ensemble, though the precentor's voice is still clearly audible above the rest:

O well it's Jumpin' Judy
O well it's Jumpin' Judy,
Boys she was a mighty fine gal.
You catch the Illinois Central,
You catch the Illinois Central,
Baby, go to Kankakee. [This expresses the desire to go north.]

O well, and yonder comes old Rosie,
O well, and yonder comes old Rosie,
Baby, how in the world do you know.
O well, I know her by her apron, O well, I know her by her apron,

---

8. Note that in the lyrics a refrain printed in italics means it is sung by the choir. Also, we have used standard and not phonetic spellings in the lyrics.

Baby, red's the dress that she wore.
Etc.[9]

It is not easy to establish exactly who Jumpin' Judy is, in spite of her many appearances in this sort of song. Perhaps she is the personification of hard work, but that is admittedly a stab in the dark. The name Rosie—truly beloved—also appears regularly. The word "old" is a reference to the faithful beloved. It does not mean that she is old, but refers to a well-established relationship, the name "Rosie" having a familiar ring.

Children's Songs/Nursery Rhymes: "Satisfied"

Children will play, irrespective of their situation. Slave children too, play. There was little in the way of toys, but an abundance of song. The repertoire consequently embraced both African children's songs and Western children's songs, and included all sorts of combinations of the two. This is still the case today, for there is after all nothing more traditional than children's songs.

The songs were sung whilst playing, mainly during so-called ring-games such as "The farmer's in his den."[10] The next example has both melodic and in its delivery strong Western (i.e., Anglo-Saxon) characteristics. It is striking how well these children sing. The child sitting in the middle is sung to by the others, and "Sally Walker," for that is her name, has to make a hip movement at the end of the verse to indicate which child is to replace her:

Li'l Sally Walker,
Sittin' in the saucer,
Cryin' for the old man,

9. *** *Murderer's Home*, Nixa NJL 11.

10. I traced the melody from a similar Dutch song called "In Holland staat een huis," back to a spiritual. Perhaps it was derived from Dutch children's games—on the record *He Shut the Lion's Mouth*, Vi 38507, Elder Richard Bryant, vocals and orchestra.

To come for the dollar,
Rise Sally rise,
Put your hands on your hips,
Let your backbone slip,
And shake it to the East,
And shake it to the West,
And shake it to the very one you love best.[11]

Once you have heard this song it should be obvious which source Armstrong used when he wrote "Georgia Grind" in 1926.

A song such as "All around the maypole" is also clearly of Anglo-Saxon origin, but there are many others whose flavor is much more African. They have a typical responsive form whereby a game-leader-cum-precentor (usually an older girl) is answered each time by the children's choir singing the response. The lyrics also are in line with the artistic tradition characteristic of black Americans (which I will refer to in the coming chapters), and smack of self-mockery and irony—a sort of humor unfamiliar to Europeans. Here is a typical example:

I'm going up North
Satisfied
An' I would tell
Satisfied
Lord I am
Satisfied
Some people up there
Satisfied
Going to bring you back
Satisfied
Ain't nothing up there
Satisfied

11. ** FoW EFL 1417, *Negro Folk Music of Alabama*, secular. For children's songs also: *Ring Games*, FoW FP 704.

9

What can you do
Satisfied
Mamma cooked a cow
Satisfied
Have to get all the girls
Satisfied
Their bellies full
Satisfied
I'm going up North
Satisfied
Etc.[12]

There are also adult versions of this type of song to be found away from the cities. A game called "Liza Jane" often played at parties involves couples dancing in a circle while a solitary male performs the most amazing dance steps in the middle. He has to try to "get" one of the dancing women, whose partner is then banished to the middle. There is also a jazz version of the folk song to accompany this dance.[13] The lyrics go like this:

Come my love and go with me
L'il Liza Jane
Come my love and go with me
L'il Liza Jane
O Miss Liza, L'il Liza Jane
O Miss Liza, L'il Liza Jane

I got a house in Baltimore
L'il Liza Jane
Streetcar runs right by my door
L'il Liza Jane
Chorus.

12. Ibid.
13. *Celestin's Tuxedo Jazz Band*, Storyville SEP 308 (EP).

I got a house in Baltimore
L'il Liza Jane
Brussels carpet on the floor
L'il Liza Jane
Chorus etc.[14]

The connection between African-American music and the stories told
by blacks to their children might not be immediately clear, but anybody
who has witnessed a black storyteller in action (or a black preacher, as
we will see later) will recognize that the intonation and rhythm used
come close to music. It is a sort of rhythmic prose, like a recitative.

Many of these stories are related to African and, strangely enough,
also to Indian tales such as those heard in South America. The latter
creates a problem for us, which we will not discuss here.[15] An important series of stories has been preserved for us, thanks to Noel Chandler
Harris who wrote them down in 1880 from oral tradition. We are not
confronted here with Western misrepresentations as Schulte Northolt
contends[16]—the stereotypical image of a simple man, grateful for the
privilege of being a slave, an idealized image fostered by the plantation
holders of the Southern States. These are real black folk tales that can
still be heard in remote parts of the South.[17]

The following is part of the "Tar-Baby" story, the writer having
tried to reflect the dialect characteristic of that period. If the words
are pronounced out loud, the intention becomes clear. The fox has
made a little figure of tar that he uses to bait the hare. This tar-baby
is placed on the road and the fox lies in wait in the bushes:

En he didn't hatter wait long, kaze bimeby here come Brer (Brother)
Rabbit pacin' down the road—lippity-clippity, clippity-lippity—
dez ez sassy ez a jay-bird. Brer fox, he lay low. Brer rabbit come

14. Natalie Curtis-Burlin, *Negro Folk Songs*, Hampton series IV, New York, 1919.
15. See leaflet with FoW EFL 1417.
16. Dr. J. W. Schulte Northolt, *Het volk dat in duisternis wandelt* (Arnhem,
1957), p. 163.
17. A.o. on FoW EFL 1417.

prancin' 'long twel he spy de Tar-Baby, en den he fotch up on his behime legs like he wuz 'stonished. De Tar-Baby, she sot dar, she did, en Brer Fox, he lay low.

'Mawnin!' sez Brer Rabbit, sezee—'nice wedder dis mawnin,' sezee.

Tar-Baby ain't sayin' nothin', en Brer Fox, he lay low.

'How you come on, den? Is you deaf?' sez Brer Rabbit, sezee.

'Kaze if you is, I kin holler louder,' sezee.

Tar-Baby stay still, en Brer Fox, he lay low.

'Youer stuck up, dat's w'at you is', says Brer Rabbit, sezee, 'en I's gwineter kyore you, dat's w'at I'm gwineter do,' sezee.

Brer Fox, he sorter chuckle in his stummuck, he did, but Tar-Baby ain't sayin' nothin'.

'I'm gwineter larn you how-ter talk ter 'spectubble fokes,' sez Brer Rabbit, sezee. 'Ef you don't take off dat hat en tell me howdy, I'm gwineter bus' you wide open,' sezee. Tar-Baby stay still, en Brer Fox, he lay low. Brer Rabbit keep on axin' 'im, en de Tar-Baby, she keep on sayin' nothin', twel present'y Brer Rabbit draw back wid his fis', he did, en blip he tuck 'er side de head. His fis stuck, en he can't pull loose. De tar hilt 'im. But Tar-Baby, she stay still, en Brer Fox, he lay low.

'Ef you don't lemme loose, I'll knock you agin,' sez Brer Rabbit, sezee, en wid dat he fotch 'er a wipe wid de udder han', en dat stuck. Tar-Baby she ain't sayin' nothin', en Brer Fox, he lay low.

'Tu'n me loose, fo' I kick de natal stuffin' outen you,' sez Brer Rabbit, sezee, but de Tar-Baby, she ain't sayin' nothin'. She des hilt on,

en den Brer Rabbit lose de use er his feet in de same way. Den Brer
Fox, he sa'ntered fort', lookin' des es innercent ez one eryo' mammy's mockin'-birds.

'Howdy Brer Rabbit,' sez Brer Fox, sezee, 'you look sorter stuck up
dis mawnin',' sezee, en den he rolled on de groun', en laughed en
laughed twel he couldn't laugh no mo'.[18]

The story goes on to tell how the hare, in spite of being in a tight spot,
manages to get free by bamboozling the fox. Almost all these stories
have the same moral, of a hare who is too clever for the fox. Perhaps
they reflect the hopes of the blacks who, in spite of their weaker position, were still able to outwit the "stronger" whites.[19]

THE FIRST OF THE AFRICAN-AMERICAN CHRISTIAN SONGS IN NORTH AMERICA: "GO PREACH MY GOSPEL"

When black slaves arrived in North America, still an English colony in the seventeenth and most of the eighteenth centuries, they were
introduced to the Protestantism of their masters. There were various
denominations, the majority of them dissenters or Nonconformists,
i.e., Christians who did not wish to belong to the Anglican Church,
the established church in England. These people sang psalms only.

Thanks to Calvin in Geneva, the psalms were translated and set
to music, which in turn contributed greatly to the propagation of
the Reformation. They were sung briskly and cheerfully. Even Queen
Elizabeth I once made a reference to these "Geneva jigs." Since people
at first were not familiar with English rhymed versions of the psalms
it became customary to have a precentor recite a line, which was then
sung by the congregation, and so on. The custom continued even
when it was no longer necessary.

18. J. Chandler Harris: *Uncle Remus* (New York, 1933), p. 7 ff.
19. This adaptation by J. Harris of the stories in which Brer Rabbit plays the
leading role was used by Walt Disney for the cartoon film based on the story.

In the seventeenth century people began to sing the psalms slower—more solemnly and legato (this may still be heard in some old Calvinistic churches). It became so slow that it was impossible to hold a note for the required length of time. At that point "grace notes" were introduced to replace the notes that were too long. These took the form of decorative melodies that swerved very closely around the tone. Since everybody had his or her own method of application, the result was curious. The original note became frayed and obscure. The beginning of the eighteenth century in England saw an attempt to improve the standard of singing in churches. Dr. Isaac Watts, a clergyman from London, particularly devoted himself to the abolition of "lining out," in which a precentor sings the line for the congregation to repeat. He was also responsible for revising the metrical psalms and writing a large number of hymns.

Let us return to the Africans in America, who at this time were learning psalms and hymns like those of Dr. Watts, but performing them as described above. While Dr. Watts had been successful with his hymns, his efforts to improve the standard of singing had rather failed. Having a precentor sing and the choir "respond" sounded familiar to the black slaves. This was what they had been used to in their native countries—responsive singing of solemn melodies. The rhythm as basis was certainly lacking, but as we discussed earlier, for various reasons the intensive contact with biblical Christianity led to African rhythms being abandoned. These were considered pagan—after all, the gods spoke through the drums.

There is therefore much evidence that blacks, having arrived from Africa, were very fond of psalms and hymns. They simply could not stop singing them. That sort of song was in fact the most Western, European music to be found in America. Although it cannot be referred to as highly sophisticated, it was conceivable only in the context of Puritan, Christian Europe. At the same time, and without any modification, it was also African song in its purest form. There was no mutation necessary; no hybrids were involved—the music was purely African and purely Western at the same time.

It seems strange that it was the very hymns from Dr. Watts that the blacks preferred to sing in this way. They still do for, as we shall see later, it was the "songs of the old Dr. Watts," alongside other sorts of sacred songs, that remained popular—a regular feature of the blacks' church service. The precentor "lines out" a line, which is then sung very slowly, elaborately drawn out by the congregation. This sort of singing died out in other parts. It is only in the black American churches today that we can witness how the English congregations sung around 1700. Just how slowly and spun out the hymns were sung can be seen by the following hymn that took more than five minutes to sing.

This is one of Dr. Watts' hymns, which is still sung today in the prescribed fashion.

> Go preach my Gospel, saith the Lord,
> Bid the whole earth my grace receive;
> He shall be safe that trusts my word,
> He shall be damned that won't believe.
>
> I'll make your great commission known,
> And ye shall prove my gospel true
> By all the works that I have done,
> By all the wonders ye shall do.[20]

THE ORIGIN OF THE TRUE NEGRO SPIRITUAL: "I WANT TO BE A CHRISTIAN"

Dr. Watts' songs were sung by slaves (and free blacks) in the Northern states, and here and there in the South. In the South, however, there lived large groups of slaves who worked in remote plantations and who had hardly encountered Christianity. The eighteenth century in particular witnessed concern about the fate of the blacks, and a more conscious effort was made to preach the gospel to them. Baptists and Methodists were particularly committed to this work,

20. ** FoW MS VI.

but Presbyterians also made a contribution. Consequently, African Americans were exposed to the sacred song of the whites—the hymn. It was not only the Dr. Watts' hymns that were circulating; hymns by Wesley and his family were in circulation as well. The Wesley brothers were leaders of a spiritual revival movement in England in the middle of the eighteenth century. Methodism, as it was called, devoted much attention to improving and reforming the standard of hymns. They were more successful than Watts in breaking down the rusty traditions of "lining out" and note-stretching. For their hymns they often used the tunes of folk songs.

It is evident that these hymns were also sung by blacks. The words were often too difficult for them, however, as they lacked the formal education of the average Westerner, and it was this that led to the simplification of the songs. Sometimes the hymns profited from it for, once it was stripped of its poetic frills, the essentials became more evident. Songs of this sort are still sung by black Christians. They often have an attractive melody which is sung slowly, either collectively or as a solo. It is possible that the following song stems from that period:

> Lord, I want to be a Christian in my heart, in my heart,
> Lord, I want to be a Christian in my heart, in my heart,
> Lord, I want to be a Christian in my heart, in my heart.[21]

The next few verses may read:

> Lord, I want to be more loving in my heart (x 3)
> Lord, I want to be more holy in my heart (x 3) Etc.

The following variations developed:

> When Jesus comes into my heart, into my heart (x 3)
> I'm filled with joy, Etc.

21. M. Mark Fisher, *Negro Slave Songs in the U.S.* (Ithaca, NY, 1953), p. 30.

Wesley's lyrics are often constructed in four-line verses which, when set to music, require eight measures (four times two). This sort of Negro spiritual consequently consists of verses of eight bars.

At the end of the eighteenth century a great revival took place, also known as the Great Awakening, mainly in the Southern States of the United States of America. The influence of the Wesleys and others created a strong revival movement focused on a more personal, warm, authentic Christianity—biblical and primarily practical. Conversion was emphasized—a personal, direct relationship with Jesus, with a whiff of mysticism manifest in such expressions as "Jesus comes into my heart." There was also a certain moralism involved, and an emphasis on going to heaven to be with Jesus. Little attention was given to doctrine and a scriptural, solidly formulated confession. In practical terms the revival consisted primarily of camp meetings, social gatherings in large tents lasting several days. There was singing, prayer and preaching from the Bible. It was at these meetings in particular that the need was felt to make Wesley's new type of hymn accessible to everyone. That would promote the standard of combined singing. Simplicity was the key since these camp meetings were primarily attended by the lower classes.

An interesting feature of these meetings was that blacks and whites were on a par with each other, side by side and not separated. That was significant. It also made an impact on the singing, since the blacks were not only good singers with a sense of rhythm but their principle of responsive singing was a welcome addition. It worked by enabling the crowd to join in easily: the songs with tricky words and irregular word patterns were chanted by the precentor-preacher and the crowd responded with the chorus.

This is how the most well-known type of Negro spiritual probably came into being. Having said that, there are many unanswered questions in this area and there is little about the origin and the early development of the Negro spiritual of which we can be absolutely certain. In any case, the structure of this kind of Negro spiritual generally follows the pattern as described next.

Firstly, there is a verse consisting of eight bars, divided as four times two. Each set of two bars is allocated a single sentence, which is also a musical phrase. At the end of the line there is often a word or short sentence that is sung collectively which we might call a short refrain. After this verse comes the actual chorus, which we call the main chorus, also consisting of eight bars. This is sung collectively. Many variations are possible—the verse is sung twice and the chorus once, or a verse of sixteen bars is followed by a chorus of sixteen bars, for example. The main chorus is sometimes omitted. This type of song is still often sung in churches by blacks, briskly but not hurriedly. A rhythmic accompaniment such as the clapping of hands is regularly heard, but true African polyrhythms are never heard—they have barely survived in North America. The tune is always based on a simple, even meter and so is the rhythm, which is often varied, never monotonous. Rhythm, however, is never the feature of the spiritual. The following is an example:

> When I am sick and by myself, (one bar)
> *Do remember me.* (short refrain, also one bar) x3
> *Do Lord, remember me.* (all together, two bars, last syllables on long notes)

Main chorus:

> *Do Lord, do Lord, remember me.* (two bars)
> *Do Lord, do Lord, remember me.*
> *Do Lord, do Lord, remember me.*
> *Do Lord, remember me.* (see the last line of the verse)

The first lines of the following verses are:

> When I'm crossing Jordan. [which means, when I die and go to
> the "promised land," namely heaven]
> If I ain't got no friend at all.
> When I'm going from door to door.
> When I am bound in trouble, Etc.[22]

22. M. A. Grissom, *The Negro Sings a New Heaven* (Chapel Hill, 1930), p. 69.

We can be reasonably certain that one of these spirituals, "Roll, Jordan Roll," came into being around this time:

> Brother you ought to be there, (two bars)
> *Yes my Lord,* (two bars)
> A-sittin' in the Kingdom, (two bars)
> *Just to hear old Jordan roll,* (two bars)
>
> *Roll, Jordan roll, roll, Jordan roll,* (2x2 bars)
> *I want to go to heaven when I die,* (two bars)
> *To hear of Jordan roll,* (two bars)

Both the words and the music (which is a tune derived from an English folk song) are based on a song written by Charles Wesley, but it has undergone significant changes since the original.[23]

23. G. P. Jackson, *Spiritual Folk-Songs of Early America* (New York, 1937), p. 193, no. 184; Idem., *White Spirituals*, p. 264.

2

Nineteenth Century:
Development

THE DEVELOPMENT OF THE SPIRITUALS IN THE NINETEENTH CENTURY: "GO DOWN, MOSES"

In the eighteenth century the blacks formed their own church. There were many factors involved in this development but we will not discuss them at this point. What concerns us here is the songs that were sung in their services: first of all hymns, sung in the time-honored style in which the hymns of Dr. Watts were performed; moreover it is probable that many of the new hymns, those written from the late eighteenth century onwards in the spirit of Wesley, also penetrated the black churches. Here is an example of a white song of this sort, regularly sung in black churches and also popular among whites. The melody is American and dates back to the eighteenth century. The words were written by John Newton (1725–1807), who worked on a boat for fetching slaves until, under very adventurous circumstances, he became a Christian and subsequently a minister in England.

> Amazing grace! How sweet the sound,
> That saved a wretch like me,
> I once was lost, but now am found,
> I was blind, but now I can see.

Thro' many dangers, toils and snares,
I have already come,
This grace has brought me safe thus far,
And grace will lead me home.[1]

Many new hymns emerged from the black culture in North America, however. They essentially followed the pattern of the hymns of Wesley and others, but in contrast to the white hymns composed during the nineteenth century, which were seldom of a high standard,[2] many of these were particularly beautiful. This new type of black hymn, by blacks for the blacks, was called a Negro spiritual. The lyrics are often powerful, poetic though simple, and strongly biblical. Unlike white spirituals, the tunes were often far from sentimental with depth and beauty. These songs have been referred to as compositions because we believe that someone composed them—someone who functioned as a musical leader, who stimulated musical life and contributed his or her own work.[3] On the other hand we must not think of compositions as music written down once for all in musical notation and with a definite text. The composer and poet (we imagine it would have been one person in most cases) would have taught the congregation the song, i.e., the tune and the words. The song would have been performed in a traditional, very lively fashion, in responsive form. There would always have been room, however, to vary the number of voices and details in the melody, etc.

Believers have always sought comfort from events recorded in

1. Many versions including Mahalia Jackson (Vogue 103); a church, Dr. Watts-type songs, **FoW EFL 1418 (*Negro Folk Music of Alabama*, religious); †† Rev. J. M. Gates (Victor 20216; ca. 1925).

2. H. A. L. Jefferson, *Hymns in Christian Worship* (London, 1950); S. R. Cowell, "The 'Shaped-Note Singers' and their Music," *The Score* (London, June 1955); G. Woodcock, "The English Hymn," *Folk I* (London, 1945); G. P. Jackson, *White and Negro-Spirituals* (New York, 1943); and M. A. Grissom, *The Negro Sings a New Heaven* (Chapel Hill, 1930).

3. See introduction J. W. Johnson, *Books of American Negro-Spirituals* (New York, 1940).

the Bible. These stories teach us, after all, how the Lord acted with his people, and they also show us how he will act today (see Romans 15:4). It is therefore no surprise to us that blacks, in their desperate circumstances in the bonds of slavery, also reached for the Bible; for all sorts of reasons the plight of slaves in the nineteenth century was harder, more inhumane and cruel than previously. In the face of that it is astonishing—and we may praise the Lord for it—that the blacks who were already Christians remained so. Not only that but, in view of the fact that those who were responsible for the sorry condition of the slaves professed to be Christians themselves, it is amazing that large numbers of the slaves also became Christians. They particularly sought solace in the stories with a message of hope and expectation, such as the history of the people of Israel in Egypt and their subsequent exodus. Would this not have taught them that the Lord does not let his people cry out in vain when they ask for deliverance? There are cases of slave insurrections, but it seems certain that these were led by slaves who were not yet familiar with the gospel or, at least, only superficially. Attempts to liberate themselves often led only to an aggravation of their circumstances.

The song "Roll, Jordan Roll" has already shown us that Christians were making associations with parts of the book of Exodus. An even clearer example of this is "Go Down, Moses," in which we are also struck by the poetic way in which blacks were able to present a situation in no uncertain terms, using a few strokes of the pen, a few well-turned phrases. The words are recorded here. Authentic renditions from church circles are very rare, a phenomenon which we shall be discussing in a later paragraph.

Go down, Moses, way down in Egypt land,
Tell ol' Pharaoh to let my people go.

When Israel was in Egypt land,
Let my people go
Oppressed so hard they could not stand,
Let my people go.

23

When spoke the Lord, bold Moses said,
Let my people go.
If not I'll smite your first born dead,
Let my people go.

No more in bondage shall they toil,
Let my people go.
Let them come out to Israel's soil,
Let my people go.[4]

The Civil War in the 1860s brought the long-awaited answer to prayer. A bloody war was fought between the Northern and Southern States to decide the future position of blacks. After the Northerners had won the war under the inspiring leadership of Abraham Lincoln, the slaves were declared free. Now they were free as people. But the faithful Christian knows that being free from oppression is only part of the battle; freedom is complete only in the spiritual freedom found in Jesus Christ. In him we are no more slaves to sin—no longer children of the devil. This gives us reason to think that the following song is a product of the post-Civil War period. It is a lovely example of words without a direct basis in Scripture, a black Negro spiritual which is able to express the heart of the matter directly, perceptively and deeply, in almost childlike, but far from childish, words.

Free at last, free at last,
Thank God Almighty I'm free at last.
Free at last, free at last,
Thank God Almighty I'm free at last.

One day, one day I was walking along.
Thank God Almighty I'm free at last.
I met old Satan on my way,
Thank God Almighty I'm free at last.

4. Several renditions, a.o. by the Davis Sisters, **† Savoy Mg 14014.

24

What do you reckon old Satan said to me?
Thank God Almighty I'm free at last.
Young man, young man, you're too young to pray,
Thank God Almighty I'm free at last.

If I'm too young to pray, I ain't too young to die,
Thank God Almighty I'm free at last.
Oh free at last, free at last,
Thank God Almighty I'm free at last.
Old Satan mad and I am glad,
Thank God Almighty I'm free at last.
Well he missed the soul he thought he had,
Thank God Almighty I'm free at last.[5]

Liberation meant new horizons for the slaves—new opportunities and wide perspectives. It also brought many new problems, worries which partly stemmed from the uncompromising attitude of the former slave owners. Even without additional pressure from outside the liberated slaves had no easy time. Indeed, there were many for whom the temptation to stop working altogether became too strong. They sought refuge in the cities, far away from the rural areas where they had such a miserable existence, and gave themselves over to living a loose life that often culminated in crime. New opportunities had brought a new dilemma—freedom bred temptation, which bred crime, and evading crime became a tough test of faith. Many held on to the faith of their fathers, sung of in the spiritual "Give Me That Old-Time Religion." On the other hand we must not underestimate the troubles and sorrows of that time—pressure from outside and testing from within. That is what is expressed in the following song:

I ain't gonna lay my religion down, (x 4)

Ever since I've been free, (x 3)
Nobody knows the troubles I've seen.

5. Dock Reed, ** FoW EFL 1418.

Nobody knows but Jesus and me, (x 2)
Ever since I've been free.
Nobody knows the troubles I've seen.
I ain't gonna lay my religion down. (x 4)[6]

THE ORIGIN OF THE WESTERNIZED SPIRITUAL: "SWING LOW, SWEET CHARIOT"

Emancipation of the blacks was marked by a declaration of their full dignity as citizens of the United States of America. At the same time it created a problem for their liberators, because there were thousands upon thousands of slaves in the Southern States who were suddenly granted rights and had to fulfil obligations with little understanding of the implications of either. It was a difficult matter to provide for these ex-slaves, the vast majority of whom were illiterate, had no financial resources and absolutely no property. The responsibility for the new task had fallen to the Northerners and, it must be said, they approached their task with much idealism and endeavor. An example of their achievements was the founding of schools and universities, one of which was of particular importance. It was the Fisk University, established in the south in an area densely populated by blacks. At first it was probably simply a primary school for adults. It still exists and has become a very important institute for higher education.

A music teacher by the name of White became the principal of Fisk University. He heard the songs of the blacks, admired their beautiful lyrics and melodies, but decided that his pupils who were now full citizens of the USA should not sing "so barbarically," so he began to transcribe and edit their songs. He met with all sorts of difficulties however because our tone system is *wohltemperiert* (of equal temperament). Since the eighteenth century there has been a definite (though somewhat artificial) division of the octave, which has made it possible to play in any key, and facilitated the playing together of various instruments. (Bach wrote his *Wohltemperierte Klavier* for clavichords

6. Georgia Peach, † Classic Editions 5001.

and harpsichords tuned in this [new] fashion.) What the blacks sang, however, was partly determined by Western tone systems and partly founded on African systems, not in the least equally tempered, while it had its basis in natural intervals and the combined sounds resulting from them. In order to "temper" these songs fully, White proceeded to refine them as he transcribed them. The style of their adaptation for male-voice choir was reminiscent of Schubert; these Schubertian adaptations became White's Negro spirituals.

Some years later the University ran out of funds and someone had the bright idea of letting the choir go on tour. By early in 1870 the "Fisk Jubilee Singers" had already staged many concerts, the tours of the Northern States and Europe having been very successful. So much so that almost all spirituals known nowadays are the same as those first sung by the Fisk Jubilee Singers for white audiences: "Deep River," "Go Down, Moses," "Swing Low, Sweet Chariot," "Nobody Knows the Troubles I've Seen," "Little David Play on Your Harp," and so on.[7]

The success can be accounted for by the fact that these songs were not difficult for white audiences to digest. The Schubertian style appealed greatly to them. In this way these often beautiful melodies and catchy or haunting lyrics were displayed in a way that was most agreeable to the Western palate.

Apart from the musical aspect there was another factor that undoubtedly contributed to the success of the choir: the words spoke of faith, oppression and liberation. Imagine for a moment that you were a member of the audience of that time. There on the stage a performance is being given by people who have been subjected to all sorts of wrongs, for generations—and then listen to the beautiful, haunting music. Would there have been a dry eye during "Nobody Knows the Troubles I've Seen"? Indeed, the success of these songs is definitely linked to a certain feeling of sympathy towards these oppressed and sorely tested folk. The great popularity of the spirituals cannot be attributed to the real religious spiritual but to these songs,

7. J. B. T. Marsh, *The Story of the Fisk Jubilee Singers* (Boston); G. D. Pike, *The Jubilee Singers and their Campaign for Twenty Thousand Dollars* (Boston, 1873).

arranged for Western ears and concert stages and awakening all sorts of sentiments.

This is also why we know renditions of the spiritual "Go Down, Moses" from this setting, while it is hardly sung in church these days. This spiritual originates from the Fisk area and it is even possible that it was not known at all in other regions. But more importantly, in the living musical tradition of the blacks who keep producing new songs, a song like this will be forgotten because the content no longer has much bearing on the present circumstances. Only in the concert tradition of Fisk have these songs, while they are an enduring memorial to slavery in the past, been preserved artificially.

A few soloists have emerged from the universities where students strive for emancipation and complete equality with the whites. These soloists—Marian Anderson, Roland Hayes and Paul Robeson, for example—have in their own way contributed to the further westernization of the Negro spiritual. For them as blacks the Negro spiritual had become a kind of obligatory encore piece for every recital or concert. But even if they considered these songs as part of a tradition that still moved them deeply, things are different for a more recent generation of blacks. They often enjoy these songs less, and certainly do not appreciate that they more or less have to sing them: "They remind us too much of the period of slavery."

This leaves black people in a quandary. On the one hand they want to disown the things belonging to their own folklore, art or custom in order to be accepted by whites, while on the other hand whites keep on telling them that their spirituals are the only authentic contribution they have made to the world.

We called this type of spiritual "Schubertian." Indeed, people like Roland Hayes conveyed these songs with so much emotion, rallentandi and accelerandi, so much gesture and emotionalism of a romantic nature that the authentic character of this originally Christian church song is completely lost; pathos and romanticism are after all foreign to this kind of song, which has a steady beat—an expression of peace and certainty—and conveys an emotion of a very different kind. No, White's version, and those of his successors, did not only create technically perfect songs, they also translated them into a language with a completely different attitude to life, into a type of romanticism of which the roots are foreign to Christianity.

The words to the song "Swing Low, Sweet Chariot," made famous by the Fisk Jubilee Singers, mark the end of this chapter. This spiritual, written prior to 1860, is interesting and important enough to contemplate more deeply.

> *Swing low, sweet chariot,*
> *Coming for to carry me home,*
> *Swing low, sweet chariot,*
> *Coming for to carry me home.*
>
> I looked over Jordan and what did I see
> *Coming for to carry me home?*
> A band of angels coming after me,
> *Coming for to carry me home.*[8]

This imagery is most unusual. It is very probable that it is derived from the story of Elijah, who rode to heaven in a chariot. It is an image that apparently had a profound impact on the imagination of the blacks because we come across it often in various ways. Somewhere along the line the chariot was replaced by a train, and it is evident that the "gospel train" evolved from this idea. There is a whole range of variations on the theme: "If I Have a Ticket, Lord, Can I Ride,"[9] "The Gospel Train Is Leaving,"[10] and it also makes its appearance in sermons.[11]

THE BACKGROUND TO THE TRUE SPIRITUAL: "DOWN ON ME"

The nineteenth-century Christianity which emerged from the evangelical churches in Anglo-Saxon countries has often been accused,

8. Fisk University Jubilee Quartet, †† Victor 16453; ca. 1910.
9. Rev. T. E. Weems and congregation, †† Col. 14254-D; ca. 1926–1927.
10. Rev. J. C. Burnett, **** Fontana 467064 TE.
11. E.g., *Noël à Harlem*, ** Ducretet-Thomson 260V069.

and unfortunately not always wrongly, of speaking only of heaven and life in Christ without tackling concrete problems. People were ushered towards Christ as a way out of their problems, but no attempt was made to take action at root level. Of course, this is not the whole picture. These congregations were made up of the lowest social ranks. The simple and poor people had little say in matters outside the church and could do little else than accept their lot in faith and with hope for a new earth. The alternative would have been to take the revolutionary path alongside their socialist fellow sufferers. If anyone is to blame, then not so much the evangelical Baptist and Methodist groups but rather the Anglican and Reformed churches, whose members were generally from well-to-do circles. But it is very well possible that much more was done by these people for social improvement than often assumed, perhaps due to socialist propaganda.

Be that as it may, there seems to be no justification for accusing the blacks of escapism, having their hearts set on heaven, far removed from earthly realities, in a sort of Christian stoicism. The Scriptures teach us to face up to difficulties and trust in God. That, in many respects, is what the blacks did. It is this aspect which emerges from their songs: joy, happiness, a love for others and hope for the future (including the future on earth). They did anything but deny their troubles, even in the face of the most awful circumstances imaginable.

The spiritual "Down on Me" is a classic example:

Down on me, down on me,
Looks like everybody in this whole round world down on me.

Mary and Martha, Luke and John,
All God's prophets dead and gone,
Looks like everybody in this whole round world down on me.

Ain't been to heaven, but I've been told,
Gates is pearl and the streets is gold,
Looks like everybody in this whole round world down on me.

God is God, God is God, rain is rain,
God's a man don't never change, ["God is a man" here refers to
the personal character of God]
Looks like everybody in this whole round world down on me.[12]

This song shows a recurring feature of spirituals: they show us that focusing on the scriptural hope of salvation in Christ Jesus is anything but stoical. The joy that emanates from their songs, and particularly in the delivery, is a testimony to the depth of that joy and to how vital and real that faith and hope in the work of their Lord and Savior was and is. In view of the circumstances of these people, in view of their songs and attitude, is it fair to accuse them of escapism? For those who are familiar with the arrangement and performance of these songs in the spirit of the Fisk Jubilee Singers only, this will not be easily recognized. It is sentimentality, escapism and sorrow which emanate from those versions; the vital, religious spirituals express strength, joy and a sense of reality.

SECULAR FOLK SONGS DURING THE AGE OF SLAVERY: "HERE, RATTLER, HERE"

Although many black Christians sing exclusively spirituals, they also have a large repertoire of what we call folk songs. Some sing them, some do not, but it cannot be said that these songs do absolutely belong to a non-Christian culture. They are the property of all blacks whether they are members of a church or whether they are no longer Christians (in the strict sense of the word). It is necessary to make this distinction because the difference between being a member of a church and not being a member of a church is very marked in African-American culture, and mutual contact is virtually nonexistent in some black villages. Church discipline is strictly adhered to, particularly with regard to conduct. One dance too many on a Saturday evening may provide sufficient cause for action.

12. LiC X, by Dock Reed.

Some of these secular—at least, nonreligious—songs are work songs, some are solos—hollers—which we will come back to later, some are songs to be performed on social occasions (e.g., "Saturday Night Hoe-Down"[13]), some are dance songs (like "Liza Jane"), while solid instrumental music, which played a significant role in the later developments, is also evident. The song "Here, Rattler, Here" dates back to the days of slavery. It deals with a subject that is reminiscent of the story of Uncle Tom's Cabin. It is about a black slave who escapes and is then tracked down and chased by bloodhounds, one of which is called Rattler. "Here, Rattler, Here" is the refrain which is sung by everyone together, while the verses are solos. It is another responsive song.

> Oh, b'lieve to my soul there's a nigger gone,
> *Here, Rattler, here,*
> Oh, b'lieve to my soul there's a nigger gone,
> *Here, Rattler, here.*

> *Here, Rattler,*
> *Here Rattler, here*
> *Here Rattler, here*
> *Here Rattler, here.*

The words of the song continue (somewhat shortened):

> Oh, he went right through the corn.
> I heard the old horn blow.

> Go and get the dog man,
> Go and get the dog man.

> Run that nigger to the riverside,
> Run that nigger to the riverside.

13. *** FoW MS V.

Go and call old Rattler,
Call old Rattler.

Oh, he set so long with the sympathy,
Oh, run that nigger right lost his mind.

Oh, he run that nigger till he went stone blind,
Oh, cross the river to the long leaf pine.

Oh he run so far he didn't leave no sign,
Oh, got a baby here, got a baby there.

Oh, trip this time, I'll trip no more,
Oh, going to the North where you can't go.[14]

The African Americans also sang all sorts of ballads. A very popular one, is about a bad man called Stackolee. It is difficult to say how old it is, but it may have been written after 1870.

Stackolee was a bad man, everybody knows,
Spent about a hundred dollars, for just one suit of clothes,
He was a bad man, that mean old Stackolee.

Stackolee and Billy Lion, fighting on the floor,
Stackolee pulled the trigger, of that smokeless forty-four, [a revolver]
He was a bad man, his name was Stackolee.

Billy the Lion said: 'Stackolee, please don't take my life,
I've got two little babes and a darling little wife,
You're a bad man, your name is Stackolee.'

'Well, what I care for your two little babes, and your darling little
      wife,

14. LiC VIII by Moses Piatt.

You done throw my Stetson hat, now I'm bound to take your life,
I'm a bad man, my name is Stackolee.'

'Well', the judge said: 'Mister Stackolee, Mister Stackolee,
I'm gonna hang your body up, and set your spirits free,
Cause you're a bad man, your name is Stackolee.'[15]

Minstrel Shows: Jim Crow

We can be certain that a considerable number of this sort of folk
songs existed prior to 1860. Not only do we have the testimony of
many that were resident in the South at that time, but the impact of
the songs on Western popular music was also considerable. Minstrel
music particularly owes its emergence to true black music, though
they bore little resemblance to each other. It was popular music, composed by whites, and seldom profound.

As to the origin of minstrel music, it is set to date from 1828
when Daddy Rice put on a cabaret with his group in Baltimore,
Pittsburgh or Louisville. Jim Crow owned the farm behind the concert "hall" (which consisted of a number of tents) and his slave, who
was named after his master as was customary, had a clubfoot. Rice saw
this slave tending the cattle, stumbling around and singing:

Wheelabout, turn about, do just so
And every time I wheelabout, I jump Jim Crow.

Rice proposed that the slave appear in the show. The show was promptly
threatened with a boycott, so Rice borrowed the slave's clothes and,
having blackened his face, performed the slave's "dance" and its accompanying song. It brought the house down. From this originated the
cabaret routines in which whites impersonating blacks performed qua-
si-black songs and dances: the black and white minstrel shows.

15. Mississippi John Hurt, †† Okeh 8654, 1928; and Woody Guthrie a.o., ***†
"Stain Gang" Stinson SL 87.

This is also the origin of the subsequent expression "Jim Crow Regulations" for those rules that segregated black Americans from whites in public places in the Southern States.

Stephen Foster was responsible for the most popular and indeed often charming products of the minstrel show scene. He appeared in Christy's Minstrel Show and, prior to that, composed white American folk songs, some of which have become classics: "My Old Kentucky Home," "Swanee River," "Old Black Joe," "Camptown Races" (mainly played as a cowboy song) and the well-known "Oh Susanna."

The minstrel shows, which toured the Northern States, did not really produce any music that was directly related to authentic black music. Still, the existence of minstrel music is testimony to the fact that the influence of black music was present early on, and that black music was recognized as something remarkable.

Secular Hollers: "Whoa Black"

Blacks who worked as slaves or those who did manual work in poorly paid jobs after 1865 often sang while they worked. Some still do. When they needed to convey a message to someone working further away, they would sing out the message. Those two functions produced the "holler," a call, a song, a free melodic expression, sung exclusively as a solo. Although references to faith and the Bible may be heard, they are not typically religious in content but of a rather secular nature.

These hollers, often very beautiful, provide a distinct musical expression of great originality alongside the spirituals and, later, the blues. They are almost always sung very slowly and solemnly, thereby enabling the voice to be fully exploited, and falsetto is often heard. The melodic lines are very capricious, moving from phrases in spoken verse to drawn-out melodies, only to switch suddenly to a faster passage, a rest or something like a scream. There are pieces that resemble yodels albeit in slow tempo.

Where did the holler originate? This sort of music possibly has traces of African influence, but it seems more likely that it is connected with the church songs we discussed earlier, sung in the way of the psalms and hymns of Dr. Watts. When these are sung solo, the result is very similar to the holler and we may suppose that churchgoers sang their favorite songs alone, whether working at home or on the land. We hear a succession of spoken and sung parts, the melodic structure of the latter being very capricious, strung out and free. If we listen to Suddie Griffiths, for example, who sings hymns that date back to the nineteenth century (and appear in nineteenth-century Baptist hymnbooks),[16] the relationship becomes very evident. The holler may therefore amount to little more than the time-honored hymn, but now fully secularized. The way in which it was sung would have been that of a hymn, the words freely composed, springing from the singer's circumstances, but as to content it was definitely not a church song.

This holler was sung by a farmer to his draught animal whilst ploughing the land. A recording of the music (by Lomax) is still available.[17]

> O . . . a-whoooo . . . whoo . . . oo (etc.)
> Sometimes I plough the old grey mare,
> And then I plough the cuddy,
> When I make my fifty cents, Lord,
> I carry it home to Rosie.

Spoken:
> Come here Old Mule.

> Whoo . . . Whoo . . . Lordy Lord,
> Somebody stole my old coon dog,
> Boys I wish he'd bring him back,
> He run them big ones over the fence,
> Boys, and the little ones thru the crack.
> Hee, whoo . . . whoo . . . (etc.)

16. ** FoW MS VI.
17. *** *Murderer's Home*, Nixa NJL 11.

Spoken:

> Right Old Flat Tom, we're going to make some corn this year boy.

> I been rollin', rollin', rollin',
> Boys we gotta make that money,
> We're gonna take it home to Rosie.
> Whoo . . . whoo . . . whoo-a'whoo . . .
> Black gal wear the brogan shoe,
> The yellow gal wear the slipper,
> I don't care what Old Flat says,
> We're gonna ride in a Lincoln Zephyr.

Here is another example. The farm-laborer in question would have been lying on his back in the shade during the very hot hours of the afternoon. Then he starts to sing—a holler, of course. He sings to himself, as it were, meditating aloud. It is not a story, neither a ballad, but an utterance that flows from his situation. On the other hand he may not be singing of his present circumstances at all but be making it up, though not just anything, as we will discuss later. Who is to say what the origin of the tune is? Unlike the previous example, which reminds us of a white folk song as sung by a cowboy, the tune is vaguely reminiscent of a spiritual. Rich Amerson of Livingston, Alabama, sings:

> Well I said come back here black woman
> Ah-umm, don't you hear me crying, oh Lordy!
> Ah-hum, I say run here black woman,
> I want you to sit on black Daddy's knee, Lord.
> M-hmm, don't your house feel lonesome,
> When your biscuit-roller gone.

> I'm going to Texas mamma,
> Just to hear the wild ox moan,
> Lord help my crying time I'm going to Texas,
> Mamma to hear the wild ox moan!
> And if they moan to suit me,

I'm going to bring a wild ox home.
Ah-hum, I say I got to go to Texas mamma.
Etc.[18]

It is evident that the singer lets his thoughts take over, alternating between fantasy and reality.

There are many more examples we could show here. The song of the assistant pilot, the man who is employed to take soundings by throwing a plumb line into the Mississippi[19] and who then sings the measurements to the captain on the bridge. Then there is the song of the foreman instructing his workers, who are unloading railway tracks. The holler is a type of song that is freely rhapsodic, with variable lyrics, springing from circumstance and the inspiration of the moment.

THE ORIGIN OF THE BLUES: "BLUES AT SUNRISE"

After the spiritual came the blues, another preeminently African-American music style that originated in the nineteenth century, probably between 1880 and 1900. Its roots can be traced to the Mississippi basin, the land along the river where so many blacks live and work. The blues was not invented by city slickers or university students; rather, it is a pure form of folk music.

It would not however be true to say that the blues suddenly came into being, just like that. Nothing happens just like that, and something as well balanced as the blues certainly cannot simply be called forth. It was, we think, the brainchild of artists, a sort of compilation and refinement of all the existing black folk music. The primary constituent has to be the holler, but folk and work songs are also main ingredients, while instrumental music like that of the string bands (which we will be discussing later) may well have influenced the style of accompaniment. While it is certainly true that artists shaped the blues, we must realize that these were no sophisticated,

18. ** FoW EFL 1417 – Ruby Pickins Tartt discovered the singer Rich Amerson.
19. LiC VIII.

trained composers in the Western sense. We suppose that the artists who forged the blues were real folk artists, wandering troubadours who accompanied their own songs on the guitar or mouth organ whenever they were able to find an audience. We encounter the spirit and character of these people beautifully in Fenton Johnson's poem:

> There is music in me, the music of the peasant people.
> I wander through the levee, picking my banjo and singing my
> songs of the cabin and the field. At the *Last Chance*
> *Saloon* I am as welcome as the violets in March. There
> is always food and drink for me there, and the dimes of
> those who love honest music.
> Behind the railroad tracks the little children clap their hands and
> love me as they love Kris Kringle.
>
> But I fear I am a failure.
> Last night a woman called me a troubadour.
>
> What is a troubadour?[20]

A troubadour of this kind used many different sorts of folk music to make a new art form—the blues. This means that the blues cannot be referred to as the common property of all blacks. The blues sung by ordinary people is almost always derived from the work of these troubadours, and this is plainly evident later, when the influence of gramophone recordings can almost always be demonstrated.[21] We may also see blacks from rural areas, who have not yet mastered the complex structure of the blues, translating the song back into a holler.

There is a nice example of this in "Black Snake Blues." This was first sung by Blind Lemon Jefferson, one of the best-known folk artists, and highly esteemed by blacks. The first few bars of his song (later

20. Langston Hughes, Arna Bontemps, *The Poetry of the Negro 1746–1949* (Garden City, NY, 1953).

21. Cf. e.g., LiC IV, McKinley Morganfield (and text on leaflet).

recorded around 1925[22]) are a sort of drawn-out hum, reminiscent of the holler, but the song in its totality is very definitely a blues song:

> Oh . . . ain't got no mamma now,
> Oh . . . ain't got no mamma now,
> She told me late last night, You don't need no mamma nohow
> [The typically black expression "mamma" means
> "beloved," as does "pappa."]

Horace Sprott, a simple farmhand from rural Alabama, tells (in 1954) he had heard Blind Lemon Jefferson singing this blues song. He even recalls how it went and proceeds to demonstrate. It is the same song, the same lyrics, but the first line is not repeated; it lacks the twelve-bar structure and it is sung in exactly the same way as a holler.[23]

There was probably much experimentation at first and we may be able to detect remnants of this in divergent variations and in structurally simpler songs,[24] but the blues as a finished product has a highly original, fixed structure. It is constructed on a simple, gentle 4/4 time, harmonically based on a simple pattern where tonic, dominant and subdominant alternate. The "blue note," a minor third or seventh within the otherwise major tonality is often heard. These strange blue notes help to give the blues its own character; they also show that this music originates from a milieu in which our *wohltemperierte* musical system (or music system of equal temperament) was little known. (We will gladly leave the music-historical complications of this to the experts.)

Unlike the sixteen-bar scheme of white popular music and the eight-bar scheme of the spiritual, the blues uses a twelve-bar structure. This is then divided up into three parts of four bars. A phrase that is sung during the first four beats is repeated in the second four, while

---

22. **† Jazz Society AA 513 (78 r.p.m.); London AL 3508 (small LP).

23. * FoW MS IV.

24. E.g., "Another Man Done Gone Down," by Vera Hall, LiC IV; Joe Williams, "Baby Please Don't Go," †† Bluebird B 6200, 1934.

the third four bars close the verse with a line which, together with the first phrase, forms a sentence. The blues is thus based on an AAB pattern. The tune and lyrics form a close bond. Irrespective of the number of syllables, each line contains a number of strongly accented points that form the supports for the melody. These supports often occur on the first and third beats of the first bar, on the first and third beats of the second bar, and always at the end of a line. This last beat almost always coincides with the first beat of the third bar. The line for the vocalist therefore contains just two-and-a-quarter or two-and-a-half bars. The musicians then fill in the remainder of the line. There is almost always a caesura in the vocalist's line—a rest which coincides with the position of the comma. Here is an example, although it must be said that the accentuation rarely falls precisely on the beats. Furthermore, there will be all manner of small deviations from this pattern to ensure that the audience remains enthralled.

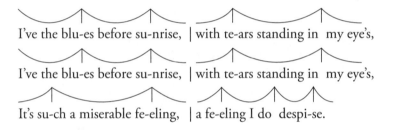

The second strophe:

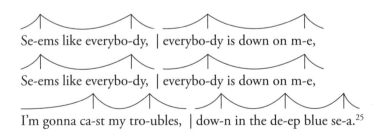

25. **** Fontana 462021 TE. In this analysis I have borrowed a lot from an unpublished study about the blues of the late Drs. F. G. Boom. Cf. the LP *Nothing but the Blues* that I compiled: **** Fontana 682073 TL.

The harmonic pattern is repeated in each strophe and the melody remains almost identical. The tension is built up during the first two lines, reaches its climax at the end of the second line and then disperses in the third line. The third line rounds off both the lyrics and the melody. Each strophe forms a complete unit. This example features all sorts of little tricks which are characteristic of one of the best blues singers available on record, Leroy Carr. He composed this blues music and wrote the lyrics. The repetition of the word "everybody," strongly emphasized in the second strophe, is particularly beautiful. His language is very poetic. For instance, look at the following line:

> Sun rises in the East, and sets well in the West,
> Sun rises in the East, sets well in the West,
> It's hard to tell, hard to tell, which one will treat you the best.[26]

The singer is wondering here whether it is the beginning or the end of the day that is best for him in his troubles.

The blues song is meditative. Barely more than two bars are sung for every four played. The rest is given over to instrumental music by the guitar, perhaps, or other accompanying instruments. The guitar is, however, the most characteristic instrument of these blues singers-cum-troubadours and together with the Spaniards they may be called masters of this instrument. Big Bill Broonzy was such a master and his music has been recorded on a number of LPs.[27] The meditative aspect is strongly enhanced by the instrumental parts.

So the blues is the song of secular African-American culture. No black Christians would sing the blues; the content of the songs would be considered incompatible with their faith. The content is indeed curious. The songs tell of worries and troubles and presuppose a rather immoral lifestyle. It must be said, however, that this is partly due to the past, the slavery, when the owner was at liberty to sell his slaves

26. †† Bluebird B 5877, 1935.
27. **** Vogue LD030; ** Philips B08102L.

42

irrespective of their family and to bring men and women together as he wished. The blues emerged from an impoverished world, a world of people who stand on the very bottom rung of the social ladder. It would hardly be fair to blame blacks for this, as the Jim Crow regulations made progress almost impossible.

It remains remarkable that while the main subject matter of the blues is love, the songs are seldom or never coarse or vulgar. Sex is certainly referred to and taken for granted, but the blues is rarely "dirty," and sexual relations, as such, rarely or never besmirched. That only happens with a certain type of blues, sung in nightclubs and intended for white ears. (We shall come to it later.) The blues is based on poetic fiction, as is the case in European songwriting. In the case of the latter, falling in love and flirting are central. It is widely recognized that the rather sturdy singer on the stage, declaring his love for the pretty miller's daughter as he sings Schubert's cycle of Die schone Mullerin ("The Pretty Miller-Girl"), has not actually fallen in love with this particular girl. In the same way the worries, troubles and strife which the blues singer laments, are not necessarily part of his personal experience. The subject of the poetic fiction of this black music is abandonment: the abandoned singer tells of how his beloved left him, and how he has got the blues, which proves how much he loved her. An appeal to return, a desire to contact her is often included and, at the same time, a desire to escape from the torment. Travelling as migrant workers was indeed characteristic of these poor people and the music speaks of a permanent state of migration. This is confirmed by the incidence of geographical knowledge of the Southern States in these songs. Finally, besides a healthy dose of characteristic humor, there is a certain amount of optimism, as in this traditional line, which is often heard: "The sun's going to shine in my back door some day."

Here are one or two examples of blues lyrics. Firstly, the "Midnight Hour Blues" by Leroy Carr:

> In the wee midnight hour, long before the break of day, (x2)
> When the blues creep upon you and carry your mind away.

While I lay in my bed, and cannot go to sleep, (x2)
While my heart's in trouble and my mind is thinking deep.

My mind was running back to the days of long ago, (x2)
And the one I love, I don't see her anymore.

Blues why do you worry me, why do you stay so long, (x2)
You came to me yesterday, been with me all night long.

I've been so worried, I didn't know what to do, (x2)
So I guess that's why I've had these 'midnight hour blues'.[28]

There are few blues songs that deviate from the above in content. The following example is a particular exception. The background is that "grades of skin color" were prevalent in the USA—a sort of apartheid or segregation. School clubs were structured according to skin color[29] and the males, in their search for a partner, strove for the "bonus" female whose skin was lighter than their own. It is also useful to know that African Americans were not particularly fond of South Americans, whom they referred to as "monkey men."

So glad I'm brownskin, glad I'm brownskin, chocolate to the
        bone,
So glad I'm brownskin, chocolate to the bone,
And I got what it takes to make a monkey man leave his home.

Black man is evil, yellow man so lowdown, ["yellow" here refers
        to light brown]
Black man is evil, yellow man so lowdown, I walk into these
        houses,
just to see these black men frown.

28. See note 25.
29. Anonymous, *Belle Bradley: Her Story* (New York, 1953).

I just like Miss Lillian, like Miss Lillian, I mean Miss Glynn you see,
I like Miss Lillian, I mean Miss Lillian you see,
She said: 'A brownskin man is just all right with me.'

Yellow man won't quit, black man just won't behave,
Yellow man won't quit, and a black man just won't behave,
Got a pigmeat mamma crazy 'bout brownskin baby ways.

I got a yellow mamma, got a yellow mamma, she always got a
      pleasant smile,
I got a yellow mamma, she always got a pleasant smile,
But that brownskin gal with her coalblack dreamy eyes.[30]

THE BACKGROUND TO THE BLUES: BLUES AND TROUBLE

There are other aspects of the blues worth mentioning before we bring the subject to a close, because it is evident that, in contrast to Western entertainment music, which abandons the concept of everyday reality, blues music is very realistic. This comparison is important because popular music, cabaret music, schmaltz intended for home listening, dancing to or otherwise, has replaced the folk music of the West. It has become the new folk music—the music of the "folk," as it were. It is barely conceivable that entertainment music would sing of the somber side of life. A reference to a valley of tears may occur in a sentimental song, but that same sentimentality removes it from everyday reality with little elaboration of the situation. I am convinced that the realism in African-American music can be partly attributed to biblical preaching. Its influence is evident, even when the church has been abandoned by the songwriter. Christianity is not opposed in these lyrics; in fact there are many songs that show that writers were familiar with the Bible and, although they may not have lived up to it, considered it to be the truth. One well-known example is the traditional line, "The Good Book [the Bible] says you got to reap just what

---

30. Barbecue Bob (= Robert Hicks), †† Col. 14331-D.

you sowed." The Bible does not teach us to escape from reality and neither does it teach us stoicism. It does not teach us to say "all that misery does not bother me," but to face up to problems and hardships, to look to God for help and to expect it from him. The Scriptures teach us to break with superficial escapism, pretending there is nothing wrong. In the light of this we can understand the true-to-life realism of the songs, including the secular ones, of the blacks.

This spirit is anything but self-evident. Would it not seem more appropriate for the indigent blacks in their songs to seek escape from reality, to sing of their wishful dreams?

The blues and spirituals certainly share a similar realistic approach. We have already talked about "Down on Me"; this is another spiritual:

> Wait and see what your brother will do:
> Before your face have a love for you.
> Behind your back scandalize your name,
> Just the same you have to bear the blame.[31]

Can we imagine a European folk song like this?

> Death is awful, death is awful, death is awful,
> Spare me over another year.
> This is the way that death begins,
> You stretch your limbs and close your eyes,
> Death is awful, death is awful,
> Death, spare me over another year.[32]

That was a spiritual. The following line is characteristic of the blues:

> Blues and trouble, seem to be my best friends (x2)
> When my blues leaves me, then my trouble begins.[33]

31. LiC III.
32. **** FoW FP 38, Dock Reed and Vera Hall Ward.
33. Snitcher Roberts, *Snitcher's Blues*, †† Okeh 8781, 1930; and the Fontana record mentioned in note 23.

Sometimes the blues cites a piece of proverbial wisdom like this. Another example is the recurring notion which Snitcher Roberts put into words like this:

> When I have money, I have friends from miles around, (x2)
> Ain't got no money, then my friends cannot be found.

> Some give me a nickel, some give me a lousy dime, (x2)
> Some people say: 'Baby, you was never an old friend of mine.'[34]

One of the most curious examples of this attitude can be heard in the "Moppin' Blues" by Big Bill Broonzy. It is a song which shows that in spite of their circumstances, the blacks did not display rampant revolutionary sentiments. It also shows that they had not yet learned to express the concept of human rights. They were not aware of society's obligation to provide for them. What they did express was great joy and openness—cheerfulness under the most testing circumstances. There was no escapism—they faced the difficulties positively; no bitterness, in spite of everything. A song like the following one shows the strong influence of scriptural preaching and its effect on a milieu which was anything but churchgoing. It also shows the secret of these people, how they were able to survive during all those years of oppression and poverty.

The joy that can be heard in the song is definitely real, and the chorus betrays no pretense—no superficial que sera sera. It is a typically Western thought, anyway, to assume that happiness and cheerfulness are superficial, and that melancholy, sadness and seriousness are the only deep emotions.

The singer tells how he is sweeping a building out, alone. He has nothing, no house, no money, nothing to lose apart from his "moppin' broom"—his broom. Still, the chorus confirms, "I'm the happiest man in town." As always, the blues is played in a major key, apart from the blue notes (i.e., minor notes in an otherwise major key),

---

34. Idem.

although this example is played particularly briskly. Each strophe contains twelve bars, but the structure is unusual. In fact it is probably an early form of the blues, dating back to the time before a structure was established. Each line contains two bars.

I've got the moppin' blues, (x5)
But I'm the happiest man in town.

You know I can't lose (x5)
Nothin' but this moppin' broom I knew.

I'm all alone, (x5)
But I'm the happiest man in town.

I ain't got no money, (x5)
But I'm the happiest man in town.

I ain't got no home, (x5)
But I'm the happiest man in town.[35]

THE BLUES AS SUNG BY MA RAINEY ET AL.: "BACKWATER BLUES"

Besides the mainly male, itinerant troubadour blues singers, there were also some women who played the blues. They were the core of the travelling shows—groups who toured from one place to another and held their gigs in tents. Bands of this type had already existed for some time in America—the minstrel shows, as we have seen, had been around a while—and it was understandable that black groups like this would also develop to perform for exclusively black audiences. Also blues were sung at these gigs where the climax of the evening was provided by the likes of Ma Rainey. She was regarded as a great artist by her own folk, and rightly so, for the many records we have of her music bear witness to this fact.

35. **** Vogue LD030.

Usually accompanied by a small orchestra/band—she did not play the guitar, unlike most troubadours—she sang blues which she had composed herself, or drew on tradition. Her orchestra/band always comprised of a piano and a guitar, and was often joined by a trumpet, clarinet and trombone. The passages that were not sung—generally the last two bars of a four-bar line—were taken over by the instruments. Ma Rainey and other singers of her genre had no formal music education and their voices were not "trained" according to Western standards. But that in itself does not make them natural voices. Here too we find a certain artistic, deliberate style of singing that builds on the tradition of the hollers and uses the voice in a very distinctive way. This style of singing is varied, not based on the violin like our Western singing tradition,[36] and the potential of the voice is fully tapped. The rendition is always based on the text, for the singer as well as for the musicians; madrigalisms, i.e., direct illustrations of the text, often occur: when she sings "moan" for example, the trombone will make a moaning sound; when she says "laugh" we hear the trumpet laughing; while other words like "rain," "whistlin'" (of a train), and so on are also depicted by the instruments. The tempo is usually gentle, never very slow, never sentimental, the rendition always powerful but at the same time never wild, rough or uncontrolled. The only way to recognize these characteristics is to listen to the music. This is no simple matter for us Westerners because the songs have their own style, which is anything but Western or Schubert-like, and equally little redolent of Africa. This art form is pure African American; it is a new art form, completely the creation of North American blacks.

To give you an idea of the impression that "Ma" (this was her nickname, and it testifies to her popularity) Gertrude Rainey made on her audiences, let me quote a poem by Sterling Brown, written prior to 1932. Ma Rainey's golden years as an artist were between 1900 and 1930; her stamping ground was almost exclusively the Southern States.

36. Cf. M. W. Stearns, *The Story of Jazz* (London, 1957), p. 276.

49

When Ma Rainey
Comes to town,
Folks from any place,
Miles aroun',
From Cape Girardeau,
Poplar Bluff,
Flocks in to hear
Ma do her stuff;
Comes fliwerin' in,
Or ridin' mules,
Or packed in trains,
Picknickin' fools . . .
That's what it's like,
For miles on down,
To New Orleans Delta
An' Mobile town,
When Ma hits
Anywheres aroun'.

Dey comes to hear Ma Rainey from the little river settlements,
From Blackbottom cornrows and from lumber camps;
Dey stumble in de hall, jes' a-laughin' an' a-cacklin',
Cheerin' lak roarin' water, lak wind in river swamps.

An' some jokers keeps deir laugh's a-goin' in de crowded aisles,
An' some folks sits dere waitin' wid deir aches an' miseries,
Till Ma comes out before dem, a-smilin' gold-toofed smiles,
An' Long Boy ripples minors on de black and yellow keys.

O Ma Rainey
Sing yo' song;
Now you's back
Whah you belong,
Git way inside us,
Keep us strong . . .

O Ma Rainey,
Li'l and low;
Sing us 'bout de hard luck
Roun' our do';
Sing us bout de lonesome road
We mus' go . . .

I talked to a fellow, an' the fellow say:
'She jes' catch hold of us, somekindaway.
She sang "Backwater blues" one day:
"It rained fo' days an' de skies was dark at night,
Trouble taken place in de lowlands at night.
Thundered an' lightened an' the storm begin to roll,
Thousan's of people ain't got no place to go.

"Den I went an' stood upon some high ol' lonesome hill,
An' looked down on de place where I used to live."

An' den de folks, dey natchally bowed dey heads an' cried,
Bowed dey heavy heads, shet dey moufs up tight an' cried,
An' Ma lef de stage, an' followed some de folks outside.'

Dere wasn't much more de fellow say:
Shejes' gits hold of us dataway.[37]

This is the well-known "Backwater Blues," inspired by a Mississippi flood and later made famous by one of Ma's pupils, Bessie Smith, who never bettered her teacher—just occasionally equaled her. "Backwater" refers to the water which, having burst through a dike elsewhere, floods the area from the land side.[38]

37. Sterling Brown, *Ma Rainey, Southern Road* (New York, 1932), pp. 62–64.
38. Records of Ma Rainey reissued on London, a.o. **** London AL 3502.

The First Brass Band Music: "I'm Going Up the Country"

Socially there was not much going on in the plantations; the odd party was held. But 4th July—Independence Day—was earmarked as a day of celebration. There were barbecues, and musical accompaniment was guaranteed. Slaves were often used as musicians in the brass bands. They played patriotic songs like "Hail Columbia," "President's March," "Hail to the Heroes Whose Triumph Have Brightened" and "The Star-Spangled Banner," but also less distinguished pieces like "Yankee Doodle" and "Wait for the Wagon."

After the Northerners won the Civil War, the slaves were freed and these blacks began to play their own music—spirituals, folk songs, early blues, etc.—on the instruments they had kept. They played mainly for dance parties, and the dances that were performed to this music were the real folk dances of the rural areas.

Such bands cropped up all over the South and, as we shall see, contributed to the emergence of jazz. In the 1950s they could only be heard in very remote areas such as rural Alabama, for example, where Ramsey made recordings of the Lapsey Band and the Laneville Johnson Brass Band in 1954. These musicians are farmers who play at rural dance parties while they are waiting for the harvest. The Lapsey Band bears the name of the plantation where their ancestors, more than a century ago, were slaves. The Laneville Johnson Brass Band was created through the amalgamation of the Laneville and the Johnson Bands.

The musicians play exclusively by ear on old brass instruments like the cornet, the horn, the valve-trombone, and on drums they inherited from their ancestors, instruments that would not be out of place in the nearest museum. They have a traditional repertoire that consists predominantly of spirituals and folk songs, such as "Precious Lord, Hold My Hand," "Take Rocks and Gravel to Build a Solid Road," "Preaching Tonight on the Old Campground," "Dixie" and "Going Up the Country, Don't You Want to Go."

Their music is rough and little refined, but how would these amateurs have been able to refine their technique? Still, it seems to me that Ramsey's recordings, while they provide us with a valuable addition to our archives, are qualitatively misleading; the oompah of the horn, which sets the rhythm, has been recorded a bit too loudly in comparison with the other instruments.[39] This is not surprising since the recordings were made at night, in the open air and in poor weather conditions.

String Bands: "Hootchie Kootchie"

It is hard to say when the string band came into being. It possibly started on Saturday evenings, after the slaves had had a day off. They would dance and sing, make music and tell stories to each other. On the other hand, the custom to play like this may have arisen only after liberation. In any event, string bands seem to have been around as far back as we are able to trace. They are small, informal bands composed of amateur musicians. All manner of stringed instruments are played, guitar and banjo being the first to come to mind. One indication that this form of music has existed for a long time is the fact that the banjo—an instrument developed by the blacks—is now considered an old instrument, one that existed in the days of slavery and was used way back in the minstrel shows as an instrument to give the black parody its couleur locale.

There is little material to give us an exact picture of the string-band music of the nineteenth century. The few later recordings provide little insight as most of the musicians in question will have been exposed, remotely at least, to the development of jazz. We suspect that the character of the music played in the nineteenth century was not unlike the white folk-dance music that still exists today in the Appalachians—remote parts of Carolina and Virginia. These square dances were played on fiddles, five-stringed banjos, guitars, dulcimers (dating back to the seventeenth century) and accordions.[40] So the black string bands played a rendition of white folk music, which in

39. FoW MS I.
40. † Traditional Recordings, (Col), TPL 1007.

turn was reproduced by whites in their minstrel shows—the cakewalk, for example, which was an early form of ragtime.

The most important recording is once again to be found in the Folkways series,[41] recorded in Vicksburg, Mississippi. Old examples are very rare, because record companies seldom recorded music by amateur bands. We believe that the Dallas String Band, possibly a professional group who made famous the "Dallas Rag,"[42] provides us with quite a good example of this sort of music.

RAGTIME: "MAPLE LEAF RAG"

Although the 25 years after their liberation were in many ways not easy for the former slaves, they did have more opportunities and discrimination did not take on its really ugly forms until after 1900.[43] In any case, African Americans began to feel their way in the world of music. It is quite understandable that the very first music they took hold of was minstrel music, particularly banjo music, which is distantly related to string-band music.[44] They tried to improve the music by arranging it more in line with the musical practice of their own background, and to develop it as a characteristic pianistic art.

This is a brief outline of the origins of ragtime. Shortly after its birth, between 1895 and 1900, it became the rage in the USA and, inevitably, its commercial viability destined it for a very wide audience looking only for rhythmic entertainment. We must not forget, however, that the musicians, mainly from St. Louis and surrounding areas—such as Scott Joplin and Tom Turpin—were real artists with serious ideas and ambitions. Their music was far from straightforward and their use of the piano was particularly rich and versatile. Piano rolls, published at the beginning of the twentieth century for mechanical pianos, give only a faint idea of the achievement of these

41. *** FoW MS V.

42. *** FoW FP53 (Jazz, vol I, the South).

43. Cf. R. W. Logan, *The Negro in the United States* (Princeton, NY, 1957), p. 39 ff.

44. A late example from before 1920 is HCJ - Fred van Eps, *Ragtime Creole*.

musicians, also in an artistic sense, though it is sufficient to convince anyone who really wants to hear.[45]

Ragtime is composed music that is published as sheet music. The fact that all of the important ragtime composers were black (with the exception of Joseph Lamb) may be considered as further evidence that ragtime indeed had its origins in African-American music. We have already mentioned Scott Joplin, who even ventured a ragtime opera.[46] A striking characteristic of ragtime is the prolific use of the syncopation, but it was written of Joplin that,

> although syncopation remained an essential component of the musical resources he used, he pushed it aside to some extent. His phrasing is longer, his harmonies more complex. He uses more modulation and often more than one key within a sixteen-bar strophe. Three features of his art particularly stand out: greater freedom of the left hand, the attempt to make the beat more implicit than explicit, and a renewed or at least greater interest in matters of form.[47]

Joplin's ragtime, in contrast to popular ragtime, was not reduced to a formula, i.e., a particular type of melody with much syncopation, a definite rhythm produced by the left hand (referred to in the trade as "pumping"), in pursuit of a stereotypical construction.

We would like to refer briefly to musical structure here, because it helps to explain some of the typical features of later New Orleans jazz. Firstly, the sixteen-bar form is central, constructed of a four-bar phrase, which is repeated, and repeated again (note that the basic chords of the repeated phrases may vary), plus a counter melody of

---

45. *** London AL 3515 and HCJ.

46. Literature about ragtime: R. Blesh and H. Janis, *They All Played Ragtime* (New York, 1950; second ed. 1959); G. Waterman, "A Survey of Ragtime," *Record Changer* XIV:7 (New York, 1956); G. Waterman, "Joplin's Late Rags," *Record Changer* XIV:8 (1956). These articles have been reprinted in M. T. Williams, *The Art of Jazz* (New York, 1959).

47. G. Waterman, "Joplin's Late Rags," *Record Changer* XIV:8 (1956), p. 5.

four bars. The following structure however, occurs more often: a four-bar phrase, which is repeated followed by the counter melody, plus a repeat of the first phrase. These sixteen bars are then usually repeated and are followed by a new sixteen-bar section, which also is repeated, and so on, leading to the common pattern of AABBAACCAADD, or more frequently AABBC-CDD (each capital letter represents a sixteen-bar section). The various themes are not in contrast to each other; there is no mood change in the piece as a whole, neither does the tempo change (no accelerandi, just as in other African-American music). The meter is always even, mostly 4/4. Little research has been carried out in this field so far. There must be much of aesthetic value among the large amount of sheet music published in the course of the first decade of the twentieth century waiting to be discovered. The following poem, published by Stark, has been reproduced with permission. Stark published a lot of work in this area (including all Joplin's work), continually emphasizing aesthetic significance as opposed to commercial imitations. He said, for example:

> Publishers are known to hold that the best songs never become hits. The pieces which are all the rage in the cinemas and bars are songs with a twist to draw attention or a dog barking, a cat mewing, hooters or ships' whistles [this was pre-1920, these things were still a novelty], and by the second hearing they sound as flat as a pancake. Sales techniques are also far removed from our idea of how the 'art divine' should be propagated.

He then continues by quoting this poem:

> Full many a gem of purest ray serene
> The deep unfathomed caves of ocean bear,
> Full many a flower was born to blush unseen,
> And wash its fragrance in the desert air.
>
> Full many a mushy, gushy song—and vile
> Is sold by methods—sure the devil's own,

Full many a gem of art and love—the while
Lies silent, sadly waiting to be known.[48]

This poem is entitled "Maple Leaf Rag," taken from the title of Joplin's debut piece from 1897, which is also his best-known work.

48. Blesh and Janis, *They All Played Ragtime*, pp. 253, 254.

3

Twentieth Century:
Pre–World War I

New Orleans around 1900: "Eh La-Bas"

A new cultural phenomenon, a new style or new art does not suddenly spring up out of the blue. Neither can we explain the new on the basis of a single factor; that would be insufficient for more than a fleeting manifestation. If the new is to be awarded a permanent place in the annals of history it will have to prove itself in depth and breadth—depth, to make a deep impression on the audience, and breadth, to remain solidly founded, even if one contributing factor changes.

The above applies to the birth of jazz in New Orleans around the turn of the twentieth century—it cannot be accounted for by a single factor. It was neither the brothels of this port nor the Storyville bars that led to the birth of jazz. The fact that so many jazz writers get wrapped up in the red-light district of New Orleans can be attributed to a craving for colorful sensation, for lawless sleaze (albeit "written" sensation and sleaze). Historical truth does not benefit from such cravings and they do not explain anything. Economic and social conditions did sometimes lead to black musicians seeking employment in the brothels, but the very notion that a real jazz band, with music that is so far from sentimental and sweet, would actually have found

59

its niche in a brothel is so obviously misguided that we have to refute it out of hand.

The music flourished and there was a profusion of enthusiastic musicians (often more semiprofessional than professional), which can partly be attributed to the fact that instruments could be bought very cheaply from the junk shops in New Orleans. The army, which had fought in Cuba against Spain, had shortly before been disbanded, and with it the military bands. This paved the way for the poor, who in this case were blacks, to get hold of instruments which they otherwise would not have been able to afford. This does not, however, explain the birth of jazz music. Let me explain what happened in New Orleans during the first ten to fifteen years of the twentieth century.

The original name for New Orleans was La Nouvelle-Orleans, and it was the capital of the colony of Louisiana, founded by the French during the reign of Louis XIV. This area was bought by the Yankees at the beginning of the nineteenth century, but it retained its French character for a long time—Roman Catholic and French-speaking. It is remarkable that this city, with one of the key ports for the slave trade, freed blacks long before the Civil War and that there was little racial discrimination. Colored people were socially divided from whites, belonging to different classes, but that is where the differences ended. After 1865 the coloreds began to fare quite well and the Creoles (of mixed descent) in particular formed a flourishing middle class. The old French families and the well-off Creoles lived in the Vieux Carre, the old city. The culture of the Creoles was French, not only in terms of their language but also in terms of morals and customs.

Those who could afford it sent their children to be educated in France and, even though they were only part-French, they called themselves French and looked to France for their roots. Music played an important part in their lives. French opera held a central place in their culture and both amateur and professional orchestras were of a high standard. Creoles also had a great love for marching music, which had flourished during the Napoleonic era. New Orleans was no different from the French provincial towns in this respect.

The Creoles lived in a part of town called Downtown. To the

west, on the other side of the road, lay Uptown, the home of the Anglo-Saxon Americans who had come to live there at a later time. In the poorer neighborhoods lived blacks who had left their rural homes for the cities, where they hoped to make a living as casual laborers. The musical traditions of these country folk lived on in the blues, string-band music and folk music, but also in the spirituals that were sung in the Baptist Churches.

Both Creoles and blacks had been doing quite well after the Civil War. Access to the higher positions was not closed and many held important positions, right up to the State Parliament. This changed in 1890 when discrimination became harsher, even in these parts.[1] As a consequence both the Creoles and the blacks became impoverished. Creoles were forced out of their positions as a result of boycotts and discrimination, while blacks were increasingly socially and economically deprived. Music formed an escape route with many opportunities to play at parties, weddings, festivals, picnics with dancing, and so on. It was a well-established custom that Downtown Creoles played in Uptown. The number of blacks from rural areas who sought employment from the Uptown whites also kept growing. Competition was born—the contrast was sometimes sharp but it made contact possible—and an exchange took place of their respective heritages.

The Downtown Creoles provided the music strictly according to the French palate—they were technically capable and good at reading scores at parties, while the blacks, possibly in order to honor their own culture as opposed to that of the Creoles, played more American music. They took greater liberties in their interpretation of the printed notes (going so far as to pretend that they could not read music), and there were many features typical of their own tradition that gave the music its own character. Occasionally they played the blues (Bolden apparently being the first to do so in 1896).

The musical flavor that the Creoles introduced to the mixture of styles—the socioeconomic situation created a necessity to merge

1. See note 43 of the previous chapter and also S. B. Charters, *Jazz: New Orleans 1885–1957* (NY: Belleville 1958), p. 3.

in many areas—was very significant for the new music which was to emerge, namely New Orleans jazz. A typically French playing style can sometimes still be detected in the clarinet pieces—tunes like "High Society" (an old French march) give their origin away. Grace and lightness were generally regarded as the Creole-French contribution, while their extensive knowledge of the theory and technique of music must not be underestimated and will certainly have been important to jazz musicians.

We mentioned that Creole-French elements can sometimes be detected, but besides that some of the old traditions are still alive in New Orleans as well. Kid Ory was able to play old songs like "Blanche Touquatoux" in 1945, sung in the French dialect Creole patois. Then there is "Eh La-Bas" ("There Downtown"), recorded in New Orleans in 1944,[2] which has a strong flavor of the French chanson. Old French quadrilles are occasionally still danced.[3]

BLACK MUSIC IN NEW ORLEANS: "219 BLUES"

African Americans who came to New Orleans later brought their own traditions with them—including their spirituals, blues, folk songs and work songs. We hear a reverberation of the latter in Oliver's "Snag It."[4] Some of the stylistic eccentricities of the trumpet are reminiscent of the way black preachers deliver their sermons; the taste for rendering a melody together, while each one is free to sing his or her own version—not unisonant or homophonic, but with a sort of restrained polyphony—to some extent resembles the way Dr. Watts' hymns were (and still are) sung, and dancing songs such as "Liza Jane" and children's songs such as "Sally Walker," even though they have been transformed (e.g., Armstrong's "Georgia Grind"[5]), have survived through jazz.

Buddy Bolden occupied a prominent place among blacks. He was

2. † American Music 513.
3. Charters, *Jazz*, p. 22.
4. ITJ.
5. † Odeon 279.790, recording of 1926. Various reissues.

a Baptist and a regular churchgoer—though we can hardly call him devout. He was born in New Orleans in 1868, but his family is said to have come from Tunica, a place west of New Orleans known for its brass bands. It is not impossible that he introduced some, if not a considerable amount, of that tradition to New Orleans.[6] Bolden was musically well educated and played the cornet. His musical career began in 1895 as leader of several bands in the parks of Uptown, Johnson Park and Lincoln Park, where people danced in the open air.

Bolden was a very popular musician, but the great influence he had on many young people, including a certain Bunk Johnson, is even more significant. The band in which he played in 1897 consisted of the following instruments: clarinet, cornet, trombone, guitar, double bass and drums. It seems possible that he was the first to have introduced this now traditional formation of New Orleans ensembles.

It is also significant that he was the first, or one of the first, to include music of black origin in his repertoire, in particular the blues, or related music. Bolden's "Take It Away," played later by Jelly Roll Morton,[7] his "Bucket Got a Hole in It,"[8] and many others, have sixteen bars but the pattern of the melody comes very close to that of the blues and does not have the structural characteristics of ragtime.

There was something else which set the blacks[9] apart from the Creoles. Initially, they would have made it their duty to emphasize the difference between their own style of music and the other, more French, style. That is also the reason why blacks set out to use their instruments in their own special way—to achieve sounds the others were not able to produce. As a result they developed their own taste in instrumental style that was in keeping with their own traditions. We have already mentioned the French clarinet style, which continues to be recognizable. This contrasts starkly with that of black roots which

6. Leaflet FoW MS I.

7. * HMV B 9216 (and reissues) (tape recording 1939); **** General 589, piano solo (reissues on LP by Vogue and M.M.S.).

8. A rendition by George Lewis Orchestra: ** Blue Note BLP 7027, 1955.

9. We use the word *blacks* to distinguish them from the French-oriented Creoles, although many of these English-speaking Protestants were also black people.

has strong vibrato and a stronger attack of tone. Besides using the normal mutes many more tricks were devised for the trumpet. The use of the mute to create a "wa-wa" sound was particularly revolutionary. It is said to have been the brainchild of King Oliver. Another trumpet player who has also been credited with the honor of being its inventor is Mutt Carey. He came from New Orleans but later moved to Los Angeles and wrote as follows:

> Joe Oliver and I were the first to use mutes and that sort of thing. We were both freak trumpet men. I have to give Oliver the credit for starting it off. Joe could make his trumpet sound like a holy roller meeting [referring to a sect whose singing was often intense and emotional]. That man could do anything with his horn![10]

To sum up, we can say that the fact that the blacks began to emphasize the characteristic features of their own music, so as not to lose ground in competition with the Creoles, led to a characteristic approach that maximized the potential of the instruments. This use of the instruments found its way into jazz music, which was just developing around that time. Intonation, tone modulation and vibrato are all characteristic non-Western, pure African-American elements in this music. Also phrasing, the pattern of melodies, rhythm and, as we shall see, structure differ in jazz from Western music.[11]

The first Creole musician to play the blues was Jelly Roll Morton. I will come back to him later but he is important to us here because he made a recording of the first blues he ever heard, the "219 blues," sung around 1900 by Mamie Desdoumes, a female vocalist from New Orleans. "Two nineteen" is the number of a train, also "two seventeen" and so on:

> Two nineteen took my babe away, (x2)
> Two seventeen will bring her back some day.

10. *Heah Me Talkin' to Ya*, p. 50 (see the bibliography for full title).
11. Cf. Winthrop Sargeant, *Jazz: Hot and Hybrid* (New York, 1946).

Stood on the corner with her feet just soakin' wet (x2)
Beggin' each and every man that she met.

If you can't give a dollar, give me a lousy dime, (x2)
I wanna feed that hungry man of mine.[12]

Brass Bands in New Orleans: "Just a Closer Walk with Thee"

Buddy Bolden often played in the brass band parades that were so popular in New Orleans. Any excuse was sufficient for staging a parade. These bands, however, also had, and still have, a special task: to play at funerals, a typical custom of New Orleans.[13]

Spirituals were sung in the house of mourning where the deceased lay. When it was time for the funeral, the procession was led by a brass band that usually consisted of an E-flat clarinet, two trumpets, an althorn, a trombone, a tuba, a drum and a bass drum. They played spirituals like "Nearer My God to Thee," "Just a Closer Walk with Thee," and so on, in a slow and stately tempo. On arrival at the graveyard the band stayed outside and the family followed the coffin to the graveside. When the mourners returned, the drum sounded a roll, the band set up and began to play as soon as the party stepped outside. The music was slow till they reached the corner of the graveyard, but then became fast and lively. The "second line," adults and children who walked alongside the band, followed along the pavement. There were many brass bands that played on this sort of occasion, but the Excelsior Brass Band and the Onward Brass Band were particularly well known. (The Eureka Brass Band and the Young Tuxedo Brass Band still play as of this writing.) Many later jazz musicians owe a significant part of their education to these bands, King Oliver being one of them.

---

12. **** Vogue V 2119 (and reissue on LP of Vogue).
13. ***† American Music: *Babe Dodds No. 1*; Young Tuxedo Brass Band, *** Atlantic 1297, 1958; Eureka Brass Band, ** FoW FA2462, 1956.

Jelly Roll Morton in New Orleans: "King Porter Stomp"

Ferdinand La Menthe, also known as Jelly Roll Morton, was born not far from the Vieux Carre in Downtown, New Orleans around 1885. He gave the following account of his roots—like an ancient legend, accompanied by ceremonial piano chords:[14]

> As I can understand, my folks were in the city of New Orleans long before the Louisiana purchase (when the land was bought by the Yankees), and all my folks came directly from the shores of France, that is across the world in the other world, and they landed in the new world years ago.

> I can remember the time of my great-grandfather and my great-grandmother. My great-grandfather was Emile Pechet. He was regarded as one of the greatest jewellers of the South. My great-grandmother was Mimi Pechet. She travelled great distances (as a nanny you see), and she died aged about a hundred when I was grown up. As long as I knew them, they were not capable of speaking a single word of American or English.

> My grandmother was called Laura. She married a French colonist called Monette, who was a wholesaler of liquor. That was my grandfather—and neither of them spoke American or English.

> My grandmother gave birth to Henry, Gus, Neville and Nelusco, her sons, all with French names, and three daughters, Louise, Viola and Margaret . . . Louise married F. P. La Menthe, also a colonist and regarded as one of the leading building contractors in all the South. Now Louise was my mother, mother of me—Ferdinand Jelly Roll Morton.

14. Originally LiC, reissue on ****† Circle LP (L14001), recently another reissue: **** Riverside 9001.

Of course you will be asking yourselves where the name Morton comes from, because it's an English name. Well, I'll tell you. I changed my name for reasons of business when I began travelling around. I didn't want to be called 'Frenchy' . . .

My first instrument consisted of two chairs and a tin can. It sounded like a symphony to me, because the only music I heard in those days (around 1890) were classical compositions. The next instrument I tried was the harmonica when I was five . . . We always had musical instruments at home, including the guitar, drums, piano, trombone, etc. We had a whole lot and there was always somebody enjoying playing . . . When I was seven years old I was regarded as the best guitarist in the neighbourhood, and sometimes I played in a string band—there were a lot of them around at the time. The small combinations of three instruments, consisting of double bass, mandolin and guitar played serenades late in the evening . . . Of course my family never imagined they had a musician in their midst. They always thought of a musician as a hobo . . . apart from the musicians of the French opera, where they often went. Actually it was at a recital at the French opera that I hit upon the idea of taking up the piano . . . One day at a party I saw a gentleman sit down at the piano and I heard him play a good piece of ragtime.[15]

Here you have a glimpse of the beginning of the musical career of the man who was to create the jazz-piano style. His story shows the various factors that played a role. He must have been a good pianist as early as 1900 or thereabouts. Besides a semiclassical style of music he will have been thoroughly acquainted with ragtime. He also made early acquaintance with the blues, as we have seen.

About 1902 he composed the "King Porter Stomp," which has the structure of pure ragtime. We know it only from the many later versions made for the gramophone, so that it is hard to imagine how he would have played it. But the piece as we know it shows clearly how

15. Text printed in Lomax, *Mister Jelly Roll*, p. 3 ff.

the approach differs from real ragtime; it has a very free left hand, a much freer, less jumpy melody and a more fluent rendition. The structure of the various themes also differs somewhat from that of standard ragtime. The phrases consist of eight bars, repeated, making a total of sixteen bars per theme. Jelly Roll (the American word for "Swiss roll") Morton even gave a demonstration of the difference between ragtime and jazz—the style of piano playing which he introduced or, at least, developed—using the "Maple Leaf Rag"[16] to illustrate his point. This shows the very varied and richer rhythm—although a steady 4/4 time is retained—and the extraordinarily beautifully phrased rendition of the themes.

The tango became popular around the turn of the century. This dance with its characteristic rhythm was conceived either in Havana or in Argentina by black laborers from Central America. In either case it is clearly a mixture of African and Spanish musical heritage: the tangana is an African dance, but the Spanish element dominates the melody. Jelly heard tanganas and later confessed that he found them difficult to play well and that he was not very keen on the tunes. This led him to compose a few of his own, which constitute some of the most beautiful music he has written. They are in fact quasi-tangos, with a jerkiness and excessive dance music quality characteristic of the tango, restructured to produce a fluent beat that is closely linked to the very beautiful melody. The themes themselves are just fascinating. Of these gems—which are even more beautiful than Albeniz's quasi-tangos, and others—"Mama 'Nita," for example (probably composed on the West Coast where he married Anita), and "Tiajuana" (a place on the West Coast)[17] are just two examples.

Finally we would like to mention his "New Orleans Blues" from 1904, among the first blues ever to have been played by a Creole. Here too Jelly handles the structure very freely, dividing the twelve-bar strophe into a sort of introduction consisting of four bars and a

16. Same series as in note 14, ****† Riverside 9003.
17. Recordings of piano solos of 1923: **** London L 3559; recordings of 1937 on LiC, ****† Riverside 9004.

long phrase of eight bars. There are four themes, of which the first three are vaguely reminiscent of the tangos we have just mentioned, while the last one is played in the more usual jazz rhythm. Each theme is played twice. The structure of the piece, the actual composition, was very important to Jelly. Although variations were permitted within the given framework, there was no essential deviation from the fixed sequence of the themes and their structure. We can best compare this approach, common to all jazz that originated in New Orleans, with the procedure sometimes followed in Europe in the seventeenth century: the composer wrote the themes and supplied the general instructions, while the performer was free to add the embellishments and to choose the instruments. The way Jelly went about it becomes clear if we compare the two recordings of "New Orleans Blues" (under the title of "New Orleans Joys")[18] recorded in quick succession in 1923. Although they differ in detail, the overall structure and the themes remain the same, so that the total impression is very similar. He had to play the piece quite quickly here, or it might not have fitted on the small 78 rpm disc. (Later, in 1935, he played the piece again in essentially the same way, but at a much slower pace.[19])

In 1905 Jelly composed the "Jelly Roll Blues," which was published in 1915 in Chicago[20] where he was then based. Its structure is similar to that of "New Orleans Blues," except that the first four bars of each theme are regarded as a break. This is a typical feature of jazz, which Jelly paid much attention to and valued greatly. The steady rhythm is interrupted for one or two bars in order to allow a free passage to be played with the upper hand. In the band's version of 1926, Morton either leaves the breaks to a solo instrument or he plays them himself on the piano.

Jelly Roll Morton did not have an easy character. Many aspects of his performance can be explained by his high ideals and the

18. **** London AL 3559 and ****† AFCDJ A09.
19. See note 17.
20. Piano solo 1923 **** London AL 3559, tape recording **** RCA LPM-1649-C.

great demands he placed on his music (and thus also on other jazz musicians), and by the fact that he refused to acknowledge that he was subject to racial discrimination. He tried to live as if it did not exist, seeking recognition for himself as a Creole. In his study of Morton's background and the childhood influences and memories which molded his character, Lomax discovered the extent to which his race—and class-consciousness affected his view of the music world.[21]

Jelly Roll Morton was very creative and talented—one of the most important musicians to have shaped jazz and a driving force behind its development. As the creator of the jazz-piano style and composer of countless important pieces of music, it would be impossible to ignore him and we will certainly be coming back to him later.

THE DEVELOPMENT OF EARLY JAZZ: JACK CAREY

Jack Carey, Mutt Carey's brother, was a trombonist who founded a band in New Orleans around 1913. It was made up of two clarinets, a trumpet, a trombone, a double bass, a guitar and drums. He composed a number of pieces for his band, the Crescent Orchestra, including a piece which was known to black musicians as "Jack Carey" and to white musicians as "Nigger No. 2" (we will come back to this shortly). The composition has been, and still is, widely known and loved as "Tiger Rag." Jelly Roll Morton claimed to have composed it and it is difficult to confirm or refute this. However, it is undoubtedly difficult to argue with his analysis of the composition, where he shows that the succession of themes is derived from a French dance suite, beginning with a quadrille.[22] Acquaintances of Carey have suggested that Mutt Carey took the themes from an old music book of French dances.

Carey's band was one of the first to have played in New Orleans during the time between 1910 and 1920. Oscar Celestin's and Edward Ory's bands also played there. Members of the latter included Oliver

---

21. As described in his book, *Mister Jelly Roll*.
22. **** Riverside 9001.

and the clarinetist Johnny Dodds, for a while. Several circles of close friends arose from this time—something which was to be of great significance to the history of jazz. There was Clarence Williams' band, who went on tour in Texas with Sidney Bechet and Freddy Pechard's group, the Olympia Orchestra, which was dominated by a number of Creoles including Alphonse Picou, who devised the clarinet solo in "High Society." In 1907 the band was still playing a lot of legitimate Western (i.e., French) dance music. Some time later during 1913 Keppard went on a nationwide tour, from San Francisco to New York, with an orchestra called The Original Creole Orchestra which included the clarinetist George Baquet. This band opted for jazz.

Jimmy Noone, Babe Dodds, Johnny St. Cyr and Bunk Johnson also played in New Orleans, in various combinations, while after 1915 musicians like Louis Armstrong, Paul Barbarin and many others from the younger generation joined them. (I have mentioned only the names of those who were to become famous.) There was a great surplus of musicians as is often the case when art is flourishing, as for instance during the seventeenth century in the Netherlands. Many of those mentioned were semiprofessional and depended on earning their income as laborers or traders; they performed occasionally for a ball, party, picnic or per part-time contract at one of the dance halls, clubs and so on.

What kind of music did the bands play then? Initially it was ragtime, compositions originally written for the piano and subsequently arranged for bands. They were published in *The Red Back Book of Rags*[23] and other publications. It seems that after 1900 this part of the repertoire began to lose its significance. There were also the "tunes of the day," the popular songs. The New Orleans musicians were primarily concerned with their own interpretation of these songs, which formed a welcome starting point for performances and gave the audience what they wanted. The songs were pleasant enough. Good

---

23. Compare Scott Joplin's *Entertainer* (*** London AL 3515) and Bunk Johnson's rendition of the same piece on the basis of such an arrangement (* Philips B 07009 L).

examples of this are "When You and I Were Young" and "Maggy."[24] Then there was the blues, particularly Jelly Roll Morton's "Jelly Roll Blues," "New Orleans Blues," etc. Original compositions like Bolden's "Bucket Got a Hole in It," and "I Wish I Could Shimmy Like My Sister Kate" (possibly Louis Armstrong's composition), published by Clarence Williams, were also played in the sixteen-bar structure. Finally, musical compositions based on marches were played, the best known of these being "High Society."

In all these cases—with the exception of written ragtime—there was a particular melody, or melodies, plus the chords. These constituted the material that each band used for its own arrangement—it was a question of what it did with the material. Most important was the given tune (or tunes); the chords were secondary. Improvisation in the true sense of the word, namely to create a new tune ad lib based on the given chords, was uncommon. What took place was not improvisation, but "embellishing around the melody,"[25] the word improvisation was not even used yet! The musicians often played without the help of sheet music, or without referring to a written score. This was called "faking."[26] Still, a definite discipline by way of an agreement as to when the band was to play ensemble, solos, breaks and so on was certainly present. This agreement can also be regarded as a framework, even though everything within it was determined with much more care than in the "composition" that was the starting point for the performance. A certain amount of freedom was definitely present in the rendition, but only within the given framework or there would have been chaos, or a succession of solos only. This did happen later in jazz music, but it would have been unthinkable for early New Orleans music, which was primarily geared towards ensemble.

What was the quality of the music? Sometimes good, sometimes mediocre, depending on who was playing, of course. Neither would it have been very sophisticated at all times. But we must be careful here

---

24. ***† American Music LP645.
25. *Heah Me Talkin' to Ya*, p. 77.
26. Cf. Ramsey & Smith, *Jazzmen*, p. v.

because we must not apply Western standards in our assessment of quality. We must not expect to find refined modulations, for example, since there was no demand for it; neither can we expect subtle compositional solutions because this music was not designed for the concert hall, and also because these musicians lacked the relevant education. With such expectations we are barking up the wrong tree. This music was not Western music, played in a rough and crude manner; it was the birth of a new kind of music, African-American music, which bears no historical, spiritual or technical relation to Western classical music (from Mozart to Brahms and Cesar Franck).

It has often been said that this music was loud and wild, but we must try to put this in its proper context. This criticism was expressed by people who had no understanding of these new sounds. The first time I heard Bach's second *Brandenburg Concerto,* the first Bach concerto that I consciously and attentively listened to, I heard only loud and apparently unconnected sounds. This was due to the fact that I did not understand what I was hearing, I did not know when musical sentences started and when they stopped—I had nothing to go by, no grip on it. The same applies to early jazz. To the untrained ear it was incomprehensible. There were no guidelines for arranging the strange and new sounds to make sense, which was why it was called "wild." So, was it not hard and loud? Let us agree that a trumpet cannot sound louder than it can be played, and that this maximum volume is more often reached in our concert halls than in performance by a good New Orleans jazz band.

The objections about the music being loud and wild confirm that this was indeed a new type of music—a new style that simply could not be compared with the contemporary dance music of the time or with Western marching music (i.e., the types of music that bore the closest relation to jazz music with regards to theme and structure). It is a remarkable fact that the prominent jazz musicians had enjoyed a good education. They all knew their music through and through, and there is as little truth in the romantic notion that naturally talented musicians suddenly caused this music to spring into existence out of the blue, as there is in other similar cases.

In case we need to prove our point further, here is a quote from Babe Dodds, the most important drummer in the history of New Orleans jazz. He got his nickname because he was the younger brother (by twelve years) of the clarinetist Johnny Dodds. Babe Dodds said:

> When I was only fourteen, I was obsessed with the idea of playing in my brother Johnny's band . . . I had been playing since I was a little lad and I thought I was good. But Johnny's answer was, 'Buzz off, kid! Learn to play percussion first and don't bother me before you can.' I took his advice and went to music school—I called it school—four years long and I soon realized that my drumming had been completely wrong. I had to start all over again and completely unlearn everything I was used to doing. This is how I got the basic rudiments of drumming. When I was nineteen I was quite a well-educated musician, at home in all sorts of drumming techniques. I went back to my brother for a job and he got me my first professional engagement—with King Oliver in the famous King Oliver Band, where Johnny was playing the clarinet. Maybe I should point out something important about my brother for the connoisseurs. Johnny had respect for good musicians and good music, but he loathed musically poor musicians attempting to play jazz.[27]

EARLY WHITE JAZZ: "CLARINET MARMALADE"

It is 1917 and the Original Dixieland Jazz Band plays in New York to great applause. They arrived there after having spent some time in Chicago without much success. They were white boys from New Orleans. Since about 1910, possibly earlier, a number of white bands had been playing the new music or, at least, were trying to produce something which resembled the music of the Uptown blacks. They stayed more with ragtime. However, their tempo was faster and

27. *Heah Me Talkin' to Ya*, p. 37.

74

their music was rhythmically weaker—partly due to their white background, no doubt, where rhythm was not a natural part of their cultural heritage.

In 1917 they had so much success that their music was recorded for gramophone records. The first jazz "on record." The story goes that Kempler had already been approached by the record companies but that he had turned them down, partly because he was afraid that others would "steal" their music. In any case, these records are the earliest documentation for us; they give our story a solid foundation so that we do not have to reconstruct it or to form an opinion based on all sorts of assertions. We can hear it for ourselves.[28]

It is immediately evident that this music—even at the time of writing, more than forty years later—still sounds fresh and new. It may come across as wild because we have to get used to the tempo, which is often fast, and because the rhythm is not very marked (we will come back to this in the analysis of the New Orleans jazz of the African Americans); we somewhat miss the firm structure which, after all, also this music demands.

If we really concentrate, however, we hear that the music is anything but rough and uncontrolled. There are often subtle dynamics, there are accents and contrasts, there is a fixed structure within the given framework and there is polyphony between the clarinet, the trumpet and the trombone. These are all characteristics which we recognize from black New Orleans jazz, though there are differences. Black jazz music is much more tranquil, more distinctive and transparent, with more artistic balance than white jazz. You sometimes get the impression that the white musicians are overdoing it with regard to the tempo or in the fierce attack of the tone, though their music is never out of tune, coarse, chaotic, noisy or unmusical.

The setup was the same as that of the black bands: trumpet (La Rocca), clarinet (Larry Shields), trombone (Ed Edwards), piano (Ragas) and drums (Tony Sbarbaro), but note the absence of the saxophone.

28. **HMV DLP 1065.

They played ragtime compositions like "Tiger Rag," which we already mentioned, and original compositions in this vein like "Clarinet Marmalade," "Sensation Rag," and so on, and occasionally a blues number like "Bluin' the Blues,"[29] which was strongly reminiscent of Morton's "Jelly Roll Blues," and others.

HANDY'S BLUES: ST. LOUIS BLUES

"Handy, Father of the Blues." You may have heard this phrase, or seen it in print, countless times. But what is it? A story? A mistake? A slogan? It is an advertising slogan for a publishing company named Handy!

Handy was born in 1873 in Florence, Alabama. He had a musical education, sang popular songs in a quartet and in 1896 he became the leader of Mahara's Colored Minstrels. This was a touring band that had a very varied program—from Shakespeare to the latest hit—including "coon-songs," the imitation black songs. Handy played the accompanying music in the orchestra pit and also overtures like *William Tell*, selections from operas like *The Mikado*, and pieces such as "Dichter und Bauer" which was renamed "Poet and Peasant" for this purpose. In 1903 he became the leader of a dance band called The Knights of Pythias Band and Orchestra in Clarksdale, Mississippi.

One evening at a ball, Handy was playing the quadrilles and other contemporary dance music. Then someone requested: "Play some of your own people's music" Handy tried a sort of minstrel song but the man was not satisfied. He proceeded to pull in a three-piece string band from outside and it began to play "rough backstreet music with a lot of repetition, which earned them more than the uniformed band's combined salary for the whole evening."

This is a quote from Abbe Niles' foreword to Handy's publication, *A Treasury of the Blues*. Niles, acting as W. C. Handy's official historian, writes, "It was still hard to believe that there would be anything at all of commercial value in that disorganized musical

29. See note 28; cf. **** RCA LPM-1649-C.

by-product," and indeed it took about another ten years before Handy was fully convinced.

It is striking that this musician was able to observe and listen to the music of his black counterparts as a complete outsider. He claimed to be very interested in the music, but more as a curiosity—as something fascinating. Only very gradually did he dare to stray from the secure path of light music in the Western vein.

What did he do next? Niles continues the account:

> Then Handy came along, who started to draw inspiration from the folk music he had already heard so often—folk songs that were rough and without much meaning. It required a musician to take responsibility for putting something of lasting value into this music. Without this man, W.C. Handy, the blues would not have permeated the national (American) consciousness so quickly, nor would it ever have formed an integral part of it as is now the case.[30]

That "lasting value" is chiefly pecuniary, by the way, as there are hundreds of records where the "ordinary, rough and little significant" blues is sung by folk troubadours with a beauty and quality such as no production of Handy even comes close to approaching. Without Handy the blues would indeed probably not have permeated popular music, but whether his diluted product is indeed worth the effort remains to be seen. "Handy, Father of the Commercial Blues," that is the truth.

Perhaps he was not even that. It is a fact that the first blues to be published was issued by Stark—Artie Matthew's "Baby Seal Blues" in August 1912; next came Hart A. Wand's "Dallas Blues" in September 1912, and third was Handy's "Memphis Blues," three weeks later. The strange thing is that Handy had already composed the piece three years earlier but apparently could not or did not want to publish it.

At best, Handy is a folklorist, someone who tries to present contemporary folk music in a way that makes it more accessible to a

---

30. W. C. Handy, *A Treasury of the Blues* (New York, 1949; second edition), p. 18; see also W. C. Handy, *Father of the Blues: An Autobiography* (New York, 1947).

"better" audience of "higher cultural standing." His blues, for example, always has a sixteen-bar introduction, which is in fact given more emphasis than the twelve bars of blues that follow. The type of blues we discussed earlier, however, the living blues of the troubadours, exists as a permanent reminder that there is no need for improvement or refinement of this very subtle and deep folk art, and that its commercialization by a handy and well-trained musician does not automatically imply that the art itself has profited.

Let us consider the full implications of this. Westernization does not necessarily imply improvement, and presenting something in such a way that it becomes socially acceptable does not automatically imply that it has become good and pure and art.

However, this is the impression of Handy that the film *St. Louis Blues* presents, historical distortion aside. In the film Handy's father, the preacher who cannot accept his son's career as dance musician, is persuaded that his son is doing something meaningful when his work, the "St. Louis Blues," is performed by a big symphony orchestra rather than a jazz or dance band, fit for the best class of people in Washington. This may have contributed to the aspect of social acceptability (albeit a very dubious aspect), but in that sort of setting the blues is twice sold short—first it is commercially westernized and second, "dignified" as classical! "Handy—*Stepfather* of the Blues"!

Handy's version of the blues, which was also taken up by others, based on authentic black music or personal inspiration, was identified by its subject matter and titles. In very many instances it uses place names like Memphis, Dallas, St. Louis, Beale Street (a street in Memphis), something that seldom occurs in traditional blues. The Handy blues is furthermore far less realistic. With all the sharp edges smoothed the music is also less authentic—less articulate. In spite of the use of the blue note (i.e., a minor third or seventh in a piece which is otherwise major) which is so typical of African-American music, the character of this type of blues (most of which is sheet music) relates more to white popular music than to real African-American music.

4

The 1920s

POST-1918 NEW ORLEANS MUSIC IN CHICAGO: KING OLIVER ("SOUTHERN STOMPS")

During the First World War there was a great shortage of industrial workers due to the large numbers of whites serving in the army or navy, while there was an increased need for production. One of the consequences of this was that blacks from the South headed for the industrial centers in the North because there were well-paid jobs to be had in the factories. This provided them with the opportunity to break away from the South, with its apartheid, its nasty "Jim Crow" attitudes and its impoverished living conditions, for a better future in the North.[1] Chicago was a particularly attractive destination and the black population there doubled from 50,000 to 100,000 during the war years.

It was this fact, rather than the closing down of the red-light district in New Orleans, that encouraged also many musicians to move to the North. They came to offer their music to the blacks who were already resident there and relatively well off. Freddie Keppard, Jelly Roll Morton and many other musicians from New Orleans performed there for varying periods of time between the years 1914 and 1918.

Joe Oliver, whose trumpet-playing in New Orleans had won him

1. H. C. Cayton & St. Clair Drake, *Black Metropolis* (London, 1946).

the title of "King," also arrived in 1918. Until 1920 he played in a number of different bands, of which the members were almost exclusively people from New Orleans. He formed his own band in 1920 and played in Los Angeles in 1921–1922 with a slightly different lineup—and his good friend Jelly Roll Morton on the piano. He returned to Chicago in 1922 to form the band with which he was to become famous. It is hard to overestimate the significance of this band, which only made minor changes in the lineup until 1924. Many musicians came to listen to them and gained a thorough knowledge of the content of New Orleans style. Whites came to listen too, and the effect this music had on them requires further discussion. Last but not least, in 1923 they cut a series of gramophone records that will remain significant because of the superior quality of their music. These records have continued to win admirers and still inspire those with a heart for the music of New Orleans. We may be grateful for the first recording of real black music in 1923. Only two such recordings were made prior to this—one by the Ory Band and the other by Johnny Dunn's band. These records immediately sold well and were often played—the original editions are very rare and the fact that they are almost always in bad condition is evidence of this.

The band always featured top musicians with King Oliver and Louis Armstrong on cornet; Johnny Dodds on clarinet; Honore Dutrey on trombone; Lil Hardin on piano; Bud Scott on banjo; Warren "Babe" Dodds on the drums; and bass saxophonist Charlie Jackson[2] joined in for some numbers, thus doubling the trombone contribution.

In spite of this lineup and in view of later conceptions of jazz, it would be quite wrong to classify Oliver and co. as "great soloists," as Coeuroy does;[3] it would be even more inappropriate to call them great "individualists." Those who take the time to listen to these records[4]

2. About the recordings, where they have been issued and the musicians involved, very accurate information is to be found in W. C. Allen and Brian A. L. Rust, *King Joe Oliver* (NY: Belleville, 1955).

3. A. Coeuroy, *Histoire générale du jazz* (Paris, 1942).

4. **** Philips B O7435L, **** Col. 1065, and Riverside 12–101.

will discover that the emphasis falls entirely on ensemble, although there are the odd solos. A significant part of the records consist entirely of ensemble playing.

The majority of the pieces they played were original compositions, written by Oliver, one of the other band members or other African Americans who were working in the same or a similar style (like Jelly Roll Morton, Richard M. Jones, Thomas A. Dorsey, etc.). They also played cover versions of classics like "High Society," but hardly ever played contemporary popular music and never schmaltz. The extraordinary impact of this band, which is still evident, is indeed partly due to their good choice of repertoire. Their music sounds fresh, even now [at the time of writing], never old-fashioned or outdated.

The themes are usually longer winded than those of the average ragtime with its core of four bars which are continually repeated. Instead, the themes are more often constructed of phrases of eight bars (which are sometimes divided into two sub-phrases of four bars). Thematic units of twelve bars also occur regularly. This adds to the richness and renders this music superior to the schmaltz of those days, which stuck to the time-honored basic melody of four bars, repeated and embedded in a larger structure of sixteen bars. The fourth theme of the "Chime Blues,"[5] to which we will come back later, is a good example of this. Be that as it may, there is a legion of beautiful and elaborate melodies; listing them would serve little purpose.

A comparison of the different recordings of one particular piece, for instance "Riverside Blues," "Dippermouth Blues," "Snake Rag" or "Mabel's Dream" can show us that this band did not improvise; the various versions of each of these pieces hardly differ from each other. Small differences can be attributed to the working method we discussed earlier, in which each musician has some freedom to occasionally play a note differently, within the largely predetermined framework, as long as the arrangement (mostly unwritten) is not affected.

The musicians have their own particular styles of playing. This is one of the reasons for the ease, freedom, suppleness, which yet preserves

5. **** London AL 3504.

the purity of style that each of the musicians produces. Individualism, on the other hand, with musicians vying to be "in front," does not occur. Each individual is completely committed to the rest of the band and tuned in to hear the other members. The starting point of each performance is the melody or melodies, as many compositions consist of several themes. This melody is varied, interpreted, played in the band's own style, but never abandoned in order to improvise on the given chord progression. If there is more than one theme, as is the case in "Chimes Blues," each theme is rendered in a different way, partly to ensure clarity but also to retain the clear structure of the whole. The first theme of "Chimes Blues," for example, is played ensemble and subsequently repeated identically (as always); then the second theme is played homophonically (and repeated); the third theme is played (twice) by the piano; the fourth theme is introduced by the trumpet (the first ever recording of Louis Armstrong playing solo) and then repeated note by note, and the rendition is finally concluded by a repeat of the second theme. Compare this recording of Oliver with later versions, e.g., that of "Mournful Serenade" by Jelly Roll Morton's quartet,[6] (the same sequence of themes, each one repeated), and with that of George Lewis and his band who, as late as 1955,[7] played an identical rendition of the different themes. The framework for the authentic New Orleans' compositions seems to be quite tight and any variation in personal style for cover versions remains strictly within that framework, while the melody, which can be clearly followed, is retained.

We have discussed ensemble work several times. It is now time to focus on it, because it is the heart of this New Orleans music. It is pure polyphony. The schematic structure is thus: two trumpets render the theme in unison and in pointed rhythm, the trombone provides the foundation in long, legato phrases while selecting notes from the base chords, while the clarinet ad libs above the trumpets. The clarinet and the trombone also base the structure of their phrases

6. **** HMV B9221.
7. ITJ.

on the given theme. On occasion they may play the theme, while the trumpets depart from the theme both melodically and rhythmically. The clarinet sometimes plays the same rhythm as the trumpet, possibly with a different melody, matching note by note, before releasing itself for a countermelody that creates a more open polyphony. Part of the theme is sometimes played by the trumpets, while the clarinet and trombone play freely at first before continuing the tune with a few bars together, in parallel, and the trumpets now play a rhythmical countermelody. It is important to realize that the parts that are played freely, simultaneously with the actual theme, are not just erratic tunes to a haphazard beat (as we so often hear in later Dixieland jazz) but they too are melodically sound. Compare the two different versions of "Riverside Blues" because the recordings differ so much technically. In one case the countermelody stands out and it becomes apparent that it is just as rich as the main theme, which is more clearly conspicuous in the other case.

The reason we are devoting so much attention to this is to emphasize that this pure polyphony expresses a resourcefulness and ingenuity that cannot possibly be produced by simply playing or improvising. It was at this point that later imitations failed. They took over the pattern we mentioned at the beginning of this discussion and assumed that the rest could be improvised during the performance itself. They underestimated the austerity of the framework and were therefore oblivious to the freedom it provides.

What role do the rhythm instruments—piano, banjo and drums—play? They do not constitute a separate section that thrashes out the beat like a pounding-machine. Instead they join in with the whole, using their varied manner of rendition to support the theme in their own way. Anyone who has heard Babe Dodds' drum solo[8] knows what a rich melody he is able to elicit from his instrument, and those who have heard his discourse about his manner of playing[9] cannot fail to admit that he uses his intelligence in his music,

8. ***† Blue Star BS95 (1946) and other issues.
9. ***† American Music, *Baby Dodds Album No. 1.*

constantly searching for the right way to support his band, selecting just the right tone to provide that firm basis that allows the polyphony even more freedom. There is no tapping out of the beat, although his drumming always retains the strict, strong beat which constitutes the bonding element for the rest of the band. Banjo and piano together support the trombone in laying the harmonic foundation; they too play a very capriciously varied rhythm which nevertheless helps to provide a steady beat.

In searching for other musical equivalents we should not compare this music with the later swing music, with its strong beat, its tight and sometimes sharp rhythm, but rather with the basso continuo as used by Bach. It gives a similar fluent support to the work of the melody instruments—nowhere marking the beat as tightly as a metronome, and always following the melody. It is a lively and warm rhythm, loose and dynamic. The set tempo, like Bach's, almost completely lacks accelerandi and rallentandi, though there is of course a certain rubato in the rendition of the melody instruments, where we find a free rhythm with agogic accents.[10] We have mentioned Bach's name here and, indeed, this music is similar to his; not only in its structure with the emphasis on the polyphony, but particularly in atmosphere and nature. Listen to "Where Did You Stay Last Night?" and compare it with Bach's sixth Brandenburg Concerto. The resemblance is remarkable. The same type of polyphony, the same sort of rhythm, but the comparison has to be taken further than establishing a musical resemblance; the atmosphere is similar—the same serenity the same joy, the same lively sharpness, the same lack of any romanticism or rhetoric, the same fortitude. It is striking that Oliver also feels it necessary to repeat a theme, thus enhancing the solid serenity and flexibility. Finally, common to both there is pure joy, not exuberant, not wild and uncontrolled, but a deeply rooted cheerfulness.

10. *Accelerando* means an increase in tempo. *Rallentando* means a decrease in tempo. *Rubato* denotes that part of the melody is to be slightly overstretched or played slightly too quickly. *Agogic accent* is a subtle extension of the note in order to emphasize it within the melody.

The cheerfulness and openness here is as little superficial as in Bach's music. The view that only the tragic, the serious in the sense of somber, the sad, is really deep and meaningful is a typical Western, Romantic mistake. It may be true to those who no longer recognize the Christian beliefs or no longer accept them, but the Bible teaches a different view. A joyful disposition is the fruit of a real understanding of the word of God. Joy is not superficial—on the contrary, it is very deep. It is only to those who find depth and real truth in the tragic, the ruinous, that joy is an escape, a denial of reality; and this type of joy is then expressed in a wild letting go of oneself.

Oliver's joy is deep and real. There is no sign of escapism—just a peaceful solidity for the joy to rest on. Why would that be? What is behind that great inner affinity with Bach's music? How can there be such a conformity of musical structure? These people hardly knew Bach's music, if at all. What they heard of Western music was popular amusement pieces like Suppe's "Dichter und Bauer," or possibly one or two compositions by other nineteenth-century composers. Dutrey played cello music as part of his practice routine, for instance! This therefore rules out any immediate factor being responsible for this remarkable state of affairs. We believe it can only be explained by a common spiritual background. Bach's was very positively Bible-believing Christianity.

What about these blacks then?[11] Most of them were not church-goers, nor were they devout. On the other hand, they did not have a negative attitude towards God and his word, nor towards the church; they were not against it, not anti-Christian. Louis Armstrong, not a devout man by any means, still deems it necessary to mention in his autobiography[12] that he enjoys going to church and does so if possible. A few letters Oliver wrote shortly before he died, at an indescribably difficult time, speak for themselves. In 1937 he wrote this to his sister: "I am still out of work. Since the hotel closed I haven't produced a single note. But there is much to thank God for. Because

11. Also compare Grossman & Farrell, *The Heart of Jazz*.
12. Louis Armstrong, *Satchmo: My Life in New Orleans* (New York, 1954).

I have food and can sleep . . . It seems that each time one door closes, God opens another." Two months before he died, when he was to undergo surgery: "Perhaps I will never see New York again. Don't think I'm scared because I wrote that. I'm trying to live closer to the Lord than ever. I have a feeling that the good Lord's going to take care of me."[13] This attitude made it possible for the fruit of the blacks' own Christian culture to leave its mark on the work of these people. We can typify many aspects of this black culture as early Christian; these people too stood alone, with their faith in their hearts and the Bible in their hands, just as the churches in Ephesus or Corinth to whom St. Paul wrote.

The African-American culture was characterized by a heavy emphasis on developing its own Christian lifestyle, and real scriptural joy was one of its characteristic traits. If these musicians had been hostile towards Christianity and broken with their roots it would not have been possible for their music to carry this mark of deep joy, often despite their circumstances, the fruit of Christian faith.

This is how their musical affinity with Bach is ultimately to be understood. This is why their rhythm, which we compared to the basso continuo because it serves a similar function, and the polyphonic musical structure, which these blacks had independently rediscovered, bore such resemblance to the music of Bach.

Still, this music remains a miracle. Its high quality, its integrity, its nature we must ultimately simply accept for what it is: partly the result of the genius of these musicians, who put the aspect of playing together as a group before any individualistic presentation of technique and ability and partly to be attributed to their realization that freedom only exists in alignment to a given structure, to the theme and to the style of the other musicians.

Is there no African element in their music? We think there is very little. We have not been able to trace the roots of this art form in traditional African music, with its characteristic polyrhythm. Indeed, polyrhythm is hardly perceptible anywhere in the USA; it is not a

13. Ramsay & Smith, *Jazzmen*, pp. 89, 91; idem., *Heah Me Talkin' to Ya*, p. 169.

characteristic of African-American music, which is neither Western nor, to be sure, African. African polyrhythms are produced by super-imposing a variety of rhythms in different meters. The polyrhythms we sometimes find with Oliver are of a completely different nature. Within the structure of 4/4 time the melodies, which are played by the instruments with their own rhythms (and agogic accents), can develop a polyrhythm because one of the instruments may be slightly "ahead of" or "behind" the others. This helps create the lively sense of suppleness in this music. However, it is not typically African in character. Neither can this music be explained in any way in terms of the context in which it was played. It has nothing to do with red lights and gangsters, nor with the nightclub ambience of New Orleans or Chicago.

This section's title referred to "Southern Stomps." It is the title of one of the most beautiful pieces recorded by King Oliver's Creole Orchestra. It also characterizes the significance of this band, who played New Orleans music, devised by African Americans from the Southern States, particularly from Louisiana. Only when they started to play in Chicago, however, were they able to make an international impression and to become a force in the twentieth century that simply could not be ignored. But even though this music was played in the twentieth century, in the Western world, its nature was determined by factors which in no way reflected the Western world of the twentieth century. New Orleans jazz was born in the same period as Picasso's modern art and the Expressionism of Klee and Mondrian, but the music and the art are in no way connected. There is no line of con-nection to be found, however thin, between New Orleans music and the modernist Parisian art scene.[14]

The fact that music was played in the Western world which did not belong to the West, was bound to lead to unusual problems. As soon as jazz became influential and was adopted by others, tension arose—misinterpretations followed, and subsequently a fundamental restructuring of the music into something which could be referred to

14. So we do not agree with C. Delaunay, *De la vie et du jazz* (Lausanne, 1946).

as Western and contemporary. This process of tailoring it to the world of the day completely determined the development and profound alterations that we shall be analyzing next.

Post-1918 New Orleans Music in Chicago: Other Bands, Morton ("New Orleans Joys")

Oliver's band was not the only New Orleans ensemble playing in Chicago. As is often the case in times of cultural growth and activity overproduction was rife in New Orleans. There was an increase in demand for this type of music by the black audiences in the Northern States whose numbers were steadily increasing, so the most obvious solution for the New Orleans musicians was to seek employment in the North. Some of their music has been recorded. "Play That Thing" by Ollie Powers' Harmony Syncopaters is a particularly special recording, featuring Tommie Ladnier's superb trumpeting and Jimmy Noone on the clarinet. Even though the general characteristics of New Orleans jazz are not lacking, this is a group with a completely different style.[15]

Another recording made in 1923 is that of "Wild Cat Blues" and "Kansas City Man Blues" by a band led by the pianist, composer and publisher Clarence Williams.[16] Thomas Morris played trumpet; Charlie Irvis or John Masefield, trombone; Buddie Christian, banjo; but the leading role was certainly taken up by soprano saxophonist Sidney Bechet. His very dominant style, personal but sometimes too individual and to the fore, partly due to his instrument which in itself produces a dominant sound, was at its best here. This band's jazz closely resembles Oliver's in many respects, but the splendid balance that typifies Oliver's work, which hinged on the fact that all the instruments were of the same caliber, is less perceptible here. Still, it remains joyful, honest music, controlled, and with a great sense of inner calm despite its outward intensity.

Sidney Bechet had not long been back from a tour of Europe,

15. †† Anthologie du jazz AFG 7, *** London AL 3524.
16. †† Okeh 4925, 1923. *** Fontana 682.055 TL (*Bechet Memorial Album*).

including Paris, before he made this record. Europe had been exposed to jazz earlier, for the Original Dixieland Jazz Band had visited London in 1921 and the Jim Reece Europe band had done a tour of France prior to that. If Morton is right, one of the numbers they played was "Jelly Roll Blues." What made Bechet's visit memorable was that it gave rise to the first serious review of jazz. It was no one less than Ernest Ansermet, the famous conductor, who in 1919 felt compelled to comment on a concert staged in Paris by the band in which Bechet played.[17] He wrote:

> The first thing that hits one when listening to the Southern Synco-pated Orchestra is the surprising perfection, the exceptional taste and the enthusiastic performance of the band . . . It is only in the area of harmony that the blacks have not developed their own means of expression . . . They seem to have a style of their own and their form is solid, abrupt, rigorous, with an ending as brusque and relentless as that of Bach's second *Brandenburg Concerto*.

Anyone who has heard "Wild Cat Blues" referred to above will know how accurately and perceptively Ansermet was listening. He closes his article with a special comment about Bechet:

> Meeting this very black, fat young man with his white teeth and narrow forehead is quite an experience. He is very glad if you appre-ciate what he does, but he cannot tell you a thing about his music except that he goes his own way. Just think—his own way may be the main road that the whole world will walk along tomorrow.[18]

Jelly Roll Morton was also in Chicago in those days. He recorded a number of his compositions—records that are always worth listening

17. Bechet, who recently died, had been recorded many times. His best, apart from the ones already mentioned, are the recordings from 1925 together with Arm-strong under leadership of Clarence Williams. See the Fontana LP, note 16.

18. This whole article has been incorporated in M. T. Williams, *The Art of Jazz* (New York, 1959), p. 3 ff.

to (there is nothing outdated about this music), in spite of the fact that the difficulties in recording techniques for the piano in those days are clearly audible.

We have already discussed the recordings of "New Orleans Joys." If we listen to Morton's recordings of "Froggie Moore" and "London Blues" and then compare them with the rendition of the same pieces by Oliver's band,[19] the importance to the musicians of the structure of the piece and the themes implemented becomes abundantly clear. The latter number in particular is one of the most beautiful that Oliver made and is a typical Morton composition in its curious structure. Each new chorus (a closed part containing the theme or a variation of it) of twelve bars consists of a four-bar break, followed by a four-bar theme and finally by a four-bar refrain, i.e., a recurring short, closing theme. The first two groups of four bars keep on changing themes and each theme is rendered twice.

The performance of these bands was very influential, but it was especially the gramophone that was to play a very important role in the propagation of the music.

White Jazz in Chicago: "Tin Roof Blues"

At the beginning of the 1920s a white group from New Orleans was playing in Chicago. They had taken the place of the Original Dixieland Jazz Band, who had left for New York. They were young people who in New Orleans had been listening to black music whenever they could. They obviously did not go to the black neighborhoods, or other places that were accessible to blacks only, but they could hear this music at parades and open-air performances.

The Brunies brothers were the core of this group of enthusiastic youths. Leon Rappolo, of Sicilian origin (at home his family played only the music of their native country), learned to play the clarinet because it was impossible to gain a place in a brass band with a violin.

19. Morton's piano solos on **** London AL 3559; Oliver's band on **** Philips B O7435L and HCJ.

After the Dixieland Band, they were the first to record something of the music that could be heard in Chicago. The band was called New Orleans Rhythm Kings. Paul Mares, the trumpeter, later said:

> In 1922 we spent a number of successive weekends in Richmond, Indiana making recordings for Gennett. We were so set on making gramophone records that we accepted the first offer that came our way so as to beat the other bands to it . . . The band certainly played good music. We only had two different tempos: 'slow drag' and 2/4 time. We did our best to imitate the black music we had heard at home. We did the best we could, but of course we couldn't play 'real coloured style'.[20]

The records that were made then are still worth listening to.[21] The repertoire seems somewhat more old-fashioned than that of Oliver— more real ragtime (e.g., the "Maple Leaf Rag"), and also numbers which are strongly reminiscent of the entertainment music of that time. Nevertheless, their playing was thoroughly musical. They strove for pure polyphony and often achieved it; the solos were tasteful and often captivating. The music sounds different from that of the Dixieland Band, which was more spirited, but also less calm, more jumpy, with a lot of staccato. This music was more fluent, calmer and more tuneful, though that sometimes made it too sweet, too weak. It is as if white musicians face a dilemma in trying to imitate their black counterparts: either wild and turbulent, or calm and then too sweet and, indeed, depending on their taste, either the one or the other manifested itself. These white youths do not seem to have possessed the inner calm that can express itself forcefully in a joyful outburst. Certainly one of their mistakes was to include a tenor saxophone in the band. This particularly affected the quality of the recording—lack of clarity in structure and little clear definition of tone. The instrument, popular among dance bands in those days, was not suited for

20. *Heah Me Talkin' to Ya*, p. 116.
21. ** London AL3536.

the New Orleans ensemble. The blacks—who had created this sort of music with their fine taste and intuition, did not include it in their lineup. They opted for clearly contrasting parts: clarinet, trumpet, trombone, so the saxophone was of no use to them.[22]

Their "Farewell Blues" has become famous—it was the theme song of a Dutch dance band for years. Their "Tin Roof Blues" also became famous. It was indeed a beautiful composition, which borrowed one of its themes from Oliver's "Jazzin' Babies Blues." Brunies' trombone solo has become a classic; no band would perform the number without including it. Rappolo's solo is also very musically and melodically refined, but this is possibly the very factor that made it less suitable for direct reproduction.

This band's music proves one thing: while they were busy trying to approximate black music, these musicians were not performing wild and uncontrolled improvisation; on the contrary, they were producing a very gentle, fluent basso continuo upon which the music, played in an orderly and calm fashion, was based. This assures us that original New Orleans jazz was not wild or rough; it utterly belies the theory that the music was loud, noisy and without nuance. That view, as we have seen, stems from a lack of understanding and ignorance of the structural laws which apply to this music. As a result people could not make sense of the sounds that reached their ears.

The Development of Jazz on the White Scene: "Riverboat Shuffle"

If we investigate the significance of original New Orleans' jazz music in the early 1920s, it becomes apparent that the few records produced at that time made a tremendous impact. A handful of musicians spread over a small number of bands caused almost all dance bands to change their tone within a short space of time.

---

22. The bass sax from Oliver's band served to double the trombone contribution and Bechet employed his soprano sax as a clarinet. The alto and tenor saxes are the very instruments that obscure the sound in this sort of band.

Listen to the early recordings of the New York dance musicians who called themselves Original Memphis Five.[23] Listen to the very calm music that jazz musicians like Phil Napoleon and Miff Mole were able to produce; it will certainly have been easier on the ears of the audience than the sharp sounds of the Original Dixieland Band. But note too how in the polyphony and strict structure of this music the influence of New Orleans music is unmistakable.

Dance bands that included at least one jazz-oriented musician soon appeared and proceeded to play music which, although it was far from being pure jazz, had very clearly undergone exposure to it. A good example of this would be the California Ramblers.[24] Ted Lewis, besides his own humorous numbers which are also interesting (though not with jazz in mind), also let his band play some pure jazz in the New Orleans Rhythm Kings' tradition, and some of the best white jazz musicians (e.g., Muggsy Spanier and George Brunies) found their niche there. Ted Lewis was perhaps the most musical and as yet unsurpassed American singer of all time.

Paul Whiteman also needs to be mentioned here. He was a successful band leader in the 1920s who managed to equip himself with the aura of someone who had created jazz, and then have people believe that he indeed had done so. How he did it, remains a mystery. The first thing I ever heard about jazz (probably around 1932) was that Whiteman had invented it when the pane of glass from a swing-door shattered. How this myth ever came about is baffling, because if you listen to the recordings by this band their music is the most boring, soulless dance music, though sometimes played in clever arrangements. On the odd occasion you hear a couple of bars of Bix Beiderbecke, the talented white cornetist who spent the last years of his life playing with this big band—bored and in despair.

I want to continue with Bix and other second-generation whites. Firstly, we must mention the Austin High School Gang, a gang of youths from a School of Advanced Vocational Training in Chicago

23. HCJ.
24. Ibid.

who became so enthusiastic when they heard the New York Rhythm Kings' recording of "Farewell Blues" and other records that they went out and bought the instruments to try and produce similar music. As we shall see, their music was to assume great historical significance. They listened to the records and some of them (still mere boys) soon became professional musicians. From their recordings it becomes very clear that their music is fashioned after the example of the young men from New Orleans, the New Orleans Rhythm Kings, and of the blacks. Muggsy Spanier's music in those days, for example, was decidedly reminiscent of Armstrong's.[25]

Bix Beiderbecke was born in Davenport, Iowa, where as a boy at home he played his cornet along to Original Dixieland Jazz Band gramophone records. He was still young when he arrived in Chicago. He did not stick it out long at school—his time was almost entirely taken up by music. He soon became a serious contender with (and friend to) the boys of Austin High School. His first real contract came at the end of 1923 with the Wolverines, one of the most important bands on the white scene of that period. Bix can be heard playing his remarkable style in recordings by this band,[26] which confirms that those who tell us that he was very good are not making it up.

In 1925 he joined Frank Trumbauer's band, which was in fact nothing more than a dance band. The music they played, as we are now able to hear on the record, was anything but fantastic. On the contrary; it sounds a bit old-fashioned now—a bit sweet, too tame. Still, Bix got the chance to play his own music, inspired by and based on the work of black musicians like Oliver and Armstrong. We can hear this on a number of records made by a small group of musicians from the larger band, and apparently inspired by Armstrong's Hot Five, which we still have to deal with. Bix's personal performance, primarily characterized by a very individual tone and intonation, and a special method of phrasing, stands out very well on these

25. Ibid.
26. Ibid.

recordings.[27] It is a pity that the other musicians just fall short of his caliber, with the exception of the clarinetist, Don Murray, an otherwise forgotten musician who is certainly worth listening to. The most important recordings of this group are undoubtedly "Jazz Me Blues," "Royal Garden Blues" and particularly the very beautiful "Riverboat Shuffle."

Bix's music was very significant. He later joined Paul Whiteman's band where he was permitted to play the odd four-bar solo in its over-commercialized performances. Even though the band's arrangements were sometimes clever, there is no way in which they can be regarded as captivating, and Bix came to grief.

His creative ability was repressed, his artistic consciousness was overtaxed and, finding solace in alcohol, he perished. His life was to become a legend, his name one that would inspire countless musicians, his tragic lot a prototype of the fate that awaited (and still awaits) so many jazz musicians; but his music, as we said, made an enormous impact, particularly in the white scene. At this point we must specifically make mention of a circle of New York musicians— Red Nichols, Miff Mole, Joe Venuti, Eddie Lang and others—who, as we have seen, had already been exposed to the influence of the Dixieland Band and other similar bands around 1920. They too made many records under the name of The Five Pennies, Miff Mole's Little Molers, The Louisiana Rhythm Kings, etc. Their music is sometimes purely commercial; sometimes they aim higher and a very special sort of jazz emerges which has unfortunately not been able to endure the test of time. Nevertheless, their main significance is that these recordings heralded the arrival of jazz in Europe and that much early European jazz—from around 1928 until the Second World War—was inspired by these very records.

But with these recordings we have wandered a long way from the early and honest enthusiasm of the Austin High School Gang with talented musicians such as Muggsy Spanier, Jimmy McPartland and

27. * Philips B O7020, *The Bix Beiderbecke Story*; * Philips BO7226L (only "Goose Pimples").

Frank Teschemaker—far from their ideal of playing this new music in their own way, seriously and artistically sound. The enthusiasm of the circle of Red Nichols, amongst others, was great and we can soon get carried away writing about these young people, but it must not distract us from the fact that they drew from very different sources than the black music of Oliver and others. Their music emanates from their enthusiasm for it, attempts to grasp and equal it, but ends up being flawed because it strives to grasp something that is not really their own. We miss the inner peace, the naturalness and stylish confidence. Perhaps the most pure is Bix Beiderbecke, for the very reason that he dared to be himself and to play music that did not pretend to be black. His phrasing and his treatment of melody is purely Western.

In any case, these white musicians did work that was preeminent in the history of jazz; we shall return to their contribution at length in a future chapter.

BLACK FOLK SONGS IN THE 1920S: "JOHN HENRY"

It is evident that during this time African Americans in rural areas and in the cities sang folk songs. This sort of music was not performed by artists or blues singers, who rendered their own type of song, so it was seldom or never recorded. It was not until later—in the 1930s—that it was recorded, noncommercially. We do know something of the folk songs of this period, however, because it had been studied for some time. The most important book dedicated to the subject was Odum and Johnson's Negro Workaday Songs that was published in 1926 and recorded the results of research in North and South Carolina, Tennessee and Georgia. It included discussions of the Race series recordings, i.e., records played by blacks and exclusively intended for sale to blacks. It was the first time they were given any consideration by researchers, an example that has unfortunately often been ignored.

The famous ballad "John Henry" is also recorded in the book. It is a typical black song—also with respect to the content—about a railroad worker who was hacking away at the rock to make a tunnel when the steam drill was first introduced. He challenged the drill and won in a contest, but paid for his supernatural effort with his life. It is a song that was sung by blacks everywhere and is also a typical folk song by virtue of the fact that there are many versions of it.[28] We have chosen the version which later appeared in J. A. and A. Lomax's book *American Ballads and Folk Songs.* We have abridged it somewhat by omitting verses.

> John Henry was a li'l baby,
> Sittin' on his mama's knee,
> Said: 'De Big Bend Tunnel on de C & O road
> Gonna cause the death of me,
> Lord Lord, gonna cause the death of me.'
>
> Cap'n said to John Henry:
> 'Gonna bring me a steam drill 'round,
> Gonna take dat steam drill out on the job,
> Gonna whop that steel on down,
> Lord Lord, gonna whop that steel on down.'
>
> John Henry tol' his cap'n
> Lightnin' was in his eye:
> 'Cap'n, bet yo' last red cent on me,
> For I'll beat it to the bottom or I'll die,
> Lord Lord, for I'll beat it to the bottom or I'll die.'
>
> John Henry started on de right hand,
> De steam drill started on the left,
> Before I'd let dis steam drill beat me down,
> I'd hammer my fool self to death,
> Lord Lord, I'd hammer my fool self to death.

28. Recordings on the record: LiC VIII (Arthur Bell, 1939); *† Asch 343–3 (Leadbelly, 1943); *** Vogue V 2074 (Broonzy, 1951); etc.

John Henry said to his shaker [a helper]
'Nigger, why don't you sing?
I'm throwin' twelve poun's from my hips on down,
Jes' listen to the cold steel ring,
Lord Lord, just listen to the cold steel ring.'

De man dat invented de steam drill,
Thought he was mighty fine,
John Henry drove his fifteen feet,
And the steam drill only made nine,
Lord Lord, an de steam drill only made nine.

De hammer dat John Henry swung,
It weighed over nine pound,
He broke a rib 'n his left-hand side,
And his intrels fell on the ground,
Lord Lord, his intrels fell on the ground.

John Henry was hammerin' the mountain,
And his hammer was strikin' fire,
He drove so hard till he broke his poor heart,
And he laid down his hammer and he died,
Lord Lord, and he laid down his hammer and he died.

John Henry had a pretty li'l woman,
And the dress that she wore was blue,
And the last words that she said to him:
'John Henry, I've been true to you,
Lord Lord, John Henry I've been true to you.'

Oh, who's gonna shoe yo' li'l feet,
And who's gonna glub your hands,
And who's gonna kiss yo' rosy lips,
And who's gonna be your man, Lord Lord, who's gonna be your
      man.

Dey took John Henry to de graveyard,
And dey buried him in de san',
And every locomotive come roarin' by,
Says: 'Dere lays a steel drivin' man,
Lord Lord, there lays a steel drivin' man.'

CHURCH MUSIC IN THE 1920S: "GOSPEL TRAIN IS LEAVING"

The gramophone industry flourished in the 1920s. It was not yet threatened by the radio and shared the general welfare of the economy. There were Race records for the blacks (see the photo insert, which shows the sleeve of a Race record). They now form an almost inexhaustible mine of information on which we can draw to learn about all kinds of black music, including spirituals.

Preach discs were also launched. These were 25 cm records, 78 rpm, with a short sermon on one side preceded by a spiritual. Much of the flip side was filled with singing. These records were made by black preachers who took several members of the congregation with them. The recordings give us a good impression of the ideas, the style of speech and singing in the black churches. The Rev. Gates and his associates Weems, Burnett, Moseley, F. W. McGee, E. D. Campbell and many others can be heard on these records.

The sermons were rendered in a typical style that developed in black churches, comparable to a recitative, a sort of musical rhetoric, often of great beauty. The congregation is not wholly silent but supports the rendition by the odd "Hallelujah," "Lord have mercy," "Amen!" and so on, or by forming a humming accompaniment. If we listen to these records it becomes clear that wild ecstasy and unbridled emotionalism are not in any way the hallmark of black religious practices. Yet it is this aspect that has been stressed all too often. The reason for this is the same as in the case of jazz music—much of it stems from a lack of clear understanding of what is happening. The character and rendition are not Western, but neither are they African, primitive or unbiblical! In their assessment some allowed themselves to be compelled by a sort of exaggerated longing to display the spectacular, the foreign, the exotic, the colorful aspects. This is why so much attention was given to what happened in strange sects, where one indeed finds trances and other such phenomena, but they occur equally in white churches of a similar sort.

The rendition is generally calm and collected, as we hear on these recordings,[29] comparable to later recordings of church services.[30] The content is orthodox evangelical and the personal contact between the believers and their Lord and Savior is strongly emphasized. The language is often rich and expressive, sometimes naive in the choice of analogy but in all simplicity deep, with biblical wisdom.

We have already said that one side of the record contains a sermon, and we would like to give you the beginning of one by the Rev. T. E. Weems that is taken from a Columbia Race record from around 1927. It is entitled "God Is Mad with Man":

My brothers and sisters, I'm going to preach to you tonight from a subject from the sixth chapter of Genesis, 6th and 7th verses:

"And it repented the Lord that he had made man on the earth, and it grieved him at his heart. And the Lord said, 'I will destroy man whom I have created from the face of the earth . . . '." Our subject is: God is enraged by man. That is why every born again child of God will live in such a way that the Lord will not be enraged with him. Because whenever God is enraged there will be problems in the country. God was enraged with people in the days of Sodom and Gomorrah, and the city was destroyed with fire and brimstone. God was enraged with Nebuchadnezzar . . . God was enraged with Belshazzar, and he sent a hand to write on the wall. So then, every time God is enraged with somebody, he brings their life to an end. That is why each and every person who is really born of the Spirit, must live as Christian and as a born again Christian, so as not to

29. **** Fontana 467064 TE; HCJ; for the rest, these kind of recordings are very rare.

30. E.g., * Ducretet-Thomson 260 V 069, 1955.

enrage the Lord. Well now, in the days of Noah there were men and women . . . who were very bad . . . and nobody would get on their knees and pray.

Many sermons were about the confidence of the believer, resting in the forgiveness of sins in the blood of Jesus Christ, and very often Christian conduct would be the subject. On the flip side we find spirituals. The renditions are strongly reminiscent of the camp meetings: the minister says his lines in a melodious fashion, clearly articulated and rhythmic, and melodically defined, and then the congregation sings the recurring chorus. An image that we often come across is that of the train—a modernization, if we may say so, of the old image of the chariot which we have already come across in "Swing Low, Sweet Chariot," and which was inspired by the story of Elijah's ascension. The image of the train is sometimes greatly expanded:[31] the ticket is faith, Christ is the engine driver, and this "gospel train" takes the believer to heaven.

Very beautiful is the song spoken by Rev. Burnett and sung by his congregation (represented here by some of them, of course): "The Gospel Train Is Leaving," a sermon with singing, the label tells us.[32] The preacher begins, accompanied by an organ: "I want you to sing concerning the unconverted Christian," whereupon the congregation joins with a chorus: "Tell me how long the train has been gone (x 3), People were coming and the train done gone." Then the minister sings again: "I looked down the road and saw them coming from the South, East, West and North, each crying: 'Tell me how long has the train been gone'" (which would be repeated by the choir). It is a clear warning not to delay, but if God calls, to hear his voice and obey (based on passages like Psalm 32:6, Revelation 2:21, and others).

During the same period there was a sort of literary and cultural revival going on among black intellectuals, known as the Harlem

31. It is curious that the image of a train was already used on a gravestone in Ely (England) dating from 1845.
32. **** Fontana 467064 TE; †† Col. 14180, 1926.

Renaissance. A few important black poets had works published which were worthwhile in every way.[33] Still we must be aware of the fact that only a few blacks were involved, striving for emancipation—complete equality with whites—by means of cultural accommodation (namely proving themselves to be equal to whites in terms of their culture, so as to be accepted by them). By renouncing their own culture, they became alienated from their own people in many respects. This was a small group and we must not treat them as representative of all African Americans.

One of the most likeable characters from that movement was James Weldon Johnson. He was born in 1871 in Jacksonville, Florida, and graduated from the University of Atlanta, Georgia. He has held many important positions, including that of secretary of the NAACP (National Association for the Advancement of Colored People) and of Professor of Literature at Fisk University (a black university in Tennessee). His first collection of poems was published in 1917, and *God's Trombones* in 1927. The latter collection are sermons by black preachers which he had condensed and turned into poetry. He tried to capture something of the characteristic features of these very rhetorical and often musical preachers using rich metaphorical language. Did we not compare their rendition with a recitative? He aptly called them "God's trombones." The following poem is probably the most beautiful one and it contains a rich and deep exegesis of Genesis 1:

The Creation by James Weldon Johnson

And God stepped out on space,
And He looked around and said:
'I'm lonely—I'll make me a world.'
And far as the eye of God could see
Darkness covered everything,

33. See Langston Hughes and Arna Bontemps, *The Poetry of the Negro 1746–1949* (Garden City, 1953); the anthology edited by Rosey E. Pool and P. Breman, *Ik zag hoe zwart ik was* (The Hague, 1958); Dr. J. W. Schulte Northolt, *Het volk dat in duisternis wandelt* (Arnhem, 1957), p. 218 ff.

Blacker than a hundred midnights
Down in a cypress swamp.
Then God Smiled, And the light Broke,
And the darkness rolled up on one side,
And the light stood shining on the other,
And God said: 'That's good!'

Then God reached out and took the light in His hands
And God rolled the light around in His hands
Until He made the sun;
And He set that sun a-blazing in the heavens.
And the light that was left from making the sun
God gathered up in a shining ball
And flung against the darkness,
Spangling the night with the moon and the stars.
Then down between
The darkness and the light
He hurled the world;
And God said: That's good!

Then God himself stepped down –
And the sun was on His right hand,
And the moon was on His left;
The stars were clustered about His head,
And the earth was under His feet.
And God walked, and where He trod
His footsteps hollowed the valleys out
And bulged the mountains up.

Then He stopped and looked and saw
That the earth was hot and barren.
So God stepped over to the edge of the world
And He spat out the seven seas—
He batted His eyes, and the lightnings flashed—
He clapped His hands, and the thunders rolled—

And the waters above the earth came down,
The cooling waters came down.

Then the green grass sprouted,
And the little flowers blossomed,
The pine tree pointed his finger to the sky,
And the oak spread his arms,
The lakes cuddled down in the hollows of the ground,
And the rivers ran down to the sea;
And God smiled again,
And the rainbow appeared,
And curled itself around His shoulder.

Then God raised His arm and He waved His hand
Over the sea and over the land,
And He said: 'Bring forth! Bring forth!'
And quicker than God could drop His hand,
Fishes and fowls
And beasts and birds
Swam the rivers and the seas,
Roamed the forests and the woods,
And split the air with their wings.
And God said: 'That's good!'

Then God walked around
And God looked around
On all that He had made:
He looked on His world
With all its living things,
And God said: 'I'm lonely still.'

Then God sat down—
On the side of a hill where He could think;
By a deep, wide river He sat down;
With His head in His hands,

God thought and thought,
Till He thought: 'I'll make me a man!'

Up from the bed of the river
God scooped the clay;
And by the bank of the river
He kneeled Him down,
And there the great God Almighty
Who lit the sun and fixed it in the sky,
Who flung the stars to the most far corner of the night,
Who rounded the earth in the middle of His hand,
This Great God,
Like a mammy bending over her baby,
Kneeled down in the dust
Toiling over a lump of clay
Till He shaped it in His own image.
Then into it He breathed the breath of life,
And man became a living soul.
Amen. Amen.

ORIGIN OF THE COMMERCIAL SPIRITUALS: "CREEP ALONG MOSES"

James Weldon Johnson also published a book of transcripts of spirituals.[34] In the introduction he tells the reader how he used to sing in a quartet in his youth. It was apparently not an unusual occupation—the number of existing quartets at that time could be calculated by dividing the entire black male population by four. These quartets sang popular songs, sometimes black folk songs but mainly Negro spirituals. They harmonized by ear and often rehearsed while waiting for the barber—hence the name "barber-shop quartets."

It seems that this custom was more prevalent among the middle class than among the rural population; it is evidence of the important

34. J. W. Johnson, *Books of American Negro Spirituals* (New York, 1940).

part music played in the lives of black people. The spirituals would have been regarded (though not by black Christians) mainly as a traditional and trusted form of music—a living legacy. Recordings were made of these quartets, particularly in larger centers with a high concentration of blacks, places like Birmingham, Alabama and Norfolk, Virginia. Their songs were not actually black folk music in the true sense of the word. Rather, their repertoire consisted of spirituals following in the tradition of the Fisk Jubilee Singers, in addition to a worldlier, somewhat popular repertoire, on the whole strongly influenced by whites. These spirituals, just like those that originated in the more academic climate of the black universities, were severed from a direct connection with the church. They provided relaxation for amateurs.

It is difficult to distinguish clearly between these quartets and another kind of quartet which, judging by the number of recordings they made,[35] must have been very popular. The Americans, with their typical realism, christened their music "religious entertainment," although it almost always referred to quartets who sang spirituals because their audiences enjoyed them and not because of any religious sympathies. They do link with the tradition we have just mentioned, but they are also strongly influenced by the current trends in entertainment music. "Creep Along Moses," sung by the Taskania Four (the name is clearly popular and not religious) in 1925, is based on a rhythm that immediately reminds us of the Charleston, a dance rhythm that was fashionable at the time. This religious entertainment is obviously hardly ever very deep. The lyrics were deliberately chosen to be neutral, chosen with care not to provoke anyone's conscience.

The Blues of Bessie Smith: "Young Woman's Blues"

While Handy was performing his blues against a background of dance music, 1923 also saw the first recording of blues sung outside this setting. It was Bessie Smith's debut, "Down Hearted Blues." This

---

35. Of both kinds, though many records were made they were not reissued and these recordings are now very rare. For that reason I will not list any record numbers.

and subsequent records were best sellers, though almost exclusively to black customers. Bessie Smith, one of Ma Rainey's pupils, sang primarily in the North, while "Ma" remained faithful to the South. This is probably why Bessie became better known.

Bessie Smith was an artist. She sang the blues in traditional fashion, striving for great sophistication of rendition and she developed the form from pure folk music to something which, though it cannot be compared with classical music by Western concert standards, is a serious form of artistic expression. She developed the form, while she sometimes added non-twelve-bar strophes, particularly introductions. Accompaniment is often left to a small ensemble consisting of a piano and one or more melody instruments. It is the musical accompaniment that gives away the folk blues background of this music which, although it was influenced by jazz, is certainly not identical to it. When Louis Armstrong accompanied Bessie Smith, his style and the nature of his performance differed from his performance with jazz bands.

A remarkable feature of this genre is that it was performed almost exclusively by women. Besides those already mentioned, there is a long line of female vocalists—almost all altos—who enjoyed success on the black scene and made many recordings (in the Race series). There was Victoria Spivey,[36] Ida Cox, Mamie Smith, Clara Smith, Lillian Glynn and many more besides.

Most of them sang their own versions of the blues—based on original folk blues. They used their own approaches to acquire their own style, both in terms of melody and of lyrics. Even though the titles of the songs might indicate that we are dealing with blues, and though stylistically—in character and nature—almost all their work is blues, the form does sometimes clearly deviate from the twelve-bar scheme. Very different from Handy, who adapted the blues to the world of entertainment music, and from Ravel, who occasionally borrowed the odd element from the blues for a Western composition, here the blues was expanded and developed without violation to the character, taste and tone of the songs.

36. *** Fontana 467063 TE. Cf. also **** Fontana 682073 TL.

Below are the lyrics of "Dyin' by the Hour."[37] Both the wry humor and the way the otherwise traditional theme is interpreted is typical of Bessie Smith's blues. This record, which includes some magnificent trumpet accompaniment by Ladnier, opens with a quote from Chopin's funeral march. This must not be seen as the profane use of a Western theme but rather as a memory of New Orleans funerals, where this music was familiar to the French-speaking population:

It's an old story, every time it's a doggone man (x 2)
But when that thing is on you, you just drift from hand to hand.

I'd drink up all this acid, if it wouldn't burn me so (x 2)
And telephone the devil, that's the only place I'd go.

Once I weighed two hundred, I'm nothing but skin and bones (x 2)
I've always laughed, but now it's nothing but a moan and a groan.

Lord, if I'm dying by the hour 'bout that doggone man of mine (x 2)
He said he didn't love me, that's why I'm dyin' and lose my mind.[38]

FOLK BLUES IN THE 1920S: "YOU DON'T KNOW MY MIND"

There were a few men who, particularly in the Northern cities such as Chicago, enjoyed parity with Bessie Smith and co. such as "Texas" Alexander[39] and Lonnie Johnson, for instance, but most of the recordings made by men in the 1920s were the work of folk musicians—troubadours. They were recruited by "talent scouts" in the South and then went to a particular city, e.g., Chicago, where they made recordings for the Race series. Then they usually disappeared again. So all we get to hear of the blues on record is the work of professional artists and never pure folk music, the sort everybody sang.

37. ***† Col. DZ 346; Philips issued a whole series of LP's of Bessie (B) 7002L/B O7005L, of which in my opinion *** B O7002L is the best.
38. **** Fontana 682073 TL.
39. ** Fontana 467136 TE.

There are countless singers with whom we can make acquaintance on these records—far too many to name, not even briefly. Many of them cut no more than a few sides before disappearing completely to their Southern homeland again. In some cases these performers were semiprofessional, having a different job besides their musical activities. That may be the reason that later on we seldom come across them again.

The blues they sing—accompanied by guitar or piano, or the odd violin or trombone, as an exception—are structurally similar to those we have already analyzed, but other forms have also cropped up in the course of time. The twelve-bar construction is retained (unlike the blues of the previous chapter). One of the variations we could call the "long-lined blues." Usually in the standard structure of the blues, no more than two of the four bars of each line is sung. In the type we are referring to here, however, the phrase carries on and lasts for seven bars. The eighth bar constitutes a rest and the last four bars are then sung again.

A good example of this, and one which confirms that this genre was developed from the older standard type, is "Lonesome Atlanta Blues" by Bobby Grant:

I'm so lonesome, I'm so lonesome, hear me crying, baby I ain't
> lying,
I'm so lonesome, I'm so lonesome that I've got the blues.
I'm so sad and lonesome, mamma, I don't know what to do.

When you have a feeling, a mean old feeling, that dirty old feel-
> ing, that feeling,
When you have a feeling that your gal don't want you no more,
You better take my advice and leave her even if it hurts you so.

I'm gonna walk down the dirt road, that long, long dirt road, that
> dirty old dirt road, mmm that dirt road,
I'm gonna walk down the dirt road, 'less somebody let me ride,
If I can't find my baby, I run away and hide.

I'm going back to Atlanta, I mean down in Georgia, crazy 'bout
    Atlanta, I mean Atlanta, Georgia,
I'm going back to Atlanta, down to the Cater Street,
If I can't find my baby, I believe somebody'll be kind to me.[40]

This song was clearly developed by expanding the ordinary structure of the blues melodically, as it were, with many repetitions.

    This type of blues often features a refrain, with the last part of the strophe as a recurring theme. Barbecue Bob's blues is one example, the first two strophes of which are quoted here. The first line is sung completely and the refrain takes up the remaining eight bars:

You don't know, you don't know, you don't know my mind, cruel gal,
You don't know, you don't know my mind; when you see me
    laughing I'm laughing just to keep from crying.

I asked my brown, can you stand to see me die; she said, man,
    I can stand to see you die,
You don't know, you don't know my mind; when you see me
    laughing I'm laughing just to keep from crying.[41]

There are even more variations and deviations than these, but the original structure always remains discernible. This folk art is, strangely enough, yet to be properly researched and analyzed; hardly any work has yet been done.[42]

    This type of the blues was sometimes sung by more than one vocalist, by two or three. The tempo was mostly faster in that case and the lyrics then assumed a different character. Instead of meditative it became a sort of satire—the kind of humor that is unique among

40. *** London AL 3535 (*Backwood Blues*).

41. †† Col. 14246-D, 1927–1928.

42. We already mentioned the unpublished study of the late Drs. F. G. Boom and Iain Lang, "Jazz in Perspective, the Background of the Blues" (London, n.d.). Also very important is the recording of a conversation between three blues singers: *Blues in the Mississippi Night*, ** Nixa NJL 8.

blacks. A good example of this is the jaunty, satirical little number sung by Walter Vincent with Chatman's Mississippi Hot Footers. He always sings the first line on his own and the refrain is then sung by a number of men together:

> Jack had chickens on the roof, every night he was missing 'bout two,
> Using that too, using that too, you ain't to get mad, your friends
> > gonna use that too.

> Jack had biscuits on the shelf, every night he found them gone,
> Using that too, using that too, you ain't to get mad, your friends
> > gonna use that too.[43]

The song continues on the subject of flowers, then a car, whisky, and even his wife. The accompaniment consists of two guitars and a violin—an instrument often played in folk music of this sort. The instruments seem to be perfectly designed for the character of the piece. This sort of derivative of the blues is rare, however, and the original form is far from becoming extinct.[44]

Piano Folk Music: Boogie-Woogie

It is no longer possible to trace the origins of the old piano folk music called boogie-woogie. Some say it originated in Texas at the beginning of the twentieth century, while others mention other places. What is certain is that boogie-woogie flourished in the Northern cities, Chicago in particular, in the 1920s. The structure is almost always the same as the twelve-bar blues, often with a sort of refrain, i.e., the last four bars remain the same in each verse.

The pianistic style of this folk art is lively, the strong, rhythmic bass of the left hand being the most striking feature. Each beat

43. †† Br. 7126, 1929.
44. **† Score SLP 4022 (Lightnin' Hopkins) and also many records of Big Bill Broonzy, recorded after the War.

consists of two notes, one of which is played low and the other higher, creating a sort of walking bass. There are many variants however, to avoid monotony. Above the bass, the right hand administers the melody which usually consists of short phrases that are often repeated. Each new strophe usually has a new variation on the basic theme.

It is the art of folk musicians who play in small cafes or at dance parties in (poor) people's own homes. The boogie-woogie is, after all, also a dance. The pianist often assumes the role of dance leader as it were, indicating (in musical fashion) the type of step or dance to be performed. These black dances have to be regarded as real folk dances, performed collectively, (and relatively) unconnected with Western duo-dancing.

A considerable number of recordings of this music were made in the 1920s. Pinetop Smith and in particular Jim Yancey later became famous, both giving exceptionally polished performances, experts at contrasting extremely quiet passages with lively ones.

It took time for this music to gain fame because when these recordings were made, boogie-woogie was virtually unknown beyond the circle of black workers for whom it was intended. In 1928 Meade Lux Lewis made his *Honky Tonk Train Blues* for Paramount, the company exclusively responsible for producing the Race records series.[45] It went bankrupt shortly after and the record became a collector's piece. A copy was later discovered by the jazz critic and connoisseur John Hammond, who subsequently tried to trace the pianist. Many years passed before he succeeded; Lewis turned out to be working in a garage in Chicago. Hammond then had Lewis record his composition once again. The flip side of this recording featured a piano solo by a white jazz pianist who was well known at the time.[46] That is why the record was bought, and it was only later that the purchasers discovered the exceptional recording on the B-side. This is how the "Honky Tonk Train Blues"—today still one of the most beautiful pieces inspired by riding in a train—became famous overnight. It also

45. ** London AL 3506.
46. ***† Parlophon R 2187: Jess Stacy.

heralded the popular boogie-woogie fashion which was predominant for some time in the late 1930s. Boogie-woogie then became quite a wild sort of music with a rhythmically monotonous beat and an extremely fast tempo.

Fortunately there were others who sought real boogie-woogie, and this is how Jim Yancey was rediscovered. He went on to record some particularly beautiful numbers.[47]

Jug Bands: "Memphis Shake"

The word "shake" in this title refers to a dance—once again, a type of folk dance. Many of the strange-sounding words we come across like "strut," "shimmy," "grind," "rock" and so on, refer to types of dancing. This particular piece, "Memphis Shake," was played by the Dixieland Jug Band,[48] one of the best examples of this strange combination of instruments. Jug bands originally were probably small rural bands, composed in rather random fashion according to the availability of musicians. The few that managed to penetrate the city scene would have been regarded as curiosities; they would also have represented the best of their sort.

These bands were in possession of a variety of homemade instruments, which is hardly surprising considering how poor these folk were. The percussion section consisted of the wife's washboard, simply but very cleverly transformed into a real instrument. The bass section was a jug, a pitcher or small storage tin into which they blew; it was apparently a very useful instrument which produced a sound somewhere in between that of a tuba and a bass ("struck" strongly pizzicato, which was a common style among the blacks). The trumpet was replaced by a kazoo, an instrument made by attaching a nozzle to a little toy tin-instrument by means of a membrane. There was also the blue-blowing, a comb with paper stretched across it, which

47. *** London AL 3525; *** HMV. DLP 1048; *** Riverside 1028. And boogie-woogie recordings on HCJ and ** Br. BL 54014.
48. †† Victor 20415.

was blown in humming fashion. The harmonica was very common to these bands and very popular among the blacks, who knew exactly how to produce the most beautiful music on it, never needing to work for virtuosity. Finally, a violin was often included. It was probably adopted from white folk music, for a great deal of white folk-dance music (square dances, closely related to cowboy songs, very rarely recorded and now virtually obsolete)[49] was led by the violin. Blacks are very adept at playing it, and their style is very different from the Western style. One of the best examples is "Hen Party Blues" by the same Dixieland Jug Band.[50]

This music should not be underestimated. The fact that Johnny Dodds plays in both of the examples mentioned above and, more importantly, is not an odd man out in the ensemble, speaks for itself.

One of the oddest bands in this genre to make recordings was Bobby Leecan's Need More Band, whose "Apaloosa Blues" is particularly noteworthy.[51] The band consists of a banjo, guitar, cello, harmonica, washboard and kazoo. Stylistically, their polyphonic music is very closely related to New Orleans jazz. This is evidence that the essence of the music does not lie in a particular combination of instruments, even if the contrasting timbres of the traditional clarinet-trumpet-trombone group does constitute the ideal synthesis for the purpose.

JELLY ROLL MORTON'S JAZZ IN 1926: "BLACK BOTTOM STOMP"

The "Memphis Shake" we just discussed appeared on the flip side of the original Victor production of "Doctor Jazz" by Jelly Roll Morton's Red Hot Peppers, which brings us to a series of records that include some of the best jazz music ever recorded.[52] In September and December of 1926, Jelly Roll Morton made these records together with

49. FoW FPl.
50. **† HMV JK 2773.
51. **† HMV B 5430, 1927.
52. **** RCA LPM-1649-C.

a group of New Orleans musicians; it was not his band—the group came together just for these recordings—a so-called "recording combination." The musicians did know each other, respected each other and were united in their feeling for style and interpretation. Jelly himself had composed a significant number of the pieces they played—"Dead Man's Blues," "Sidewalk Blues," "Cannonball Blues," "Jelly Roll Blues" and "Grandpa's Spell"—and he was able to get his musicians to play every nuance that he regarded essential. This becomes evident when we compare his own piano solos with the recordings of the band.

The musicians who made these recordings with Jelly Roll Morton all have strong recollections of them. It was quite extraordinary. The members of the band were George Mitchell, cornet; Kid Ory, trombone; Omer Simeon, clarinet; Johnny St. Cyr, banjo; Andrew Lindsay, bass and Andrew Hilaire, drums.

Simeon recalls:

The people from Victor (the recording company) treated Jelly as somebody special. And that's what he was, considering that he was the best of his sort in the whole country. And they paid us above the normal margin to work with him . . . You see, Jelly set high standards when it came to his music, and if the musicians couldn't play real New Orleans style, he went looking for others.

I'll tell you how the band's rehearsals went. He was very precise. Very bright, always very lively, but also very serious. We mostly rehearsed for about three hours for four sides. And in that time he indicated the effects he was after, like for instance an accompaniment for a solo—he would play that through on the piano with one finger and then the musicians would play it together, making it a three-part.

Johnny St. Cyr tells:

The solos were free. We played as we sensed it. Naturally Jelly had his own ideas; sometimes we listened to him and sometimes we

115

tried to make something better of it. As for me, I just did whatever he asked me to do . . . Now Jelly was a very, very nice man to make a record with, and I'll tell you why . . . He never told you exactly what you had to play, but left it to your own judgment and said, 'Take a break here' . . . and 'the clarinet has to take a break there.' That's the reason why his records show so much variety . . . If Jelly asked me 'Can you take a break here?,' I answered, 'OK.' Then he would say, 'Good, let's try it.' And when we got to that place, we took the break; as if you were saying 'OK, let me take that one.' You allowed yourself to be led by your own taste, you see. If it sounded good, then it was alright. If it wasn't so good, he would say, 'Wait a minute, that doesn't sound so good; see if you can't change it a bit.'

That's the reason why his records are so full of inventions and variations; it was because he gave his people so much freedom. Sometimes we asked him—if we had an idea, you know—and then we would ask him whether we could take a certain break somewhere.

On the subject of New Orleans music in general, Johnny also tells us:

In New Orleans we had a system of playing which aimed to play music at its most beautiful . . . Whatever you did, it had to be good. No playing out of tune. You had to keep within the bounds of the given melody, but we, old hands, were very good at making a number more beautiful.[53]

That is how Jelly got his men to play exactly what he wanted them to play, still allowing them the freedom to follow their own style within the framework of his composition.

Even when Jelly played existing compositions he was able to put his stamp on the rendition to such an extent that it would almost

53. Lomax, *Mister Jelly Roll*, pp. 192, 193, and 102.

become a Jelly number. This stands out particularly in the "Black Bottom Stomp"; he reconstructed the main theme upon which the solos were based, so that the original version, consisting of a short theme of two times four bars, four countermelody bars (quite tiresome) and four bars repeating the initial theme,[54] became a theme of four bars, the fourth of which was a break, then a repeat of the theme moving into a coda, making a total of ten bars (and the boring connecting piece was excluded).

These records, along with those by Oliver, constitute some of the most beautiful New Orleans jazz ever recorded; they are very different from those by Oliver because Jelly's own trademark is clearly evident, which just goes to show how broad and versatile this black music is—anything but a dead formula. Polyphony and variation— not improvisation—are certainly the main features which incite its striking joy, its openness and suppleness, particularly in the rhythm. These are the very characteristics that the dance music lacked completely in those days before this new music became influential. The dance music of the whites was boring, wishy-washy, superficially bright but essentially uninspiring, cool and tame. That very difference is one of the reasons why jazz, like that on Jelly's records, has been so influential; its success stemmed from the lack of spirit in the Western popular music of the time, and its imitation was an attempt to seize something of it. This would certainly explain the quick spread of the jazz playing-style, though it unfortunately led to a change of jazz character.

WHITE CHICAGO JAZZ: "I'VE FOUND A NEW BABY"

The white boys from Chicago we mentioned earlier (the Austin High School Gang, Bix Beiderbecke), who were moved by the music they heard from Oliver and Morton, Armstrong and Dodds, and others, were the first whites outside New Orleans to seriously attempt

54. †† HMV B 5173 (Johnny Hamp's Kentucky Serenaders, a dance band ca. 1925/1926).

to emulate this style. The influence of Louis Armstrong in particular, who performed with various bands as soloist, was enormous.

These boys were certainly talented and very enthusiastic, but it was inevitable that they would interpret the music in their own way. This music was different from anything they already knew—the dance music of those days and the late Romantic style in classical music. This new music seemed to spring spontaneously from the black soul, since the musicians did not play from written notes. Not realizing how traditional and fixed this music was in its structure, they considered it revolutionary.

Their music therefore became founded on an odd misinterpretation of New Orleans jazz as it was played in Chicago between 1920 and 1925. They considered this music revolutionary because they thought that it was played "just like that"—directly improvised, conceived, as it were, on the spur of the moment. Was this not part of their spiritual attitude—the desire to express themselves uninhibited, independent of any tradition, independent of any norms—enjoying themselves, just letting themselves go? Jean Jacques Rousseau, the eighteenth-century philosopher, taught that it was the things that came directly from a person, without the veneer of civilization, which were real and relevant and worthwhile. His ideals had dictated the spirit of Western culture for two whole centuries, penetrating deeply, and were adopted by these youngsters too—though they had probably never read Rousseau. This attitude of Western humanism had become generally dominant and, yes, is still dominant across a great part of Western culture.

Oliver, Morton et al., started with the melody, which was then varied. All instruments, harmonically speaking, based their chords on a bass note (usually rendered by the bass but otherwise by the piano)—the chords normally changed after a number of beats, depending on the melody that was being backed up. The "Chicagoans" (the name by which these white musicians from Chicago became known) based their playing on the chords and not on the given theme—a typically Western way of approaching music. This allowed them the freedom to improvise, to let themselves go. The mutual alliance between soloist and accompaniment remained intact because the musicians adhered to the given harmonic scheme; they were therefore able to deviate from the given musical theme.

Their approach to music was typically individualistic. The emphasis no longer laid on the polyphonically played ensemble (a significant number of Oliver's records are solely given over to ensemble music of this type), but on the freely improvised solos. They abandoned the fixed structure of the pieces with their repeats and diverse themes, and the average Chicagoan rendition opens with a (virtually homophonic) exposition of the melody, followed by a succession of freely improvised solos, bound together by the chord scheme only, and ending in a rather noisy and chaotic tutti. It is, after all, not possible to play polyphonic New Orleans jazz in an individualistic fashion; it would irrevocably lead to chaos and a wild clash of individual styles.

The music of the blacks was rhythmical. In that respect, however, it was anything but African; African polyrhythms do not occur. The best way to understand what the rhythm instruments collectively achieved is to observe the similarity with the Baroque basso continuo, as in the music of Bach. At the same time we must indicate that the rhythm of the melody, with all the agogic accents evoked by melody instruments, plays a significant role in the character of black jazz.

A series of curious associations—rhythm is African, primitive, original, real, primal, free from cultured civilization, the heartbeat of life itself—caused the Chicagoans to interpret rhythm very differently from what it actually was in this music. To them, it became a rigid meter with regular strong beats (and deviant accents like the off-beat, an accentuation of the otherwise unaccentuated beats, the second and the fourth of the bar). The Chicagoans thus became the creators of jazz as we know it: music with an individualistic character, with the accent on freely improvised solos and a rhythm that is powerful and strongly metric in character.

Their music demanded aggressive rendition; this was their way of trying to approach the joyful openness of the black music. That is why their music is often loud, not only in terms of volume but also in atmosphere and character. This vehemence, this dynamism, was achieved by creating a strong tension between the rhythm of the melody (created by agogic accents, rubato, etc.) and the clearly defined meter rendered by the rhythm section. From now on we have to draw a sharp dividing line between the melody and rhythm sections, something which was not necessary in the music of Oliver and Morton. Off-beat rhythms increased the tension. The peace and inner joy of black music have been replaced by fervor, agitation, tension and lack of restraint.

Around 1927 the Chicagoans made an important series of records, with McPartland (trumpet), Teschemaker (clarinet), Spanier (trumpet), Mezz Mezzrow (saxophone), Eddie Condon (banjo) and Gene Krupa (drums). The trombone was often replaced by the tenor sax, which reduced the transparency of the ensemble sections (if they were present at all). Teschemaker was possibly the most clear and distinct exponent of what they were trying to achieve. The way he formed tones suggests strong emotion—a wild letting go, without restraint. "I've Found a New Baby"[55] was one of their most characteristic recordings, with its fast tempo, its short-winded phrasing, and a rendition which hardly does justice to the theme upon which it is based. This became jazz as it was later almost always understood to be because, needless to say, the Chicago style made a terrific impact among the white population in America and Europe—and indeed everywhere where "jazz" was played.

Armstrong's Hot Five and Hot Seven: "Heebee Jeebees"

On 12 November 1925 the first recordings by the Hot Five were made, a combination of old friends: Louis Armstrong, trumpet; Johnny Dodds, clarinet; Kid Ory trombone; Lil Harlin, piano and Johnny St. Cyr, banjo. Together they formed another typical recording combination. Since Oliver's old band had broken up, Armstrong had been the star soloist with a number of big bands which were not playing real New Orleans music. Dodds had been playing with

55. ITJ; also *Dazzling Jazz, Traditional,* ** Philips B O7226L ("China Boy").

all sorts of smaller combinations like the jug bands, but he stuck to the strict idiom of New Orleans. Ory often played in the band that Oliver formed later on (which we shall come back to), while some of the other musicians made music for a living with one particular band, and some with various bands.

Now they had come together and were going to make records in original New Orleans style. They composed much of their music themselves, played in loose arrangements with rich polyphonic ensemble music, solos and breaks with a clear structure, always musically sound. There is no sign of individualism or loose improvisation. The music is lively, cheerful, but never exhilarant; neither is it sentimental, though some pieces like the very beautiful "You're Next," created on 26 February 1926, may be described as tender. There were still more treasures to be unearthed that day: "Cornet Shop Suey," "Muskrat Ramble" and also "Heebee Jeebees."[56] The latter was a fantastic success. Armstrong sang scat—it was the first time a white audience had heard it—a style of singing without words, using the voice as a kind of instrument. The Chicagoans and their friends loved it. As far as they were concerned another tradition had been overthrown: here people let themselves go, free from all the stuffy airs and graces. This was improvisation!

Perhaps the Chicagoans were not far off the mark because, indeed, in the scat chorus solo the seeds of something new had been sown. It should not surprise us that it was Armstrong in particular who would take that road. Was he not the highly acclaimed solo star who put up individual performances? It must have meant everything to this lad from the backstreets of New Orleans to be so popular among whites—whites who said he could improvise so well, whites whose reaction to his sometimes vehement and intense performance betrayed their pleasure, whites who reveled in his ability to handle the prescribed melodic material roughly and freely. The "new" seeds had originated from the influence of the boys from Chicago

56. Many reissues of these records, such as **** Col. 3 SX 1029; **** Philips B O7181L.

(the Chicagoans, their friends and kindred spirits), who had steered Armstrong in that direction. They learned much from Armstrong, certainly, and all Chicagoans clearly show traces of that influence, but in interpretation and spirit they were themselves in fact—inadvertently and unintentionally—influential.

This is how jazz became "hot"—fierce, improvisatory, giving an impression of letting go. The Hot Five's records, made a couple of months later in the summer of 1926, already show this trend much more strongly. "Drop That Sack"[57] particularly has a very rough, vehement introduction of a character previously unknown to New Orleans jazz. The link with the melodic theme, which in the past was always respected by the musicians and formed the basis for variation, became increasingly loose, and the music began to resemble that of the Chicagoans, though the rhythm was more fluent, less rigid.

It is interesting that in the process—which is very evident when we listen to the records chronologically—the joy and the bright tone are also lost. The music has become hard, almost relentless. And we come across something else, something we noticed earlier in white music, namely that besides the vehemence there is also another aspect, softer, dreamy, almost sentimental (e.g., "Melancholy Blues" and "Wild Man Blues," originally recorded for Brunswick[58]). The original style of New Orleans music was never that fierce, but neither was it sentimental; its rich polymorphism was founded on very different foundations.

This combination which, with the addition of Babe Dodds (drums) and Briggs (tuba), now called itself Hot Seven made a whole series of recordings in 1927, which certainly was not classical jazz in the sense that it can be referred to as a great achievement. It features some beautiful details, very nice solos—in other words this music had not suddenly lost its power and significance, but some of the real serenity, which was anything but lethargic, had been lost. Sometimes you get the impression that the musicians were playing against each

57. ** Coral 94040 EPC, ITJ.
58. Ibid.

other, rather than with each other; Armstrong was powerful and sometimes dominated the band and so was Dodds. In an attempt to salvage the unity, he opposed Armstrong forcefully. Much of the balance was lost in this way. The work of the rhythm section, certainly of very high quality, lost some of its suppleness and melodiousness—its task now became that of marking the beat. Armstrong's solos are classic examples of this sort of jazz—"hot jazz," which was in fact Chicago jazz. (The trombone solos are sometimes weak; these were not played by Kid Ory, as is often assumed, but by someone else, probably a certain John Thomas.) As we have said, besides the fierce recordings like "Potato Head Blues," "Hotter Than That" and "Alligator Crawl," there are also a couple that were suddenly very calm—approaching the sentimental—like "Melancholy Blues," which we have already mentioned, and "Wild Man Blues," recorded by Brunswick.[59]

During the session of 16 November 1926 we are clearly still in the transitional phase. Although the music is already showing the new trend more clearly, it has not yet lost the old liveliness and inner peace. Then "Skid-dad-de-dat"[60] was recorded, which acts as a sort of summary of what we have just been saying. The record may be referred to as a study of contrasts: fierce passages constantly alternating with excessively soft and calm sections. Then there is an abrupt break, followed by everyone joining in for a very quiet homophonic passage, until Armstrong strikes up a fierce trombone and leads a number of polyphonic bars, only to be interrupted by another very abrupt break. In the middle of the record, Armstrong suddenly breaks out in a raucous scat-song passage on top of a sweet theme, whereupon again a familiarly quiet and bright solo by Dodds follows. It is a curious record, captivating and of high quality, full of contradictions that express what was happening during this transitional period.

At this point it would perhaps be best for me to introduce the magnificent set of eight recordings made by the New Orleans

59. ITJ; of these Hot Seven there are many reissues, a.o. *** Col. 33s 1041; *** Philips B O7237 L.
60. See note 56.

Wanderers (or the New Orleans Bootblacks as they were sometimes known). They started up on 14 June 1926 with exactly the same members that made up the Hot Five, but without Armstrong, who was replaced by George Mitchell. These records are also particularly interesting because there is no sign of the problems we hear on the Armstrong Hot Five records from those days (like "Drop That Sack," for example, recorded on 28 May), and neither is there any trace of the hard and fast music that we sometimes find on the Armstrong recordings. It would seem that Armstrong must take the blame for those characteristics. These recordings constitute some of the best New Orleans music ever recorded. If we compare them with the Morton records we mentioned earlier (which were rerecorded shortly afterwards by a band that was again largely composed of the same members), we realize what an impression Morton had made on the music of his peers. It also teaches us how rich and versatile this sort of jazz can be. It is no use mentioning all these recordings separately. Almost every number is brilliant, with "I Can't Say"; "Too Tight"; "Gatemouth" and "Perdido Street Blues" coming tops.[61]

A study of this music illustrates again how it is always based on a given theme, both in ensemble music and in solos. I would particularly like to point out again that there is no way in which the rhythm section can easily be distinguished from the melody section. The work of the melody instruments is in itself strongly rhythmic, full of variety also in that respect, and the so-called rhythm instruments rather join in with the whole than mark the beat. Note George Mitchell's beautifully punctuated playing, and you will see what I mean. It may be that, having heard the records, Morton asked him to play. Finally I have to confess that the alto saxophonist who is introduced here (even though he does understand his job), does not complement the polyphonic passages. The clarity and transparency are clouded, not because of the material he is playing, but because the instrument itself produces a sound which does not actually befit this music.

Back to the Hot Seven: late 1927 sees the process we have been

61. **** Philips B O7428L.

talking about draw to a close; that is when Armstrong blew New Orleans jazz apart by his individualistic, improvisational, fierce interpretations. One of the last recordings the band made, the "Savoy Blues," is admittedly a beautiful piece—especially Armstrong's solo in the middle—but the polyphony had gone and the character of New Orleans jazz had changed irreversibly.

Armstrong subsequently set off again, this time with different musicians. Dodds, Ory and St. Cyr were no longer the appropriate musicians for his intentions. They were also too big for him; the records that were to come are almost always Armstrong records. He was the big man and the band permitted to accompany him was much weaker. Its members could sometimes play a short solo, but then only to give Louis another chance to dazzle. "West End Blues,"[62] recorded in June 1928, is a good example. It is an almost sentimental number, with some magnificent playing by Armstrong alternating with some weaker solos by others, and concluding with a piece that makes no musical sense and comes dangerously close to musical kitsch, amounting to a failed attempt at a nice ending.

THE DEVELOPMENT OF NEW AFRICAN-AMERICAN JAZZ AFTER ABOUT 1927: "SWING OUT"

The new formula caught on. It promised to be a success with audiences. It gave the musicians the opportunity to forge ahead without too much trouble. Like Armstrong, many blacks will have had little problem accepting this new concept of jazz. Many of them lived in Chicago and were not believers; they were very much related to the white Chicagoans in spirit. Still, the pressure accompanying these musicians must have played a significant role, because if we compare the records that were made for their own black audiences (and were released by recording companies like Paramount, who produced for the black music market) with the sort of jazz we want to discuss next, they were noticeably quieter, more cheery, calm and melodious—this

62. **† Parlo R448 and reissues.

was music from "South Side Chicago."[63] Also the records Dodds made at that time are different.[64] They retain the polyphonic element and are less improvisatory and vehement.

The music in which the new principles clearly emerge is possibly best represented by the Luis Russell Band—in essence a band founded by Oliver in 1925, which was now breaking new ground. The arrangements are very concise, limited to an introduction, the odd (homophonic) ensemble and some accompaniment of the solos. The solos certainly became the center of focus at this point.

The performances of Wat Hogginbotham (trombone), Charlie Holmes (soprano and alto saxophone) and Henry Allen Jr. (trumpet) are sometimes well worth listening to (e.g., "Feeling Drowsy"[65]), but they do lack the inherent depth which would give this music lasting value. They simply do not have the caliber of Oliver's band or of Morton's. This must to some extent be attributed to the fact that the new formula allows itself to be handled so easily. The immediate effect is good; it makes an impression and sweeps you along, rendering the creative effort that produces a top-notch performance unnecessary. Listen to "Swing Out"[66] and you will understand what we mean (and, incidentally, this is not a substandard example).

THE LATER JAZZ OF OLIVER AND WILLIAMS: "RED RIVER BLUES"

The Luis Russell Band we just mentioned performed between 1928 and 1930, at least that was the period they flourished, but now we have to go back a bit in history. The state of affairs in the 1920s was rather complex and many developments took place which are worth looking into.

Oliver lost his famous band in 1924 and the musicians dispersed to various other bands. He formed a new band but for all sorts of

63. HCJ and ** London AL 3505, etc.
64. See previous note; also *** HMV DPL 1073; ** Vogue-Coral LRA 10025.
65. **† HMV B4970 and reissues of music by this orchestra.
66. Ibid.

reasons things did not go very well. After that he played in various other bands, finally forming a band in 1925 which, in spite of regular changes to the lineup, performed successfully for about two years.

Oliver's new band was bigger than his previous Creole Orchestra and roughly looked like this: Oliver and Bob Schoffner, trumpet; Kid Ory or Higginbotham, trombone; Darnell Howard, Barney Bigard and Townes, sax and clarinet; Luis Russell, piano; Bud Scott, banjo; Bert Cobb, tuba; Paul Barbarin, drums. It was not a band capable of playing real New Orleans music.

It is our impression that Oliver, after the disappointment of his first band falling apart, did not attempt more of the same but, conscious that very few of his musicians actually came from New Orleans or felt at home in this genre, deliberately set out on a different route. Still, if you listen to the records this band made—mainly in 1926—its style is typically Oliver. The affinity with his older music is greater than you may initially think. Polyphonic ensemble choruses occur regularly, although they do not form the heart of the music.

Oliver supervised his music with the greatest of attention. He also began playing many of his own compositions such as "Snag It,"[67] which became very popular. Pieces arranged for sax or clarinet trio alternate with solos, sometimes with a quiet accompaniment, sometimes unaccompanied, arranged choruses for brass and polyphonic passages reminiscent of New Orleans jazz. The polyphony is often also present when a solo instrument is accompanied by an arranged sax ensemble. The music seldom or never degenerates into a straight succession of solos. The transition from one chorus to another, or from one solo to another, is invariably very meticulous and well-considered. There is always the musical finishing touch which time and again makes this music an adventure to listen to.

The quietness and simplicity of Oliver's music is striking. It makes us conscious of our feelings of protest towards the hot jazz trend. The rhythm is discreet, tender without being sentimental, the solos always musically sound and melodious—never violent and wild.

67. ITJ; **** Vogue-Coral LRA 10020.

A beautiful and particularly successful recording is that of the "Dead Man Blues"[68] of 17 September 1926, recorded during the fruitful months when the Bootblacks, Armstrong's Hot Five and Morton and his group were making the hit records we discussed before. Oliver's music is somewhat incongruous here—less New Orleans in style. However, if we compare this version of "Dead Man Blues" with that by Jelly Roll Morton made four days later, the similarities are remarkable and the differences seem not so essential. (Jelly and Oliver had composed "Dead Man Blues" together.) It is conspicuous that of the entire rhythm group in Oliver's version, only the tuba plays during solos, keeping time in a loose, variable manner. The solo that Oliver himself plays is a real gem, strong and powerful, never rough; in sharp contrast to the work of Armstrong in "Drop That Sack," for example.

In May 1927 Oliver performed in New York with this band with great success. He made a number of important recordings during that time, in which we hear that his interpretations did not change; to the contrary. It is serenity and melodiousness that is emphasized, and increasingly so. There are some beautiful examples from that period including "I'm Watching the Clock" and "West End Blues,"[69] one of his own compositions that he recorded in June 1928. A comparison with the Armstrong version, which was recorded four weeks later, shows the difference. It displays serenity versus dreaminess; meticulous musical supervision versus the dominant soloist with some accompaniment and little homogeneity; the equality of the various band members, even during the solos, versus the solo individualist who pushes the others aside; sticking faithfully to the thematic material versus breaking away from material and turning to free improvisation . . . and that is before we have said that Armstrong's "West End Blues" does not even fall in the category of fierce hot jazz. If we were to compare it with the latter, the contrast would be greater still.

68. ****† Jazz Society AA 539; for other releases of this orchestra see previous note.
69. Ibid.

Finally we have to point out that also Oliver did leave his own stamp on his musicians, because these records essentially sound much the same, irrespective of the lineup or soloists. Compare "Black Snake Blues," for example, from April 1927, in which Ory plays the trombone, with "I'm Watching the Clock" from September 1928, in which Higginbotham plays the same instrument. The similarity in style between the trombone parts is, both in terms of interpretation and of rendition, quite remarkable. The difference between Oliver and Morton's music—the stamp of the latter being much more outspoken—lies in their characters. Morton pushed himself strongly to the fore while Oliver remained modestly in the background, but this should not detract from the similarities in their musical ideals and (partly) methods too.

Oliver's influence is evident also in the many records his friend Clarence Williams made, with all sorts of recording combinations. Oliver himself joined in occasionally, but they mainly feature other trumpet players (like Ed Allen and or Anderson) whose style is strongly reminiscent of Oliver's. Williams too strives to make pure music, balanced and unified, melodiously simple, but never at the expense of power and without ever being sentimental. There are many examples of this, but we shall mention only the "Red River Blues"[70] in which Cyrus St. Clair's beautiful tuba playing is the first thing that strikes us, though Ed Allen's trumpet solo is also impressive. Oliver was present during this recording and can be heard contributing to another number recorded later the same day (29 May 1928) called "I Need You," where he plays the high part in the polyphonic ensemble.

What we are dealing with here is not the contrast between big band jazz and the jazz of smaller ensembles, the latter being hot jazz. No, we are dealing here with a concept of jazz that seems quite different from the original New Orleans jazz, but which is in essence more closely related to it than hot jazz is. Do not think that this

70. **** Fontana 462023TE; compare also **** Fontana 682073 TL, on which there are also two pieces of Williams.

129

music was always slow and that it was mainly blues. On the contrary, there are loose, quick numbers of a cheerful and lively character to be heard. One of these was Clarence Williams' "Cushion Foot Stomp,"[71] a beautiful and joyful piece of music—played partly polyphonically— of which the atmosphere and character is strongly reminiscent of old-time New Orleans music.

MORTON'S LATER DEVELOPMENTS: "HARMONY BLUES"

> Jelly was really ahead of his time. In fact most of what he said was above our heads. So now and then I'm starting to understand what he was getting at. He was always talking about the playing of the melody. But in those days jazz (i.e. hot jazz) was the only thing in the world to me apart from eating and sleeping and I didn't understand what he was talking about.

So spoke a trumpet player who worked with Jelly in 1929–1930.[72] Jelly Roll Morton's position in those years is summarized briefly in those few sentences. He wanted to hang on to his idea of music. He hated the new sort of jazz, "jig" music, with its free improvisation and badly thought out arrangements. He wanted to keep playing New Orleans jazz, but the musicians did not understand him—they wanted something else.

The conflict between Jelly's ideals and what his musicians wanted or were able to play can be heard clearly on the recordings he made during those years. In 1927 and 1928 he made a number of recordings which retained the same sort of character and quality as the older ones: "Jungle Blues," "Kansas City Stomp," "Mournful Serenade" (which was the same as Oliver's "Chimes Blues") and "Shoe Shiner's Drag."[73] In December 1928 he recorded the beautiful "Deep Creek Blues," one of his best records, which in fact had a less distinct New

71. ** Col. 33s 1067.
72. *Heah Me Talkin' to Ya*, p. 167.
73. **** RCA LPM-1649-C.

Orleans character and was closer related to what Oliver or Williams did in those years.

The years 1929 and 1930 saw little in the way of successful recordings, at least not of the whole band playing together. On the other hand there were some exceptionally beautiful trio recordings, such as the "Turtle Twist" from December 1929, with Barney Bigard on the clarinet, Jelly on piano and someone else drumming.[74] The recordings of the whole band often manifest something unbalanced, with the musicians playing roughly and hardly conforming to Jelly's wishes, on the basis of which he had arranged the pieces. Here and there we hear nice passages; the records are not bad, but they lack the qualities that made the earlier Jelly recordings such an experience.

"Jersey Joe" and "Mississippi Mildred," recorded with members of the Luis Russell Band in November 1929[75] are good examples of what we mean. There are some good solos—it is jazz in the positive sense of the word, certainly—but the balance, the fine musicality and also the unity is markedly lacking.

On occasion they did succeed, only really in the slow numbers when the musicians were not so fiercely jigging and could capture the atmosphere because they were still able to sense it. "Harmony Blues"[76] and "Pontchartrain Blues" spring to mind, good pieces, well arranged, with solos that fit naturally and do not impose themselves upon the listener. It is odd that the clarinetist seems a bit weak in these numbers. The reason is that Jelly was so determined to employ a certain type of clarinetist, and was so insistent that people play *his* music, that once, when there was no clarinetist available to suit his style, he wanted to prove the point to his musicians that jazz was quite capable of being played simply by sticking to the notes. So he wrote out the clarinet part and had it played by a certain Victor Houseman, a musician who was present at the studio and who could play many instruments in case a reserve was needed to cover for sick leave or

74. * HMV DLP 1044.
75. Ibid.
76. ** HMV B 10683 and other reissues.

absence. This anonymous musician's style was too classical really, for he was no jazz clarinetist, with too little vibrato and so on for what Jelly had in mind; still, the result is not unsatisfactory.

Jelly was not able to retain his position however. On one hand there was the black audience, badly affected by the depression which crippled the economy in 1929. They preferred to hear their suffering sung about by the blues singers whose records were still being released regularly by companies like Brunswick. On the other hand the more advanced musicians and the wider white audience no longer wanted this kind of music; they preferred jazz played in the spirit of the Chicagoans or they turned to the more "respectable" jazz of Ellington or Henderson, a genre to which we will be coming shortly.

So Jelly made his last recording in 1930. At that point the Victor Recording Company dismissed him and began recording vast quantities of Ellington.

As from 1929 or 1930 onwards we no longer hear Johnny Dodds, King Oliver, Morton, Kid Ory and many others on record. The musical ideals of these people were too high; not wanting to set aside their principles, they remained faithful to their own music but ran into difficulties with their supporters. Oliver and Jelly battled on for a few years before ending up dejected; Dodds lived in great poverty, while Kid Ory abandoned music altogether. It was not primarily the economic situation that caused them to disappear from the public arena, though it is true that they could have gathered a few crumbs from under the table if times had been better. The main factor that caused those who clung to their high musical ideals to sink into oblivion and poverty, however talented they were, was the change in taste, the trend towards the new type of jazz which was more permeated by the spirit of the Chicagoans. On top of that, band leaders like Jelly and Oliver hardly succeeded in playing music in the way they wanted, because the musicians no longer understood them and wanted to branch out.

This defeat must have affected Jelly badly. Not only had he aimed for high quality New Orleans jazz with its own character but he had also hoped that white audiences would accept him and his music. He dreamed of emancipation, not by assimilation—adopting the white

Western culture—but by being accepted in his own right, with his own music, with its own character.

Much is true in Blesh's verdict:

> While jazz may be regarded as the symbol of struggle and hope, swing can be seen as that of defeat. The success of blacks in America cannot be measured by the phantom of popular acclaim and even less so by the number of dollars they earned—which could not buy equality anyway. Swing—both in terms of style and in terms of the mentality which created it—has heralded the abandonment of the real Negro elements in jazz for the benefit of white elements which are more accessible and acceptable to white society. This swing [which refers to a new kind of jazz that evolved from the music that Oliver and Morton opposed], at first sight a symbol of victory, is in fact one of the failures of emancipation.[77]

THE DEVELOPMENT OF JAZZ IN NEW ORLEANS IN THE 1920S: "SHORT DRESS GAL"

The jazz music we have just been talking about was played in Chicago and New York. That is where the big recording studios were located. New Orleans lay off the beaten track—it was a provincial outback. That is why only little of the music that was played there was recorded, although enough was happening there.[78] There is only a relatively small number of gramophone records to show us that the jazz born in New Orleans itself also continued its development there. If we listen to Celestin's Original Tuxedo Jazz Band, and particularly "Careless Love" from 1925,[79] we can hear that the music they played was in essence no different from that of Oliver. The musicians were not top class—the clarinet is positively weak—but the sound, the emphasis on polyphonic ensemble work, the whole attitude of the

77. Blesh, *Shining Trumpets*, p. 262.
78. S. B. Charters, *Jazz, New Orleans 1885–1957* (NY: Belleville, 1958).
79. ** FoW FP 55.

music is as we described it when we were dealing with Oliver's Creole Orchestra.

One of the better bands was that of Sam Morgan, a skilled trumpet player, who had assembled a number of musicians capable of producing something worth listening to. Their recordings, made in New Orleans in 1927, are technically very respectable but overemphasize the saxophone, producing a very strange sound on the recordings. Still, we can hear a very captivating polyphony being performed, the basis of which—almost naturally—is the melodic material being played. It is powerful jazz though we are almost obliged to call it sweetly flowing.

Strangely enough, and deviating from what New Orleans musicians in the North were used to, a number of Negro spirituals were recorded here—because they formed a permanent part of the performances, no doubt, but possibly also because contact with brass band music was still strong. It is not worth mentioning or examining here the few recordings they made, but I will make an exception for "Short Dress Gal."[80] There is a short vocal part on this record and the refrain goes, "Don't you like that, everybody lookin', with your dress up to your knee" (no doubt this mockery was directed at the emerging trend for very short skirts). The trombone elaborates on this directly afterwards with a mocking solo—almost tender—but its purpose is to underline the gist of the text. The musician was Jim Robinson, about whom we shall hear much more later. After that comes an ensemble that extends the "short dress girl" caricature even further, this time in a quasi-sentimental fashion. There was humor in this music of a kind seldom heard before.

Whites were also still playing jazz in New Orleans, as they had been doing for some years. The Halfway House Orchestra, among others, was producing some very good work as descendants of the New Orleans Rhythm Kings. They also made some recordings but these are very rare because they were unfortunately never rereleased.

80. *** Fontana 467137 TE.

The Entrance and Development of Ellington: "Creole Love Song"

"You'd better learn to jazz or you won't make money,"[81] Henderson once said to someone who played only classical trumpet. This sentence is typical of the man. He was the leader of quite a large dance band at the beginning of the 1920s but he soon began to attract real jazz musicians. They were able to take on the solos, which attracted the audiences; they were able to play "jazz."

Fletcher Henderson tried to become Whiteman's black rival and he certainly succeeded, even if it was only because he had Armstrong, Joe Smith (trumpet), Jimmy Harrison (trombone) and Coleman Hawkins (tenor sax) in his band. Perhaps Henderson's success inspired Whiteman to take on better jazz musicians like Beiderbecke too. Anyway, their function remained the same—to be soloists and relieve the heavily arranged pieces with a hot jazz solo here and there. It boiled down to a soloist-individualist exhibition of talent, technique and strength. The arranged parts were often quite monotonous. If you listen to the old recordings you will hear that many of the hits from those days were sweet and boring, with a sudden, fierce solo to liven things up a bit, followed by yet more sax ensemble without any spirit.

When the Oliver records were released, Henderson was working on the East Coast—mainly in New York. Oliver's hits of 1926, like "Snag It," definitely made a big impression on him. The outcome of this can be heard on Henderson's best recordings, namely "Stampede" and particularly "Jackass Blues."[82] The solos are more vehement, for Armstrong had made his mark on the trumpeters; it is not for nothing that he had worked with Henderson for more than a year. The arrangement and interpretation are less "sweet," less like the style of the average dance band, than previously. This was more like real music.

81. *Heah Me Talkin' to Ya*, p. 198.
82. † Col. MZ 336. No reissues known to me. Another version on **** Fontana 682073 TL. Other recordings of this orchestra: London AL 3547 and HCJ.

At the end of 1926, Ellington's star began to rise. He came from Washington, from a completely different scene than musicians like Oliver, Dodds and so on. He came from a well-to-do family whose lifestyle corresponded with that of the higher white middle class. He had attended a School of Higher Vocational Education, taking classical music lessons, and prided himself on his immaculate clothing and fine, cultivated manners.

The following quote gives an insight into his youth: "Those ragtime pianists sounded very good to my ears. And they looked so fine. Especially when they let their left hand go. I noticed that that left hand gave the effect and that the sound was most influenced by a showy left hand. And that is why I developed a showy left hand myself."[83]

It was not long before he arrived in New York with a small band. There he made his first recordings, "Rainy Night" being one of them.[84] The lineup was very promising, many of them being the same musicians that appear in the band with which he was to become famous, a couple of years later. What we get, however, is very irritating, sweet dance music without color or spirit, with a fierce saxophone solo, sticking out like a sore thumb in the midst of all that soft and straight saxophone gurgling.

Ellington learned his lesson. "The character of our band changed when Bubber (Miley, a trumpet player in the line of Oliver) joined. He played with all sorts of mutes all evening, in a jazz-like style. That is when we came to the conclusion that we should just forget that 'sweet music,'" said Ellington himself.[85] He also learned to make good use of the musicians he had in the band. He must have learned much from the records of Oliver and Williams (1926–1927). His arrangements became livelier, the content of the thematic material (mostly self-written by this time) improved and the contrast between solos and arranged parts became less sharp, disappearing completely soon after. Ellington was creating a new sort of jazz—his own sort.

---

83. B. Ulanov, *Duke Ellington* (New York, 1946), p. 14.
84. London AL 3551, HCJ.
85. *Heah Me Talkin' to Ya*, p. 209.

Ellington can be compared with someone like Handy in many respects. He too adopted from his fellow blacks any musical or playing style he saw fit; he too approached the music from the outside, as it were, and put it in a different light. It is hard to say exactly what light, because in strictly technical terms there is little difference between the structure of an Ellington composition and a good Oliver record (big band) or a Morton number like "Harmony Blues"—and yet the music does sound different. What Jean de Trazegnies, a strong admirer of Ellington, wrote about him typifies him. He says that Ellington was different from other black musicians; he was a gentleman. It was he who saw the potential for creating an art form from the still somewhat unrefined music that blacks like Armstrong were playing—almost instinctively and for their pleasure—that was to become a credit to his people. He wanted to plane down any rough edges still evident in the music of 1926.[86]

Perhaps Ellington's position can be characterized clearly by "Creole Love Call" (recorded in October 1927). "The Duke had of course never heard a Creole love song, or anything like it. You could have heard Creoles sing out their love in Louisiana, but he had never been to the South. Still the title seemed to suit the soft, languid atmosphere of the music,"[87] wrote Ulanov, Ellington's biographer. That is true, but what Ellington had heard was "Camp Meeting Blues," one of Oliver's last records with the famous Creole Orchestra. In a beautiful clarinet solo, Jimmy Noone plays the theme that Ellington then proceeds to borrow from Oliver—without so much as an acknowledgment. But the atmosphere and the nature of Ellington's music was also different from that of "Camp Meeting Blues," although the influence of Oliver's records from 1926 is very clear here. Again, it is difficult to say why this music is different, but for anyone listening to jazz for the first time it sounds more familiar because it is more Western in spirit and character. That is of itself not necessarily bad, but the striving for effect and respectability and

86. J. de Trazegnies, *Duke Ellington* (Brussels, 1946), p. 7, 8.
87. Ulanov, *Duke Ellington*, p. 64.

the fake "primitiveness," make the music less interesting even though it may possibly be more technically sophisticated than the work of Oliver, Williams or Morton. There are some riveting solos and the work is musically sound; there is really no point saying that this is bad music. To the contrary.

The popularity gained by Ellington and his musicians was immensely important to them, especially when whites, fellow-musicians and audiences were generally so full of admiration for them. This was the way to overcome the racial barrier which had always been so hard to come to terms with, this was the way to gain acceptance. This was also the time of the Harlem Renaissance (which we mentioned earlier) and it certainly did not leave Ellington unmoved. He developed a racial awareness, and Africanisms began to play a conscious role in his music. Ellington was moved to seek "jungle-istic" effects in the trombone and trumpet parts.[88] Miley showed him the way. Oliver had been the inventor of the "growling wa-wa" trumpet style—a technique using mutes—but it had never been jungle-istic, not even when his successors in the ranks of Williams took over. It did become so when Ellington went to work on it. More than a mere musical accessory, an extension of the expressive potential of the trumpet, it became an effect intended to evoke associations with Africa.

Mills, the manager of the band, advertised performances of "primitive rhythms" and Sonny Greer, with his very extensive percussion set, was able to make the slogan seem true. The primitivism of twentieth-century Western culture which around 1905 sent artists in Paris rushing off to admire and pursue African sculpture, assisted this cause. It is all a bit reminiscent of the eighteenth-century slogans of the Rousseau followers who extolled the noble savage, so pure and genuine, as yet unspoiled by civilization.

Such views were all the more acceptable to many listeners who came into contact with Ellington's music, either live or on records, because his clever arrangements and great musical talent seemed to

88. Ibid., p. 45, 73.

give their hobby—jazz—status and an aura of seriousness. They were oblivious to the fact that they were using the Western elements in Ellington's music as an excuse for their love of African-American music.

It seems to us that Ellington was taken much too seriously here in Europe at that time. The quality of show, the commercial side, the intention to dazzle the audience one way or another, were all overlooked. Everybody was impressed by the typical Ellington tricks when he was on stage: having the band slowly emerge from the darkness into the light while they were very effectively growling out "East St. Louis Toodle-oo," their signature tune. The audiences did not realize that these were not authentic African musicians, musicians playing their own folk music, but products of a man who, having discovered what Westerners were after, cut and tailored it to their palate. Ellington later tried to make his music more serious by introducing Western forms and more modern chords. But besides that the schmaltzy pop, the commercial tunes of the day also remained in place. A good example is the recording of one of his concerts from 1952: besides the "Harlem Suite," in spirit a typical albeit a somewhat late product of the Harlem Renaissance, it included the highly commercial theatrics of the drum solo "Skin Deep" which, indeed, can only be described as shallow, as well as a variety of efficacious show solos by different soloists, technically fantastic, and the purely commercial "Ellington Medley" etc.[89]

The music itself fails to move us after we have heard it a few times. As it lacks depth and authenticity, which we need, it leaves a void. We must not forget, however, that this band, with its talented musicians and very gifted leader, produced some nice music which is certainly worth listening to. Even if we only take the recordings made before, say, 1932 into consideration (the band's best period in my opinion), we could mention "Take It Easy," "Black and Tan Fantasy," "Rent Party Blues," "Saratoga Swing," "Jungle Blues," "Sloppy Joe," "Saturday Night Function" and many others,[90] as well

89. RCA L 20099.
90. Reissued on ** Philips and ** HMV DLP 1094.

as an unpretentious piece like "Drop Me Off at Harlem," with its pure rendition and melodious charm, which is still able to inspire us.

Is it jazz? Why not? It is Ellington's version of jazz. After all, what is jazz? Quarrelling about categories or restricting ourselves to an exact definition will only lead to a futile discussion.

5

The 1930s

Jazz in Kansas City around 1930: "Kansas City Breakdown"

Between 1926 and 1930 there were big bands also outside New York and the strict New York scene we have discussed. They occasionally played in New York, but were otherwise busy playing in their hometowns or touring elsewhere. These bands played jazz in their own way—music that was adapted for bigger bands—with simple but strongly rhythmical, arranged parts including many solos, rather free and improvised but not without showing the influence of Oliver and Williams. We are specifically referring to the Missourians who certainly made some good records, like *Scotty Blues*,[1] and particularly Benny Moten's Kansas City Orchestra, a band that became very popular in the city they had included in their name and where they often performed at dance evenings for whites. As a result they started to include more strongly rhythmic music and if we follow the development of their music from 1926 to 1928 or 1929 this can be clearly heard. They began to use riffs—short melodic phrases played very rhythmically and repetitively—which turned the work of the melody section into rhythm, as it were. They also included many solos, virtually continuously.

Nevertheless it has to be said that what they produced was very

1. †† Bluebird B 6084.

musical, quiet and lively, without striving for effect, without a show of quasi-depth—direct and bright. The rhythm section of this band was excellent; it is not often one comes across rhythm played so freely, so liberated from a strict beat. Benny Moten's piano-playing was certainly a contributing factor. From 1926 there is the still rather stiff "Harmony Blues"—not to be confused with Jelly Roll Morton's composition of the same name, the lovely "Hot Water Blues" from 1928 and "Kansas City Breakdown," which has an unusual tuba passage.[2]

BLIND WILLIE JOHNSON: "JESUS COMING SOON"

By the end of the 1920s there was a lot of blues-singing available, particularly on the Brunswick Race series. It was folk music, sometimes of high quality. Spirituals were sung too, primarily in the church, of course, but also on record. But let us now focus on Blind Willie Johnson, who made a number of beautiful recordings for Columbia in 1927, 1929 and 1930.

Willie Johnson was born around the turn of the century near Temple, Texas. His father was a farmer. When he was seven years old he became blind as the result of an unfortunate combination of events. During the 1920s he became a preacher and street evangelist, which was no unusual occupation in the South. He lived in various places near Dallas, Texas, finally settling in Beaumont, a small place in Texas.

We are very grateful to Columbia for having made more than thirty recordings of him, which is all we have of him because he died of pneumonia in 1949. It enables us to study his rich art. His repertoire was very varied, including white songs like the hymns "Let Your Light Shine on Me" and "If It Hadn't Been for Jesus." It also included spirituals like "Nobody's Fault but Mine," "Mother's Children Have a Hard Time" and "Bye and Bye I'm Going to See the King," as they were generally known in the area where he lived. He also sang songs in the drawn-out style, the way Dr. Watts' hymns were traditionally

2. ** HMV DLP 1067.

sung, notably "Dark Was the Night,"[3] one of the most beautiful recordings of black music ever made. He hums the whole piece and has the guitar sing along, as it were. It is a beautiful example of the special character of African-American music. Humming is a typical African type of musical expression. Apart from that, the piece really has nothing to do with Africa at all. As explained earlier, this style of singing was both truly African and typically Western-puritanical. The way Blind Willie sings it makes it pure art—one has to hear it to understand just how much depth and beauty a simple folk singer like this was able to produce.

He also did some composing himself—songs that testify to his insight and understanding of biblical preaching. We do not know for certain whether these compositions are his, but if they are not, then the same must be said of Blind Willie *and* the composer, *and* the whole community in which they lived and worked. The following beautiful song "Jesus Coming Soon" relates to the serious flu epidemic of 1918:

> In the year of nineteen and eighteen
> God sent a mighty disease.
> It killed men by the thousands,
> Oh, Lord there is none like Thee.

That is the first verse he sings. His rendition of this sort of song is interesting because he tunes his guitar differently from what he does for a more Western song, and that is different again from what he does for traditional spirituals. He sings the latter in deep growling voice, which has a peculiar effect. At first it sounds raw, but once you get used to it you begin to understand its idiosyncratic charm, and also its seriousness and dignity.[4] The refrain is as follows:

> *I have some warning, Jesus coming soon.*

3. **** Fontana 462022TE.
4. *** FoW FG 3585.

When he sings this his wife joins in. In the next few verses he elaborates his theme, until he continues:

> God is warning the nation,
> You can't go on in that way,
> Don't walk in the ways of the heathen,
> But seek the Lord and pray.

"God Moves on the Water" is a beautiful song in the same vein. It is
about the disastrous sinking of the Titanic. He tells of how the vessel
sunk, that proud ship that was supposed to have been unsinkable. The
refrain goes: "God moves on the water." We would like to transcribe
it as "the Spirit of the Lord moves across the waters," depicting how
God breaks human pride.

In "Soul of a Man" he asks what the soul actually is. Since there
is no answer forthcoming, he concludes:

> I read the Bible often,
> I try to read it right,
> And as far as I can understand,
> It always is a burning light.

That is his answer to the question.

It is telling that, while there seemed to be so much demand for
black music and spirituals, yet Blind Willie was virtually forgotten—
except for a few collectors who valued his records as priceless treasures.
In 1954 a man who lived in New Orleans spent two years trying to
trace Blind Willie. After the recordings of 1930 no more records were
made of his work. Finally he discovered where Blind Willie had lived
and learned a few things about him, which he recorded in a documentary produced by Folkways.[5]

5. Ibid. Unfortunately not much has been reissued here. Records are very rare and
almost always in poor condition, proof of the fact that they were played a lot by the
African Americans who possessed them.

THE COMMERCIALIZATION AND DEVELOPMENT OF JAZZ: "HOBO, YOU CAN'T RIDE THIS TRAIN"

The years 1929, 1930 and 1931 were years of economic crisis. Money was scarce and there was high unemployment. Everyone had to be frugal. It meant a rough ride for professional musicians.

Only those who could satisfy the demand of the greatest number of customers had a chance of making a reasonable living from their music. So, paradoxically, it was not the small (and therefore cheap) groups who were doing well, but the big bands—at least the bands who made it their business to meet the requirements of audiences who were willing and able to spend money. That is why they played entertainment music—music which can be appreciated without any trouble, music lacking content that in no way encourages listeners to think, never confronting people with real issues but instead twittering of sweet moonshine and love stories. Rhythm is something the music does sometimes have, but though it may be exciting, it is not really deeply moving. It is rhythm bereft of real musical sense. In other words, it is music which has sold its soul to Mammon. Let us not forget that all art has an economic aspect—that it costs large sums of money to put up a concert with a solo performance, but that in itself is not a bad thing. Music is not good because concerts are held with empty stomachs and only a large dose of idealism to live from. No, it becomes good when musicians of whatever musical or cultural status can give their best without worrying at every note or change of act whether the level of satisfaction experienced by the audience or the takings at the box office will suffice. Commercial art is not bad because it is commercial, but because profits are regarded as the only relevant criteria.

They were hard times. Johnny Dodds, Kid Ory, Oliver, Jelly Roll Morton—they no longer had a chance, for they did not play according to the requirements of the majority who had money. No, it was not those musicians but the big bands—like the Casa Loma Orchestra, the Dorsey Band and also, with a generous helping of real musical talent, the Ellington Band—that survived or did well, got bookings, made recordings, performed concerts for the radio, and so on.

These were hard times for the talented musicians. You needed strong principles to refuse Mammon and public demand when your stomach was empty, particularly if you had the talent that could get you places. Armstrong was one to retain his popularity during that period. On the basis of the reputation he had established earlier, he was able to keep on performing and making records. Now he sung of the "Peanut Vendor" however, and sentimental songs like "Confessin'," a quasi-hot "Tiger Rag," a quasi-tragic "I'm Just a Gigolo" and show pieces like "Hobo, You Can't Ride This Train."[6]

What came naturally to the real cabaret artist, the singer of entertainment songs, the accordion virtuoso, the musician with a natural talent for performing the type of song that originated from Tin Pan Alley (the aptly named music publisher's world where hits were made and cleverly sold), with verve and pleasure, was an ordeal to musicians like Armstrong. They saw through the emptiness, the sentimentality. They could not believe in the music they were playing. To forget their suffering, their lot, many of them began to drink heavily; it gave them the strength to do what they had to do—keep working and remain popular.

This would explain much of the banter, which was regarded by the audience as highly witty entertainment. When Armstrong sang "I Can't Give You Anything but Love," he could not help but make a silly remark, laugh stupidly or pull a funny face. That is how he coped with the situation, deep down; at least he was still the boss and not a slave to the futile and empty songs with their meaningless lyrics.

We can also understand Fats Waller in this context. He was a very talented pianist from Harlem who followed in the tradition of James P. Johnson, whose roots were in ragtime. Fats Waller was a fine pianist who made some beautiful recordings—"Numb Fumblin'"; "Alligator Crawl"; "Viper's Drag"[7] and more—and who was also a competent

6. HMV DLP 1105.
7. ** HMV CLP 1035.

composer. If this man had had the chance, we would have been many silly jokes poorer, but much music richer.

Yes, those jokes. Take a completely hollow and fatuous piece of music with third-rate lyrics, like "Mandy."[8] It is the epic tale of a certain Mandy who falls in love with a . . . Mr. Handy. Well, it does rhyme. The plot unfolds: "Oh, don't you linger, here's a ring for your finger." Assuming the singer was an intelligent being, it would be hard not to sympathize with the urge to follow this up with "Give me a ham dinner," and then to pepper the rest with all sorts of meaningless shrieks and screams, as these are to be preferred to the nonsensical lyrics. The audience loved having the truth thrown in their faces, while they did not even understand that this was happening. Who is the artistic murderer here? We are afraid that it is Joe Public who is jubilant as long as the material is silly and rhythmic. It is a great tragedy. The musicians are not blameless either because they could have opted for poverty like Dodds and Morton did, or thrown the towel in as Ory did—but who will dare to throw the first stone?

Beginning to Look to the Past: "Apologies"

It is understandable that musicians looked back nostalgically to the past, because they found themselves in a situation where making music consisted of a succession of solos only, introduced by the whole band playing a simple little theme. The solos seemed bright and direct, but after a while they were a repetitive continuum of the same ideas. Be that as it may, the alternative was to sell themselves commercially—which amounted to selling their souls.

This is how it came about that a number of musicians, both black and white, came together in 1934 to make a few records. One of the numbers was "Apologies," the full title being "Apologies to Oliver and Armstrong," and rightly so because what they were playing was the Oliver number "Dippermouth Blues." It was a piece that they all remembered from the early years in Chicago, little more than a

8. †† HMV JF 11.

decade earlier. The recording was not a great success—the members of the group were too diverse—but it was a first attempt.[9]

That same year some white musicians from New Orleans got together. They were the leftovers from The New Orleans Rhythm Kings and a few others who had left for the North. They too played recollections of better times, including "Tin Roof Blues."[10]

It was in this vein that Bob Crosby worked on. In 1935 he formed a band that was to enjoy popularity for several years. It was a large band with a very characteristic sound, which was partly the result of Bob Haggart's special arrangements—tasteful, simple, lively and colorful. They played a sort of jazz that attempted to capture the spirit of the older New Orleans jazz in modern arrangements. The solos were always very skillfully incorporated in the whole. It was never a matter of simply performing individually; the solos always reflected the mood of the piece. Besides new pieces they had composed themselves, they also played some Oliver numbers like "Riverside Blues," which they renamed "Dixieland Shuffle." Occasionally they even did some polyphonic ensemble work.

All these people, and the Crosby band in particular, paved the way for the "revival" that was to come—the renewed interest in New Orleans jazz. The audiences were being taught without being crudely subjected to real black jazz—prepared, so that the New Orleans style would not sound unfamiliar to them later. It is therefore justifiable that besides "Tin Roof Blues," which we have already mentioned, Kershaw also included "Five Point Blues," a piece the Crosby Band played in 1938 on a record he had compiled himself called *An Introduction to Traditional Jazz*. Besides its historic value, it is a number that is certainly worth listening to.[11]

9. † HMV B8408 (reissue on RCA).
10. ITJ.
11. Ibid.

The Emergence of the Study of Folk Music:
Leadbelly ("Irene")

Around 1933, serious attention was given to real African-American folk music for the first time, not for commercial reasons but out of a historical-scientific interest. That was when Lomax began to make recordings of authentic American folk music for the Library of Congress. He took his recording equipment and workers to a number of locations where he made recordings of anything he considered worthwhile. They recorded[12] songs by real cowboys, work songs by both blacks and whites, Native American music and white folk music. America possessed more of the latter than you might think and Sharp and George Pullen Jackson had already collected much in this area, albeit in the form of text and musical notation.

Black music was also recorded: the singsong manner the sailor used to convey to the pilot the result of soundings taken, the way the overseer led the workers as they unloaded railway tracks, children's songs, spirituals, sermons, whatever he could find.[13] They also visited penal colonies where blacks were sentenced to forced labor on the plantations under conditions strongly reminiscent of the old days of slavery. They heard exceedingly beautiful workaday songs sung by groups of prisoners, led by a precentor—a prisoner just like the rest.

They heard a group of prisoners in Sugarland, Texas, singing a particular song and recorded it. It was sung while harvesting sugarcane—which was cut down with sharp machetes—while the men were traipsing side by side in a long row through the mud. The precentor sings of "Shorty George," the train on which the wives travelled to come and visit their husbands, and he asks one of the prisoners for what crime he is there. After each line the others answer in unison with a long, solemn and sad "Oh . . . o."

What's the matter, something must be wrong
Oh . . . o

12. They were (partly) issued on albums (later on LPs).
13. We have already often quoted this series, LiC.

Keep on a-workin', Shorty George done gone
Oh . . . o

You ought to come on the river in nineteen-four,
You could find a dead man on every turn row.

But it ain't no more cane on this Brazis,
Says they all grind it to molasses.

Little Boy, what'd you do for to get so long?
Said: 'I killed my rider [loved one] in the high sheriff's arms'.
Etc.[14]

In a camp in Louisiana, Lomax discovered a black man who turned out to have a fantastic repertoire of folk songs and he also had exceptional talent. Lomax had him sing for the state governor and the singer was released on parole. Lomax subsequently had him perform in many places, in order to allow the Americans to hear the rich wealth of folk music that was there for the asking in the deep South.

Huddie Ledbetter, nicknamed Leadbelly, accompanied himself on the guitar and sung a virtually endless repertoire of work songs and authentic folk songs, some typically white, some typically African American in character. Leadbelly apparently worked for a while as a sort of apprentice with Blind Lemon Jefferson, the blues singer from the 1920s. It seems that Leadbelly's repertoire embraced much more than the blues we know from Blind Lemon Jefferson. Since the selection of songs by the recording companies was so one-sided, perhaps it would be better to assume that they succumbed to popular demand.

What did Leadbelly sing? He sang a song about the cotton harvest:

Jump down, turn around, to pick a bale of cotton
Jump down, turn around, pick a bale a day. (x 2)

14. LiC III.

He sings of the man working on the land who calls to his wife to bring him water:

Bring me li'l water Silvy,
Bring me li'l water now,
Bring me li'l water,
Silvy Every li'l once in a while, (x 2)

He also sung a folk song that was to become popular and was later performed by many singers, none of whom equaled Leadbelly's rendition. "Irene" was originally a white folk song, without a doubt, but there is a black flavor to the arrangement.

Irene goodnight, Irene goodnight,
Goodnight Irene, goodnight Irene,
I kiss you in my dreams.

Sometimes I live in the country,
Sometimes I live in the town,
Sometimes I have a great notion
To jump in the river and drown.

Not surprisingly, Irene is not a lively number. It tells of how he bumped into his true love, Irene, the day after he was married to another woman, and of how he was now separated from her forever by circumstances and age difference.[15]

Lomax also made recordings of singing evangelists, not only accompanied by a guitar, but sometimes by a mouth organ too. This instrument is very popular in the impoverished outback of the South. Not only religious music,[16] but also folk music was often played on this instrument. The best known harmonica player was Sonny Terry.

15. Many recordings exist. Leadbelly is very well represented on releases of FoW, such as ** FP 14, ** FP 4, ** FP 24, etc.
16. LiC X (Turner Junior Johnson, 1942).

He was born in 1911 in Durham, Georgia. His father also played the mouth organ. Much of his knowledge of technique and repertoire he learned at the dances on Saturday evenings when the jug bands played and harmonica music was performed as well. He was familiar with spirituals from the church, but he played the harmonica like nobody had done before, the way he had taught himself. He had a fantastic technique, which enabled him to sing while accompanying himself, without any breaks—it was unbelievable that an individual could achieve such a feat. He never strove for technique just for the sake of it—his aim was always to play the music as pure and melodical as possible.

Sonny, who was blind, was discovered around 1938 and, like Leadbelly, he performed for all sorts of outfits of educated whites from academic or university background. He also played in some Broadway shows, but whatever he did and wherever he did it, he remained himself, playing only his own music. Sonny is no exception—there are many like him—but musically he is the best and richest by far. He has a varied repertoire: blues, spirituals, folk songs, with "Locomotive Blues" being the icing on the cake. It is a piece which draws its inspiration from the train—an imitation of the sound, if you like—but it is musically so fine, so full of variety that all other attempts to capture the train in music (with the possible exception of Meade Lux Lewis's "Honky Tonk Train Blues") pale into insignificance.[17]

GERSHWIN'S OPERA: *PORGY AND BESS*

If my memory serves me correctly, it is at the opening of the third act that the script of George Gershwin's *Porgy and Bess* describes the scene of the square at Catfish Row: people happily going about their business, someone playing the harmonica and others dancing and singing. The accompanying music is however nothing at all remotely like that of Sonny Terry. No, it is a Franz Lehar-esque overture that opens this part. Neither is there in the whole of this opera a single

17. *** FoW 35 (recording ca. 1950).

note of black music to be heard, not even an imitation. There are no real spirituals—not only are there no traditional ones, there is not even a single one that even remotely resembles the spiritual song of the blacks. No blues, no black folk songs—not even in a Western setting or adaptation. *Porgy and Bess* are less black than Bizet's *Carmen* is Spanish or Puccini's *Butterfly* is Japanese. Gershwin's opera is based on the book *Porgy* by Du Bose Heyward which was written in the 1920s. It is a book that was written with a typical Southern approach to blacks. It is full of stereotypical characterization. The life of the blacks is portrayed as idyllic and colorful, but blacks themselves are stupid and actually slightly ridiculous people. As the writer says, "The strange mixture of comedy and tragedy leaves an unmistakable mark on the life of the Negro in its deepest moments."[18] The writer regularly lets black people cut a laughable figure at the most serious parts of the book, the climax being Porgy's run from the police. As if there were not enough reasons for their behavior—reasons the author does take the trouble to show us, though in fact sympathy for the lot of the blacks held ransom by whites is not completely lacking. In the opera these blacks do not speak properly, of course, but utter a sort of childish gibberish. Those who have heard blacks speaking—perhaps on the Folkway documentary recordings; those who have heard the prayer of the raspberry-seller from New Orleans[19] so moving and linguistically beautiful, will know that there is no such thing as an "inferior black language." It is part of a stereotypical perception of blacks.

Certainly, blacks have their own dialect, but they do not have this stupid language which sometimes becomes almost nonsensical. Incidentally, their dialect differs little from the dialect of the whites from the South. Did anybody really believe that instead of singing of the "promised land" in one of their spirituals, they would say "primus lan'"? Those who have heard the records we mentioned earlier, by rural preachers and musicians, will know better. Infidelity crime, naive love, dirt and stench, unbelievable ignorance, faith without a clue as

18. On p. 33 of the 1930 edition.
19. *** FoW MS IX.

to what it was all about—that describes a typical black person as the book would have us believe it.

The libretto does not improve matters—to the contrary. This is a piece that we can classify as one of the last examples of the black-faced minstrel shows: whites with blackened faces impersonating blacks to amuse themselves at the expense of blacks on the one hand, and to perform some of their music butchered to the tastes of the white audience on the other hand. This was then all bundled into an opera tailored to Broadway standards, composed in the veristic tradition of a Mascagni or similar. This was essentially no different from Gershwin's so-called serious jazz compositions of the 1920s— like "Rhapsody in Blue," a rhapsody that resembles a piano concerto by Rachmaninoff—which were played by the so-called "King of Jazz," Paul Whiteman, with his big band. Their value may be debated, but jazz and black music must be left out of it. Gershwin was a very good composer of songs—very talented. "Summertime" from *Porgy and Bess became* a popular song, and rightly so because it has many outstanding qualities.

It can only be described as deeply tragic that black singers have become so alienated from their own folk that they will perform a piece like *Porgy and Bess*. Tragic, because they are betraying their own culture and doing so in an opera-type operetta, which can please only at the expense of the unaffected, Southern black whose music, religion, way of life in many respects is much deeper and more beautiful than what is depicted here. Of course, injustice and poverty coupled with its inevitable partner, impoverishment, undeniably exist, but whose fault is that? It would be more appropriate to portray blacks as they really are, to break down that patronizing, denigrating view of them; making a piece like this is no contribution at all.

If it were possible to regard this piece as just a jolly operetta—in the same way as no one expects to find real Japanese people portrayed in *Madame Butterfly*—it would not seem so bleak, but here in Europe it has long been welcomed as a representative piece of black culture. The arrival of this piece of music incited lectures to be held on black music and the nature of blacks. It can only be put down to total ignorance, an absolute lack of any knowledge of real black music and black culture.

Musically, *Porgy and Bess* may be classified on a higher plane than Al Jolson's minstrel performances like "Mammy" and "Sonny Boy" and others, but that does not detract from the fundamental similarities.

JELLY ROLL MORTON'S RECORDINGS FOR THE LIBRARY OF CONGRESS: JAZZ CAN BE BEAUTIFUL

Many people have a mistaken idea of jazz. Somehow it got into the encyclopaedia that jazz should be considered as a load of bleating sounds and poor-sounding noises—something that was even supposed to be painful to the ears. Jazz music is to be played sweet, soft, plenty rhythm. When you have your plenty rhythm with your plenty swing, it becomes beautiful.

For a start, you can't play diminuendos and crescendos if you always play as loud as you can. You have to be able to go down if you want to come up again. If a glass of water is full you can't get any more ink, but if you have half a glass, you have room to add some more water. Jazz music is based on the same principle, because jazz is based on strict musical laws . . . Jazz . . . you can apply to any sort of melody. It depends entirely on your ability for transformation.[20]

Jelly Roll Morton's lecture on jazz in the Library of Congress was attended by Alan Lomax with his portable recording equipment. Lomax invited him to lecture there and that is what he did, many times. He explained his views on the history of jazz, described pianists from the beginning of the twentieth century, explained how he developed the jazz piano style from ragtime and blues, told of the lives of the musicians, analyzed the structure of jazz and demonstrated which music was good and which music was not that good. He imitated

20. Lomax, *Mister Jelly Roll*, pp. 64–66.

pianists he had heard play more than thirty years previously, he gave us a glimpse of his artistic skill, with all his intelligence and feeling for nuance. Lomax later examined everything that Jelly said, the result being the very important book, *Mister Jelly Roll.* A large part of the recordings were released on record.[21]

Besides his anecdotes and the story of his childhood and education that we quoted extensively in a previous chapter, we can also hear a number of renditions of his compositions, unlike any he had previously been able to record. What we get to hear is a Jelly—purified and deepened. He had been through a lot, but his music had never changed, essentially. Here in the recordings of "Mama Nita," "New Orleans Blues," "Jungle Blues," "The Crave," "Fickle Fay Creep" and many others—too many to list—just as in that magnificent series of piano solos he played for commercial recordings,[22] we hear that it is not in the least necessary to give black folk music social status and an artificial character by transposing it into a Western style derived from Romantic music, and arranged in a way that damages the music's own character. On the contrary, just as much as the old band recordings of Oliver and Morton, these records prove that folk music can be developed to a high artistic standard by including all sorts of refinement and nuance, without affecting its African-American character. Jazz can be music that reaches out far beyond the simplicity of folk music, but not at the expense of the typical qualities of that folk music—its unique depth, its own idiom—they must not be denied or swapped for a more socially acceptable, Western style to which it is not suited.

As Westerners we have to accept blacks with this music. They have made an important contribution to the musical culture of this world, but we must not expect them to deny their own past. In fact, doing so would imply that we do not accept black Americans but simply tolerate them once they have sold their souls to our culture.

21. On **** Circle 14001-14012. Recently a new issue of this series came out: **** Riverside 9001-9012.

22. For General, reissued on **** Vogue LD 100, **** Vogue LDE080, and by M.M.S.

No, the ideal does not mean holding back the blacks, keeping them on the bottom rung of the ladder, because that is when they make such beautiful music. Not only would that be cruel—it would be an absolute mistake. Oliver and Morton and others prove that development and depth are certainly possible, built on the traditions characteristic to the African-American culture, without blacks having to remain paupers.

Ferdinand "Jelly Roll" Morton died in 1941 in Los Angeles in dire conditions.

THE COLLECTION OF JAZZ RECORDS AND THE STUDY OF THE HISTORY OF JAZZ: COLLECTOR'S ITEM

Teenagers and young adults in America and Europe in the 1930s realized that there was much to be discovered at markets and in junk shops for those who were willing to listen and search: records by absolutely unknown musicians. One of the releases in Europe was the Parlophon New Rhythm Style series (that included many of Armstrong's Hot Seven), which opened up a completely new world. There was also much that was not worth the trouble, of course, and there was also a lot that promised much but turned out to be empty and unmusical.

The first jazz record collectors started up as early as the 1920s, but many fared like me. It was 1936. I was at secondary school. We had a gramophone at home. Once in a while I wanted to buy a record, of course. I bought . . . a sentimental song played by a band, of whom I have forgotten the name. I bought another one, but that was disappointing too after only a short time. I had heard Ellington's "Mood Indigo" at a friend's house, so I bought it, only to discover that "Bundle of Blues" on the flip side was actually much nicer. It did not bore me so quickly. Then I bought an issue of *Jazzwereld* ("Jazz World"), one of the magazines of that era which made a serious attempt to get to grips with jazz, even if there was inevitably copious advertising of popular stars. I went to the Dutch Jazz Club (*Nederlandse Jazz Liga*) by myself one evening. It was one of the clubs to be found all over Europe (and also in America), for young people who wanted to know more of the new music. Perhaps I was unlucky, but the speaker failed to convince me of his views, and the jam session afterwards—which consisted of a number of musicians improvising in the spirit of Chicago—seemed chaotic and noisy. Nevertheless, I did meet other young people there, and they already had a couple of records too. We arranged to meet up. I went to them and discovered Armstrong. We swapped. We pillaged the markets, bought some in the shops—increasingly fewer—discovered records by the unknown Luis Russell band, and once came across a very strange record by an absolutely unknown celebrity. It was "Black Bottom Stomp" by Jelly Roll Morton's Red Hot Peppers, and it cost 35 cents (10 p) at the market! We came in contact with older collectors and, about three years later we were—I was—at home in the world of records. I was familiar with Victor, Okeh, Paramount and, besides the European releases, I managed to get hold of some collector's items—records by little or better known groups which had never been released in Europe. I got to sample and know Red Nichols, Bix Beiderbecke, and the Chicagoans. Above all I learned to appreciate Morton and Oliver—through Brunswick's daring release of an Oliver album in 1936—and soon discovered the blues, Bessie Smith first, and then countless unknown blues singers on the Brunswick Race series. Even a spiritual by the Mitchell's Christian Singers found its way into my collection. I swapped, I bought from people who ordered from American secondhand record shops, such as Orin Blackstone in New Orleans and others.

For others it will have been the same story. Delauney's pioneering *Discography* helped us to learn to identify the musicians. In America people tried to discover something about the history of jazz, to find out who was who. There were a few important books on jazz published during those years. Many of them have already been obscure for a long time. Allan Ramsay and Smith's *Jazzmen* is still valuable today [at time of writing] as a source of information and an introduction to the history of jazz.

All this work has proved to be of tremendous significance. During those years the many committed enthusiasts separated, like wheat from chaff, the material they collected, and the legacy of the past was categorized. People learned to distinguish the different trends and the foundation was laid for further study, lectures, reissues and many sensible talks given on jazz. The rewards of this, which included many reissues of old records, were to be reaped after the War.

Spirituals in the 1930s: Rosetta Tharpe ("Rock Me")

In the 1930s spirituals were still being sung in the churches and recordings made of quartets. The most important of these was possibly the Mitchell's Christian Singers. The quartet included Brown, a driver; Davis, a worker in a tobacco factory; David, a coal merchant; and Bryant, a bricklayer. They performed in churches, at evangelistic meetings, and so on. One of their records is called *Travelin' Shoes*.[23]

> They stopped ridin' by the sinner's door,
> They all cried, Sinner, are you ready to go,
> *He said: 'Oh Lardy, no no no no,*
> *Because I ain't got my travellin' shoes,* [i.e., the faith]
> *It's my duty to say no no no no,*
> *Because I ain't got my travellin' shoes.'*

The first few lines are taken up with a succession of solos sung by different voices; the refrain was sung together. Then the wagon—the "chariot," of course—stops at the door of the gambler, the liar, and finally at the door of the Christian, who is able to answer "yes yes yes yes."

This period saw church solos and particularly those by women, who performed spirituals in the same style as Blind Willie Johnson, strongly influenced by the singing style of the blues as it had developed over the previous few decades. Since secular music had progressed so

---

23. †† Perfect 0298. (Also other recordings are very rare. Unfortunately no reissues.)

much as a result of the work of Ma Rainey Bessie Smith and many others, it was inevitable that church music too would be influenced. Some female blues singers became believers and continued their music in the church, now singing spirituals. People were listening to gramophone records. An enrichment and revamping of the style of singing was inevitable. Building on the old traditions, the result of developments in the secular scene was incorporated.

A typical example of this, and one of the best, is Rosetta Tharpe. She sang "hits" in 1935 as vocalist in a dance band. We did not hear her again until around 1938 when the first records of her as a singer of religious songs were released. She had become a Christian and a member of the Church of God in Christ. She accompanies herself on the guitar. The desire to preach the word of God is very evident in her music, for example in "God Don't Like It." We should mention that orthodox Christians in America do not drink or smoke—the fruit of a Puritan lifestyle. She sings about this too:

> They tell me that this yellow corn
> Will make the very best kind,
> But you better turn that corn into bread,
> And stop that drinking moonshine. ["moonshine" is whisky]

Refrain:
> *Because God don't like it,*
> *I know I am so glad He don't like it,*
> *I know, ain't you glad He don't like it,*
> *I know it's a scandalous and a shame.*

> This ol' race is goin' to be lost,
> If it keeps on like it's goin'
> It's so weak they have a little church,
> But the preacher's drinking moonshine.

> Brother when your name is in the church,
> And you drink God's Holy Wine,

You can't walk those golden streets
All staggerin' full of moonshine.[24]

The next song, "Rock Me" by Thomas A. Dorsey, is beautiful:

Now won't you hear me swinging,
And the words that I'm singing
Washed my soul with water from on high.
Now the world of love is around me,
Evil sought to bite me,
Oh, if You leave me, I will die.

Refrain:
You just hide me in Thy bosom
Till the storm of life is over,
Oh, rock me, in the greatness of Thy love.
Receive me, and I want no more
Till You take me to You — blessed home above.

Say, I'm maintaining,
I just go on uncomplaining,
But before this time another year:
My life may all forsaken,
And death may overtake me,
But if I'm within Thee I have no need to fear.

Oh, make my journey brighter,
Make my burden lighter
Help me to do good wherever I can;
Oh, let Thy presence thrill me
let its kindness still me
When You hold me in the hollow of Thy hand.[25]

24. ****† Decca M 30270.
25. ****† Decca BM 02737.

BLUES AFTER 1935: "BIG MOOSE BLUES"

In rural areas the blues was still being sung in the original style. The influence of the Race records was certainly perceptible here and there, but essentially nothing changed. It was different in the cities. Professional singers were having a hard time and more than a few of them began to serve Mammon in their own way—by singing smutty lyrics, by emphasizing all the elements that would attract a certain kind of white audience. There were also some who fared better. After the years of severe crisis had passed, a new generation of singers emerged. The style had changed, the tempo was faster, the tone was lighter, and the accompaniment more rhythmic—like the jazz which had evolved post-1928. Nevertheless, the work of Merline Johnson ("The Yas Yas Girl") is certainly worth listening to. The blues of Big Bill Broonzy Johnny Temple and Sleepy John Estes was a more direct continuation of the music from prior to 1930—the work of Leroy Carr, Texas Alexander and others—but we will not be able to check up on it extensively here.[26]

There was also an interesting record of this genre by Sonny Boy and Lonnie, who were unknown artists. It features a blues singer, accompanied by piano and guitar, who sings of his experiences on a naval transport ship in the War. We estimate that the recording was made in 1944 or 1945. *Big Moose* is the name of the ship.

> It was in San Francisco, it was way way out in the bay,
> It was in 1943, way way out in the bay,
> Yes, just a Tuesday morning that old *Big Moose go* roll us away.

> We rolled that Pacific, sailed it both day and night, (x 2)
> Yes, some was drinking and gamblin', some was low low on their
> knees.

26. Br. 87054 LPBM, *Bad Luck Blues*, a collection album on which a number of these kinds of records were brought together. Cf. also **** Fontana 682073 TL.

Japanese bombs was falling, falling down down from the sky, (x 2)
Sometimes I wanted to leave that shiphold, but I had no place to go.

We landed in Finch Haven, New Guinea, it was on the twenty-
	fifth day (x 2)
And I said: 'Lord Lord have mercy on our poor GI Souls.'[27]

The Birth of Swing: "In the Mood"

The middle of the 1930s saw the gradual emergence of a new
style. It was a sort of Chicagoans jazz but then adapted for larger
bands. The black bands like Henderson's led the way. They played
arrangements that were strongly rhythmically oriented, in which
saxophone ensembles alternated with brass ensembles—in unison
or harmonized. Solos, free and improvised, were often played and
accompanied by riffs (short melodic phrases which were constantly
repeated and had a strongly rhythmic effect). Influences from the
Benny Moten Band and others were incorporated. The music was
"hotter," and the combined effect was a fluent, strong rhythm, harmonically rendered, peppered with fierce solos, direct, vehement and
improvised—at least that was the impression they gave.

Around 1935 the time was ripe. A white band, that of Bennie
Goodman, began to use these arrangements—particularly those of
Fletcher Henderson, like Morton's "King Porter Stomp"—and played
them with machine-like precision on the basis of a rhythm section
that strongly marked the beat. They played contemporary hits. It was
a great success, and swing was born, the new sort of dance music
which was to keep thousands of fans spellbound.

This was par excellence the dance music of the twentieth century. It was music that could capture white audiences in every
respect and give them what they demanded. It was jazz, but it was
not too challenging, fierce but not too complex, always softened and
made pleasing by harmonization or, in the case of solos, by smooth

27. **† Continental C-6053.

accompaniment. Besides the apparent spontaneity, directness, seemingly primitive release of power, without dinner jackets or tail coats and without the formality of a classical concert, there was the omnipresence of the rhythm. Everyone now had access to the popular tunes rendered in an almost ideal way—"ideal" in the sense of twentieth-century Western mentality.

Goodman created a formula—at least he was able to suitably apply the formulas the black leaders of big dance bands had worked out. It was a formula that hit the mark so well that not only was it predominant for a whole decade (until 1945) but it is still alive now [at the time of writing]. Turn on your radio and some band somewhere in the world will be playing this sort of music. It has something of the streamlining that affected design and changed the shape of such diverse products as the car, the train, the vacuum cleaner and the iron during those years. It was colorful, vehement, supple, stylized, smooth—it was swing.

Many, many swing bands were able to profit from the craze. It became the era of jazz—the era that jazz was sold using all possible modern sales techniques, with much advertising while it was tailored to the demands of the public. Glenn Miller, Dorsey, Lunceford, Barnet and also Artie Shaw were the manufacturers.

Listen to "In the Mood,"[28] the most popular piece at the time. The musical starting point is a riff-like theme that hypnotizes the masses, as it were, and forms the ideal stimulant for Western paired dancing, which is almost a duet in itself, full of vehemence and improvisation—a letting go, a freeing from the conventions, from that which a modern audience might perceive as over-rigid, stylized norms. Loose and direct, rhythmical and fierce, free and carefree—that was the music, that was the dance, that in many ways was the twentieth century.

To the musicians themselves it was often less pleasant; Artie Shaw disappeared suddenly one fine day. He did not arrive for a

28. RCA A 130212 (Artie Shaw). Recordings of swing bands also on *Dazzling Jazz, Big Sound,* * Philips B O7228L.

performance. He could no longer take the pressure. Perhaps he saw what Goodman himself once said: "Many musicians today don't know any more what they really want, do they? Perhaps I don't know either. But something happens when you realize that what you are doing isn't really music any more—it has become entertainment. It is a fine difference and it determines your playing. Your whole attitude changes."[29]

THE SWING OF BASIE AND CO.: "ONE O'CLOCK JUMP"

The swing music that was played by Goodman and his many more or less original counterparts was an adaptation of black jazz, fashioned to white dance music. When we say black jazz, however, we are chiefly referring to the jazz of Fletcher, Henderson and such—jazz that originated from Western dance music, but was very substantially influenced by authentic black jazz as played by Armstrong, Rex Stuart, Buster Bailey, Joe Smith and others. The blacks had found the formula—the whites applied it. I wonder whether a black band playing the same music as Goodman would have had the same amount of success, though it must be said that Goodman was one of the first to include black musicians in his band—two of them being Lionel Hampton (drums and vibraphone) and Teddy Wilson (piano).

Both black and white elements were very strongly blended in this type of jazz. Blacks contributed their own musical tradition—some of the joy of early jazz also added to the success of this music; the white influence lay in the cultivation of great precision in ensemble playing and, most importantly, in improvisation and in "hot" and hefty beat accentuating rhythms in the spirit of the jazz inspired by the Chicagoans. Because of the teamwork and their playing together it became increasingly difficult to hear the difference between the black and the white musicians—something that hardly posed any problems in the 1920s, the era of Bix and Teschemaker, Oliver and Morton, Armstrong and Dodds.

29. *Heah Me Talkin' to Ya*, p. 282.

Still, it is important to see that the impact made by black musicians remained very great, and indeed, it would be difficult to exaggerate the significance of the Count Basie Band in the era of swing.

Basie and his musicians came from Kansas City. Most of them had been playing there in Bennie Moten's band. When Moten died in 1935, Basie reorganized the band, but musicians from Kansas City still formed the core. We do not want to contend that they were all born there, but they all received their education and began their careers there.

Jam sessions were cultivated extensively in Kansas City. They also occurred elsewhere, but less intensively. For these jam sessions various musicians, who did not otherwise form a band, got together for the purpose of playing music together. It meant that they took turns to play the solo while the other musicians improvised a background of riffs. Thus a real Chicagoan idea became the basic principle of all jazz. It certainly became the basic structure of all Basie's music, although he could not quite manage to make the music work without any arrangements at all, while in line with other swing bands he increased the saxes to four and included four trumpets, three trombones and, of course, a four-strong rhythm section of bass, guitar, piano (Basie himself) and drums.

Jo Jones, the drummer, tells us a little about their approach to the work:

The Basie Band gave you the impression of a small band. The arrangements were almost all played from memory and it didn't matter how many of us there were—there was always the freedom and the flexibility of a small band. This was not the case for other bands from that period, however good they were in many respects. [He goes on to talk about a recording.] When we went into the studio we first decided what we were going to play, looked briefly at our notes (with some instructions and agreements about the consecutive choruses), and then there it went. We played once, twice or three times at the most, and the record was made. Some of the best sides we hadn't even discussed beforehand. We just sat

there doing something during the break and the recording techni-
cians recorded it.

On the question of whether the band rehearsed he answered:

> I don't know how to explain it, how to tell you how it actually went
> on. I have never understood how an arrangement like that (i.e. one
> which came into being simply by virtue of playing and otherwise
> only consisted of agreements) came about. What I do know is that
> we were there and we began to play, but we didn't rehearse. It all
> just went so automatically.[30]

The significance of this band in the evolution of swing and in what
was still to come was very great. "One o'Clock Jump," the band's
signature tune, is a piece of a kind that has been copied and imitated
in all sorts of different ways and one that has contributed to Basie's
impact.[31]

30. Ibid., pp. 273, 275.
31. See the Philips record in note 17.

6

The 1940s

THE BIRTH OF MODERN JAZZ: "CHEROKEE"

Swing was by definition jazz, at least if you hold that the definition of jazz is rhythm plus improvisation. That was the direction pursued by the big bands. Performances by recording combinations, the (public) jam sessions, anything that could be called jazz and stood out, fitted that definition. The scheme was the same as it had ever been: the short, riff-like theme was played first or, if a popular little tune was being played it was done in strong staccato with the same effect; then solos, one after the other, one much fiercer, heavier and more direct than the other, with the only binding element being the chord scheme and the tempo. The accompaniment was fashioned by drawing out chords or by improvised sax riffs. The whole thing was supported by the constantly pumping, beat accentuating rhythm, decorated by the drum if possible.

The audience got used to it. It had to be constantly fiercer, otherwise it was not authentic and did not keep people entertained. That is why the saxophone began bleating, the clarinet was played hoarsely and the trumpet began to cultivate high tones. It was all for the sake of effect—to suggest heavy emotion, a direct release. Was it musical? Seldom. Perhaps the audience enjoyed hearing the sax produce ugly sounds and being entertained by music that balanced precariously on the edge of its own definition. This is reminiscent of the approval of the violation of norms which the Bible talks about in

169

Romans 1:32. In this case it violates the norm which also applies to art and ultimately determines its value: "meditating on things true, noble, reputable, authentic, compelling, gracious—the best, not the worst; the beautiful, not the ugly; things to praise, not things to curse" (Philippians 4:8).

Jam sessions were originally intended for the musicians only; it was their chance to enjoy making music after having played empty music in a commercial orchestra, possibly for hours on end. Now it became a compulsory part of performances, an act of letting yourself go with great emotion. It became an empty and futile repetition of tricks which had the appearance of spontaneity; it became the cultivation of nonmusic to please Mammon or, if Mammon was not involved, a striving for the approval of audiences that yearned for sensation, for a vehemence that crushed the definition of beauty, for increasingly intense stimulation.

To the musicians this became a trial, dull, a self-inflicted void. No wonder they tried to put the soul back into music after 1940, tried to give it meaning, to restore its dignity as music. That is how modern jazz came about. It started with the formula for swing music: solos based on a certain progression of chords remained the basic materials, and the themes remained partially taken from the hits of the day. There was no more reaching for Oliver's (or anybody else's) old music. Nevertheless there was a heartbeat behind the new music—we could perhaps call it an existentialist heartbeat.

This process was described very clearly and concisely by one of the most talented and influential musicians, a man who significantly contributed to the fashioning of modern jazz, Charlie Parker, the saxophonist. He tells of how he first discovered the modern jazz concept:

> It was in December 1939. The stereotypical chord progressions which were used the whole time were boring me terribly and I kept thinking that something else would have to come. I could hear it in my thoughts sometimes, but I couldn't play it. Well, that evening I played 'Cherokee' (a popular swing number) and while I was doing it I discovered that by using the higher intervals of a chord as the

melody line, thereby adapting the chord changes, I could play what
I had been hearing in my thoughts. I came to life.[1]

Parker, however, was not the only one. There were others—all intelligent young blacks who were looking for a way to fill swing with
something other than the endless repetition of a few tricks which
had made the music so empty and so infinitely boring. Intensity and
spontaneity—fine, they had nothing against it, but they wanted to
produce something with meaning, something real; "real" being an
expression of what lived in them.

Kansas City was one of the cities where this sort of sound was
being developed. Mary Lou Williams tells the following about the
pianist Thelonius Monk:

> He felt that musicians would have to start playing something new
> and he began to do it. Most of us admired him for it. He was
> one of the original modernists, a good one, who applied about
> the same harmonies then as are being played today. But in those
> days we called it 'zombie music' and waited until only we musi-
> cians were left by ourselves and the audience had left. Why 'zombie
> music'? Because the shrill chords reminded us of the music from
> Frankenstein or other horror films. I myself was one of the first
> to produce these frozen sounds and after a whole night of playing
> a jam session (for an audience), I started playing strange chords,
> nothing but modulations, together with Dick Wilson, a very pro-
> gressive tenor saxophonist.[2]

It does not sound as if they were simply looking for new chords,
new musical approaches, but as if they were also trying to express
something in their music, something that was related to the character
of a horror film. The fact that Kansas City led the way was possibly
the result of another factor, one that was also responsible for shaping

1. *Heah Me Talkin' to Ya*, p. 315.
2. Ibid., p. 280.

modern jazz, namely that musicians there were striving for individualism more than elsewhere.[3] For modern jazz is individualist, as its proponents loudly reiterate.

A further characteristic of the new jazz was a thirst for freedom—freedom for the musician who was playing. It was realized in improvised solos in which, from then on, even the traditional chord scheme was no longer binding. It was freedom from all bonds. As Dave Brubeck volunteered:

> What is jazz? If the soloist does not have complete freedom, it ceases to be jazz. Jazz is the only form of art that exists today in which freedom exists for the individual without losing contact with the others. If we play arrangements we try to get our freedom in the middle section. We start with an arranged chorus, and then there is complete freedom for as long as the soloist feels like playing, and then it ends with the arrangement again. And if it goes well, the beginning and end are largely ridiculous, because the parts in between have come at the level where you are really busy improvising.[4]

This quote reminds us a bit of the spirit of the greatest philosopher of existentialism, Heidegger. He said that human beings in their ordinary living live in the "impersonal," an improper form of existence. One is only oneself if one realizes one's own *Dasein* ("existence"), if one places oneself in one's own freedom. That takes place here in the improvised solos.

The catchword has thus become "individualistic freedom," freedom that wants to have people really free—completely free of any ties; free too from any norms. That is why modern jazz tries to break down the laws of structure which apply to melody, and not only search for the unconventional, but also for the irrational, for elements that demonstrate the freedom of the individual. Stearn, so far the

3. Ibid.
4. Ibid., p. 361.

best historian of modern jazz and a person who is positive about its development, puts it like this: "The bop soloist (bop was the name of the new sort of jazz) now began and ended at odd moments and places by shifting the respiratory pause and so often created a long, unbalanced melodic line which ignored the regular pauses."[5]

Love does not govern here. Everyone tries to outplay the other, even in the very matter of irrationality. A musician would stop in the middle of the solo and leave it to the following soloist to pick up the pieces; another would leave the stage while somebody else was playing; and for the listeners, the audience, there was not the least bit of interest.[6]

All this was strongest in the 1940s. During the War years this kind of jazz was being developed in New York by Charlie Parker, whom we have already mentioned, by Dizzy Gillespie and by a group of musicians that regularly met together at Minton's, a nightclub in New York. These jam sessions there were decisive. After the War modern jazz soon became widespread and popular, thanks to gramophone recordings and concerts staged by these people. They were all very intelligent and skilled musicians who knew very well what they were doing and, particularly at first, were prepared to give it their all. Commercial success at that point was still more or less a pipe dream because this jazz was no longer dance music. The audience sat motionless at the concerts and there was nothing left of the exuberance that had been so fundamental to swing music.

There are reasons why jazz developed along these lines, at that time and in that scene. The petering out of swing was one reason. The new music was in many respects a backlash against swing because, although it retained many elements of swing, these musicians were looking for something opposite in character and nature. This music became "cool"—as opposed to "hot"—which means that any emotion which would otherwise have been released, was repressed or avoided. The rhythm was different—more restless, more nervous, sometimes

5. Stearns, *Story of Jazz*, p. 230.
6. Ibid., pp. 223–4.

based directly on African rhythms—in any case there was no "pumping" as there was in swing.

There were more reasons, however. The position of blacks also played a role. The race issue became very acute because of the war conditions which required them to devote themselves to American civilization. The question was, should they let themselves be used again? Building on the accomplishments of the Harlem Renaissance, blacks were no longer willing to play the entertainer for whites who found them useful when it came to popular music but otherwise gave them the cold shoulder. Blacks wanted to find their own expression in jazz, one which was different from what the whites had made of it. However, the spirit of music that was being produced at the time was, in fact, of pure Western character and was very closely related to the modern art of Picasso, Klee, the abstract painters and the thought of the modern existentialist philosophers.

Freedom, irrationality, individualism—but no joy. On the contrary, this was an escape from reality, a reality that was perceived as a strange power, a prison for those who thirsted after absolute freedom. It was also a prison that resulted from repression. And it was the suffocation of the ever boring, endless repetition of sameness, concretized in the meaningless emptiness of swing's quasi-fierce release of emotion.

This is not joy; this is hatred of the world, of reality, and ultimately of creation itself. It explains the preference for the strange chords, searing and incoherent. As for the harmonies, they were not only a further development of what was already there but they were sought for as an expression of what was on these musicians' hearts, what inspired them: a feeling of alienation, of fear, of emptiness, of their experience of reality as a horror film—"zombie music."

From the typically modern aspect of this new sort of jazz, we can also understand why it was so easy for whites to adopt—so easy in fact that they were even able to play an important role in its development. Take Dave Brubeck and Shorty Rogers' group of musicians in the western USA. It is hard, if not downright impossible, to distinguish white from black here.

You could detect now, more so than in the past, that the best and most skilled musicians were playing two different sorts of music. We have seen that this had been the case also with Armstrong and his people in 1928. On one hand there now was the fierce expression of freedom, vehement and, despite all inwardness and being locked up in oneself, extrovert, outward-oriented.[7] On the other hand there was the introversion, the inward reverie, the daydream, unattached and free from reality, quieted and literally "cool." The well-known number by Parker, "Lover Man,"[8] is a good example. It is music that appears very quiet and calm, missing all the emotion of early jazz; inside it is a direct expression of what moves the musician, his feelings of being abandoned, lonely, alienated from reality, the very consequence of his search for individualist freedom in an existentialist sense.

No, joy and warmth were banished from the lives of these musicians. Parker paid for it with his mental health and ultimately with his self-inflicted death. Others either put water in their wine or sought refuge from the tension and problems in the use of narcotics.

This jazz is a phenomenon that is essentially modern and the product of our Western world. That is why it is so well understood by young people in the West, and why it is so attractive to them. That is also part of the reason why modern Western classical composers, like Schoenberg and Stravinsky, had such a big influence on the musicians of modern jazz. This is not superficial music, not at all. It has an affinity to post-War, Western, modern art—the works of the Experimental, the Tachists, modernists who also strive for abstraction and the irrational. This can be heard in the characteristic tone forming, cool indeed (the opposite of warm), withdrawn, disconnected from reality, light and not particularly mellifluous. This tone forming alone—both in the brass and the woodwind—distinguishes modern jazz from all earlier forms of jazz. Modern jazz is also not the logical consequence of early jazz. On the contrary, it is a new form of music with a completely different content, a new spirit and a new structure,

7. E.g., Charlie Parker on * Savoy G 12000.
8. * Vogue EPL 7036.

and the only thing it has in common with early jazz is its origin, in that it evolved from the jazz scene.

Grossman described one of the characteristics of modern jazz as "playfulness."[9] What he means is that these musicians sometimes do not seem to take their music seriously, but that they appear to play with it. It does not mean that they *are* not serious. Modern jazz musicians are dead serious; they know what they want, they are very conscientious artists, and they strive to develop their music. In that respect their music is a far cry from folk music. The playfulness however points to something else, an attitude, an attitude to life that will not allow itself to be tied to anything, that always wants to remain free, to treat things without strings attached, to "play" with them. What comes to the fore here is nihilism, a lack of ability to commit oneself to anything, to be bonded and, instead, to adopt a "free of obligations" attitude that covers an inability to believe in anything, a struggle to retain personal freedom at whatever cost.

This becomes particularly clear if we bear in mind the cultural history of these blacks or, rather, that which still determines the lives of many blacks both in terms of spirit and culture, namely Christianity— the biblical message. This music is a clear refutation of it. While performing "Swing Low, Sweet Chariot," Gillespie sang "Swing Low, Sweet Cadillac." This is no naive black faith, but something that verges on blasphemy. So he frees himself "playfully" from "that old time religion" sung of by churchgoers. Another musician changed the title of the well-known spiritual about Moses to "Let My Fingers Go."[10]

All this is not unconnected with what is going on at present. The attitude of many students today is one of playing around, with "no strings attached," a general lack of interest and a certain unwillingness to devote themselves to anything. It is an international phenomenon that is seen in an extreme form among the nozems, forerunners of the hippies in the Netherlands. On one hand these young people are

9. Grossman & Farrell, *The Heart of Jazz*, p. 114 ff.
10. Ibid., p. 122. Modern jazz is well summarized on the LP *Dazzling Jazz, Modern*, * Philips B 07227L.

dangerous anarchists who, given the chance, will sometimes commit themselves to a cause with valor that verges on the romantic and with a contempt for life that is real and deep, as for example during the Hungarian insurrection (in which young students often played such an important role). On the other hand they can be apathetic individuals who care little or nothing for anything and remain unmoved by any ideal. Boredom, counterbalanced by an impatient need to rush along—these are the symptoms of the empty spirit syndrome, sometimes with explosive nihilism, boredom in the sense of *nausee,* as Sartre called it, an aversion to all being.

All this is part of our culture, certainly, in the same way that this music, which is anything but commercial, is part of our culture, but that does not mean that only those who live and behave likewise are really "in touch with the times," the only ones who really live, who understand their age. It is as meaningless as the allegation that only those who vote communist really understand contemporary politics. In culture as well as in politics many persuasions exist side by side and everyone uses their own criteria to tackle the issues of the day. The persuasions may be dignified by age, like liberalism or Christianity, or they may be more recent trends like socialism and communism; likewise, in other areas of human culture all sorts of schools of thought are found to exist alongside each other and in opposition to each other. Abstract art can exist alongside art that is Impressionist in spirit, alongside art that is related in spirit, not necessarily in form, to seventeenth-century art. Provided that these trends do not get bogged down in the repetition and imitation of earlier forms but are sustained by a living spirit that engages with the issues of our time, provided that they are tuned in to the reality of today, that they are "in touch with their time" and, as such, culturally meaningful. Whether their aspirations and their presuppositions are right is the next question, and these will have to be tested. This pursuit of the truth, however, must be based on the Truth of the living God, being God today just as he was at the time he first revealed himself to us through Scripture, and who therefore manifests himself just as substantially in his work today. The categorical rejection of everything that is produced by the secular world as inhuman, meaningless and not worthy of anything is just as foolishly dogmatic as the verdict of the moderns who hold that only modern jazz, abstract art and communism are "of our time." The latter is a violation of living reality; the former will lead to neglect of spiritual warfare and the testing of the spirits while everything is deemed to be worthless and empty anyway.

I am writing this because modern jazz as an expression of a twentieth-century existential attitude is very important and its quality and meaning as a cultural phenomenon may not be underestimated. I am also writing it to show that there may be other trends today, also in jazz, each of which will have to be tested individually as to its value, but under no circumstances should they simply be written off as old hat in the way the haughty proponents of modern jazz have done to other trends. Next we shall look at some of these other trends.

The Rediscovery of New Orleans Jazz: "Burgundy Street Blues"

> I enjoy playing for people that are happy. I enjoy seeing people happy. If everyone is in a lively mood, I get the spirit and I can make my trombone sing. If my music makes the people happy, I will try and do more. It's like a challenge for me. I like to see people around me. It makes me warm inside, and that comes out in my music. When I play melodious music, I try to convey my feelings to my fellow audience. I always have that in my thoughts.[11]

That was the voice of Jim Robinson in one of the nicest statements ever made about New Orleans jazz. It makes the contrast in spirit between modern jazz as described in the previous chapter and this New Orleans jazz abundantly clear. It is the latter that we are going to discuss now.

As mentioned before, the book *Jazzmen* appeared in 1939. It was an important book and indicated a trend that sought to put new

---

11. *Heah Me Talkin' to Ya*, p. 362.

life into the old jazz of the 1930s which had become intolerable. Just prior to that, Panassie had produced a few recordings on which Mezz Mezrow and Bechet played alongside an almost forgotten Tommy Ladnier. He had tried to establish the whereabouts of the musicians who had made recordings ten or fifteen years earlier. It transpired that they were largely living and working in poor conditions or that they had bid their music farewell and gone looking for other jobs. George Mitchell had become a postal worker in Chicago, for example. Jimmy Noone, Johnny Dodds and various others had made a few recordings just before the War.

The research that preceded the writing of *Jazzmen* included a series of interviews with the musicians themselves in order to gather information about the early history of jazz (prior to 1920 and before the first recordings were made). It turned out that much had happened in New Orleans and that many obviously important musicians had never been recorded.

The research team consequently took the train to New Orleans to carry out further investigations. They discovered that many of the pioneers—who had been paraded as almost mythical personalities in stories about New Orleans—were still alive and were playing as semiprofessionals[12] or had chosen a different trade.

The first recordings of the older of these musicians were made in 1940, under the name of Kid Rena's Delta Jazz Band which consisted of Rena (trumpet), Jim Robinson (trombone), and two clarinetists who had regularly featured in the New Orleans stories: Alphonse Picou and Louis Nelson. The recordings were not brilliant, but they served the purpose of reconstructing the past.[13]

It soon became evident however that there was also a young reserve force living and working in New Orleans—musicians who had missed the developments which had taken place in the North and

---

12. As mentioned earlier, a *semiprofessional* is someone who has another job alongside their musical activities and whose income does not depend on playing music.

13. † Esquire 10-111 and 10-112.

who were still playing straightforward old-style New Orleans music. It was jazz as it had sounded before Oliver went North.

On 16 May 1943 a recording was made of a group of New Orleans musicians. It comprised of people of Louis Armstrong's age who had remained steadfast in the New Orleans tradition. Around ten recordings were made and they belong to the best of this genre: George Lewis, who could play his clarinet so beautifully, performed his almost seraphic, lyrical music, rich in variation, musical to the very core, and of great beauty; Jim Robinson turned out to be a trombonist who was able to combine melodic invention with rhythmic accentuation in an entirely characteristic style; the trumpet player Kid Howard played a style slightly reminiscent of Armstrong's around 1925 (around that time they had played together on a riverboat that did excursions from New Orleans up the Mississippi); the rhythm section was also very competent and maintained a rhythm that was completely free of any swing influence.

It was a curious series of records. No two are the same—not in mood nor in structure. New Orleans style is richly versatile—anything but a restricted formula. Lively ragtimes like "Fidgety Feet" and "Climax Rag" stand alongside quieter pieces like "Deep Bayou Blues," and there are also lyrical numbers with a beautiful melody, warm and charming, like the spiritual "Just a Little While to Stay Here."[14]

The records were recorded in an unusual way. The musicians, who had little knowledge of recording procedures, were told that the first few attempts would just be experiments and that the actual recording would take place the next day. Their performance was therefore completely relaxed—purely for pleasure, while the recordings were in fact being made. That is why some of the numbers begin in the middle of a chorus or the recording finishes before the musicians did. It is New Orleans music at its best. The structure consisted, as we described earlier, of variations on one or more themes, polyphonic ensemble choruses alternating with solos, ensemble-playing based on the themes in a melodic rather than a harmonic sense.

14. **** Blue Note 1206 (LP).

At the same time, however, the contrast with the New Orleans jazz of Oliver, Morton and others, was also clear. In general it was the best educated, most intelligent and most enterprising of the musicians that left in the 1920s. Those who stayed behind knew little or nothing of music theory and, in contrast to Oliver and others, were not familiar with Western harmony and pure intonation within the well-tempered music system. This explains why they sometimes intonate differently and to our ears, when we have not yet understood how this music is put together, sound out of tune. If we listen closely, however, it appears to be a question of taste—a difference in musical thinking. They put melody and sound before harmonic purity. George Lewis always played the clarinet so as to produce the best sound, even when he had to squeeze his instrument somewhat in order to produce a well-tempered, pure tone. Neither do these musicians imitate the famous musicians of older recordings (for they did not know them); they have their own style. The result is fresh, New Orleans music with its own character and content. It is different from that of Oliver and as such, possibly less refined, though it is not rough or uncivilized and never barbaric or primitive. It is less Western in tone and harmony but pure and of great beauty rich in variation and melody. Most importantly, it is not overexuberant and does not unleash itself in an uncontrolled fashion—it is music of great joy, of elation, almost. They make the odd mistake here or there, but their enormous enthusiasm and pure musicality more than compensate for that.

In researching for the book *Jazzmen,* the name Bunk Johnson kept cropping up. He was a trumpet player who was said to have influenced Louis Armstrong greatly and was supposed to have been a musician of extraordinary quality. Eventually he was traced to Louisiana, where he was living an impoverished life in a small town. He was given new dentures, a new trumpet, and he played. First he did a number of recordings in New Orleans on 11 June 1942. It turned out to be something quite special, different from the Kid Rena Band. In spite of the fact that he had never made a public appearance outside his hometown and had not been active for years for all sorts of reasons, this proved to be a musician with very special talent. The recordings made a few months later with George Lewis and Jim Robinson's group[15] allow us to enjoy the extraordinary qualities of the other musicians whom we have just mentioned, and admire Bunk's playing in particular. His music was a revelation—beautiful in tone, calm, with superb phrasing, rich in melodic invention and skill of variation. "Thriller Rag" and "Franklin Street Blues" were supreme numbers, but we could quote many more.

In 1943 Bunk Johnson played with the Yerba Bueno Jazz Band in San Francisco for a while, and I will come back to that. Then in 1944 he was back in New Orleans and played with the George Lewis Group. They made a series of beautiful recordings in the summer of 1944, all under the American Music label and unfortunately very difficult to get hold of [in the Netherlands] now. They played ragtimes, old New Orleans schmaltz hits like "When You Wore a Tulip," very lyrical versions of spirituals like "Walk through the Streets of the City," in which the melody itself is repeated without variation, and a number of blues.

There is little point in analyzing all these records, but there is one that stands out as the most beautiful recording of New Orleans style made after the 1923 to 1927 period. It is a beautiful live recording of blues without a specific title.[16] Various themes are used; a particular theme of twelve bars is played polyphonically and then varied in the next chorus of twelve bars. Then comes a new theme, repeated in the following chorus in a different variation. Next there is a succession of solos (clarinet, trombone, and trumpet) based on the last polyphonically played theme. It is followed by new themes and variations, always in twos. As a binding element there is a refrain, for all choruses end with the same motif in the last four bars.

There is something else that gives all these recordings such a special character and that is Babe Dodds' drumming. He had played with

15. Releases on Jazzman and Jazz Information. Reissues e.g., *** Commodore CEP 79.
16. ****† American Music 638.

Oliver previously but he comes over better here thanks to the quality of the recordings. There were also a few records made of Dodds speaking and demonstrating how his music is structured—how the tone changes from high to low, how his support of a polyphonic ensemble is different from that of a solo, and how he also allows himself to be guided by his instrument. He ends his discourse with a useful remark aimed at drummers who think that they can just sit there and beat something out. "No," he says, "you have to use your head. What else is it there for?"[17]

"Burgundy Street Blues," a solo by George Lewis, was also recorded on the American Music label.[18] Later again Lewis played this piece several times on record, providing us with a good point of comparison that teaches us much about his method. At first it sounds like pure, free improvisation on a blues chord scheme, with a set refrain in the last four bars. If we compare it with the other recordings, however, the successive improvisation pieces turn out to be new themes which are always played in the same order. There is much more structure and coherence, consideration and musical composition in this piece than is immediately obvious. It is not a succession of improvised pieces but a fixed framework of themes, which are coherently linked with each other and are also linked by a similar sounding refrain. He once recorded this piece on a 45 rpm disc, which allows more recording space, and there this pattern becomes particularly evident. As soon as his composition has ended, he stops playing and the surplus recording space is devoted to a piano solo which indeed sticks out like a sore thumb.[19]

The Lewis-Robinson Band made many other recordings, sometimes with different trumpet players and sometimes without a trumpet player at all. In 1945 they went to New York with Bunk Johnson where they surprised the jazz enthusiasts with their lively performances of New Orleans music. They made a few recordings

17. ****† American Music, *Baby Dodds No. 1*.
18. ****† American Music 531.
19. ** Br. EPB 10006.

there including the beautiful and sharply played "Tishomingo Blues," for Brunswick,[20] and a series for Victor (released on HMV in the Netherlands), which is far less satisfactory than the American Music recordings we mentioned. It sounds as if the musicians have been wrenched from their roots, for they use a loud and heavy style—quite inappropriate in relation to their own lyrical style—to let us hear that they can indeed produce something like Armstrong's Hot Five. It was a temptation, one which for Bunk—constantly confronted with the notion that he was the great teacher of Louis Armstrong—must have been particularly hard to resist. The band split up after that, homesickness and other problems being the reason. Bunk then tried again with another group and produced interesting results. Musically however, these recordings are far below the standard of the older recordings made in New Orleans.[21]

The end came soon afterwards for Bunk, while George Lewis and his band are still playing [at the time of writing]. Bunk was still making nice recordings but in the 1950s his playing deteriorated and became too comfortable and mechanical, while he tried to conform to the demands (of the audience) for a well-tempered intonation at the cost of some of the lyrical purity of tone. Nevertheless, several numbers were fine, like those he recorded for Riverside.[22]

New Orleans style turned out not to be obsolete, not by any means a thing of the past but alive and kicking. Now that doors had opened again, many of the old guard began playing again. The trombonist Kid Ory—one of those who went looking for another job in the 1930s—also took up his instrument again. Although subsequently many recordings were made of these musicians, we shall not be following their progress further, to avoid getting bogged down in a rather dry summary.

20. ITJ.
21. Philips B O7009L.
22. HCJ. Also, for example, ** Blue note BLP7027; *** Riverside 207.

WHITE REVIVAL AND DIXIELAND JAZZ: "FAR AWAY BLUES"

The renewed interest in New Orleans jazz reached young people all over the world who then tried to copy the style. Indeed, after 1945 in almost every city in the USA, Western Europe, Australia and where, Dixieland groups, mostly amateur ones, were set up. We call this music Dixieland so as not to confuse it with the real New Orleans music we dealt with in the last chapter, and which was nothing but the old music emerging from the darkness of obscurity into the limelight.

In moving on I do not want to reject the work of a few very good bands like that of Claude Lutter in France (approx. 1947–1948), Humphrey Lyttleton's band in England and our own [Dutch] Erik Krans' Dixieland Pipers, even if some of the traits we are going to talk about were evident in their music.

In social and artistic terms Dixieland is not such a bad phenomenon. It shows that young people want to make music themselves. It gives them opportunities and no doubt much pleasure. It stimulates working together in groups and is certainly anything but a pernicious pastime. Whether they always understand the music they want to play is quite a different matter. They model their music on the gramophone records of New Orleans jazz that we have discussed in this book. Nevertheless, their interpretation of the music often comes much closer to Chicago jazz than to the real New Orleans style. This can be demonstrated if we compare a direct imitation of Oliver with the original:[23] the rhythm seems to be closely related to that of swing and has none of the basso continuo that Oliver has; at the same time they are busy improvising instead of playing variations within the melodic and compository structure. Their definition of jazz is vehemence and letting go. As far as Oliver was concerned, a break was a rest filled by an instrument; to the Chicagoans it was an excuse for another fierce outburst. The theory of jazz in the spirit of

23. E.g., Oliver's "Sobbin' Blues" with the rendition of the Down Town Jazz Band, RCA 75.159.

the Chicagoans—jazz equals rhythm plus improvisation—dominates their artistic commitment.

Naturally they also want to play polyphonically but they think they are supposed to be improvising and usually shun careful practice. If they are to avoid chaos they can do little but stick strictly to the formula: the trumpet renders the melody, the clarinet "saws" away above it, the trombone slides up and down a bit and provides a few rhythmic accents. This formula, endlessly repeated, makes each number sound just like the others without any variation in mood or expression. That makes the music boring after a while. Perhaps it is pleasant to listen to for a time but it lacks real depth and invention. Dixieland jazz might be described as New Orleans music played to a set formula, according to the spirit of the Chicagoans, which nullifies the excellent qualities of freedom and spontaneity.

There are others, however. As early as the 1930s, a group of musicians conducted by Lu Watters and Turk Murphy were experimenting in San Francisco. Around 1940 they emerged as the Yerba Buena Jazz Band. Their aim was to study New Orleans jazz, to play in that vein again, to breathe new life into it and to carry it on as a living tradition. The result was good, though it was a bit stiff, not very smooth and little differentiated at first. But they stuck to it and some of their music became more interesting and rewarding.[24]

One LP particularly worth mentioning features New York trumpeter Everett Farey.[25] It was recorded in New York in 1954 by a recording syndicate led by Bob Helm, the clarinetist from Turk Murphy's band. The small band—clarinet, trumpet, piano, washboard and bass (or tuba)—performed to an unprecedentedly high standard—one of the best records of New Orleans style music ever made by whites— with a pure peacefulness, a joyful liveliness, original themes which betray a finely tuned feeling for style and perfect polyphonic ensemble playing. Play this record and then any modern jazz record—a good one—straight afterwards. The contrast is striking. The joyful liveliness

24. HCJ and *Dazzling Jazz, Traditional,* * Philips B O7226.
25. **** London H-APB 1039: *Riverside Roustabouts.*

of the one compared with the tension—the malaise—of the other; the inner peace—anything but lethargic—compared with the nervous restlessness, the inner lack of restraint and defiance; the warm openness compared with the abstract remoteness. Two worlds are expressed, neither of them superficial, both sustained by a spirit that consciously strives for the pure expression of that which moves people deep down, but what a difference in their approaches to reality. It is not a matter of old-fashioned versus modern, old versus new, but of a spirit which openly and warmly tries to work in a way intrinsically similar to that of African Americans in their own music, as opposed to a spirit of existentialist *nausée* and alienation.

In England, Ken Coyler came close to the ideal. He was a sailor and made a trip to New Orleans where he had the chance to play with George Lewis, among others. Back in England he held tightly to the character and spirit of the music he had become acquainted with. He began his musical career with Chris Barber. When Barber developed a taste for Dixieland jazz Coyler broke with him. He went on to form his own band, whose rhythm section might be described as too stiff and monotonous but whose music is pure and fresh. One of their successes was "Far Away Blues"[26] and its title seems appropriate to the content of this chapter. After all, we are talking about the search by musicians and connoisseurs for the spirit of New Orleans jazz—lively, joyful, with unity in diversity, individuality within a collective, inner peace and vitality freedom within the confine of a set musical structure. They dreamed of matching that beauty, which was a rich fruit of black Christian culture. Perhaps the dream is so elusive because while the fruits are so desirable, the faith that generated them is often lacking.

The last remark would also explain why possibly a greater number of the combos that one finds all over the place playing modern jazz and the Dixieland bands reach a higher standard. It really is not so much a question of talent or of the technical development of these amateurs but of having a deeper understanding of what one is

26. ** Decca LF 1196.

playing—of more deeply empathizing with the music one is performing. This will be obvious when we look around a bit. In the area of
modern jazz, whites everywhere—in America and in Europe—have
clearly attained a standard which revival bands, in their endeavor to
reproduce the nature and character of New Orleans jazz, seldom or
never manage.

The same remark would also explain why, with the exception of
a few real New Orleans bands like that of George Lewis, music of a
high standard and of a quality that is comparable to that of the old
jazz of New Orleans is played only in the form of spiritual songs in
church these days [around 1960]. That is our next focus in the next
chapter.

COMMERCIAL SPIRITUALS SINCE APPROXIMATELY 1940: "THE WHEEL IN A WHEEL"

Earlier in this book we spoke of the development of a genre
of commercial spirituals of the 1920s—religious entertainment that
existed alongside real church spirituals and the westernized spirituals
styled on the ideal of Romantic concert singing. This genre continued to exist through the years, its nature allowing itself to pursue the
trends in dance music as they came and went.

It is therefore logical that swing would influence these quartets
and small choirs at the end of the 1930s. A new technique was developed for this: the rhythmic element was more strongly emphasized
and riffs were implemented. The so-called short refrain (a short phrase
sung ensemble at the end of each line, after every two bars) was des-
ignated a place "under" the music as it were, and was then repeated
throughout. The rendition of the precentor was more drawn out—
more rubato—and more typical swing phrasing was introduced. The
so-called long refrain or chorus of eight bars was often dropped or
included only incidentally, and then it was sung in an equally light
rhythmic manner with accents typical for this type of music.

The nature of these ensembles was often reflected in their flowery
names, like the Dixiaires, the Sensational Nightingales, the Southern

Sons, the Swan Silverstone Singers and the Dixie Hummingbirds. Just occasionally we hear more serious names like the Selah Jubilee Singers, the Golden Gate Quartet and so on. As choir music this is not technically bad, but it is sweet, light, rhythmically playful, mellifluous with many jazzy effects and, as a result of the infinitely repeated phrase that serves as a riff, eventually monotonous and boring. The lyrics often have little content and are mainly traditional, for you cannot confront people who might enjoy listening to the music with harsh biblical truth. They might be open to a bit of edification but they do not want depth and height, and neither do they want to be confronted with admonitions or unpleasant thoughts. In fact the audience wants to "suit their own desires," to hear "what their itching ears want to hear" (2 Timothy 4:3).

This genre is still very popular in the USA today[27] and can perhaps be attributed to the great revival of interest in religious matters. It is a fascination that the Americans themselves have described with the pithy expression "a religious boom," though no one would dare to measure its depth or to guess how serious it is. The music makes it clear that while there is real conversion, there is also much chaff under the wheat.

New Church Choral Song: "On Calvary"

We have just mentioned that, aside of the spiritual singing in church, the 1940s saw the emergence of a new kind of spirituals as far as technique was concerned. It was admittedly completely removed from the church environment, but churchgoers inevitably became acquainted with the new form of quartet singing through gramophone records, radio broadcasts and perhaps because a singer from one of these "religious entertainment" choirs had become a Christian and started attending church. Whatever the reason, by the end of the 1940s the new style of spiritual was being sung by quartets in churches all around. But here the innovations were grafted onto the

27. Part of * Vogue 30.056, for the rest e.g., Fontana 462047, etc.

old living tradition of church song; more importantly, this music rediscovered its soul: those who sang it also meant what they sang.

This is already evident when we look at the texts. "Religious entertainment" would produce songs that were not unpleasant for the audiences, with more or less neutral lyrics, those that made general reference only to love or heaven. In the case of the church quartets the lyrics would stay much closer to the sometimes pointed truth of the gospel—the word of God is, after all, a double-edged sword.

As a result, the nature of the music changed as well. While the commercial spiritual was often light and rhythmically strong, it also became monotonous in its endless repetition of the same rhythmic motifs (riffs). This technique was ultimately rather limited. The church quartets, however, immediately strove for greater freedom and movement, to bring more variation into the music, to do justice to the lyrics and to let the melody speak. The result was, to put it briefly, that a completely new art form emerged, much richer than the music from which it originated. We call it a new art form, because we are dealing here with quartets and small choirs that never improvise but sing well-thought-out arrangements (rendering "framework compositions," as was the case in New Orleans jazz) that disclose a wide range of possibilities. It is an art form which, having arisen from their own traditions, was in no way westernized but rather deepened and developed what had remained largely dormant in black culture up to that time. This new development, which began to flourish in the 1950s, produced music of a quality that could compete favorably with the best black music ever produced. The character of this music is very closely related to New Orleans jazz, which should not surprise us if we consider how Christian traditions as to lifestyle and attitude made itself felt in this jazz.

In examining the technique of singing the new style of spiritual—sometimes called "gospel singing"—we shall begin with the use of the voice. It falls back on the old traditions of hymn singing—of Dr. Watts—and of the hollers and the blues. This very characteristic use of the voice is sometimes called "crying" or "shouting." In Rosetta Tharpe's method of singing, for example, this synthesis of older singing techniques was already evident. It is a very clear sound that is produced, a sort of calling or even screaming, though it is anything but that because it can also be heard in the softer and even in the pianissimo passages. The rich, full sound is certainly linked to the way it is produced, by no means similar to classical or opera singing, but more the full application of all the properties of the human voice. If you want to call it unnatural, then that is fine, but it would be wise to take into consideration that the Western manner of classical singing is much further removed from the natural use of the voice. What actually happens here is a sort of cultivation of the natural voice. Training certainly plays a part—there is no greater misunderstanding than the idea that this sort of music emerges of its own accord, without practice or study.

In the structure of the music the main principle is that one solo voice is accompanied by the rest of the quartet, who sing rhythmic phrases in full harmony. We call them phrases, because in contrast to the commercial spiritual it is not a short motif that is taken, but a longer phrase that is performed with strong rhythm. By analogy with older jazz we have to say that this is more a matter of "stomping" than of "riffs." Above this fabric of sound there is also often another voice, which in quick passages outlines the text of the next line in a way that reminds us of the recitative-like manner in which sermons are recited by black preachers. This means we can always hear beforehand what is about to be sung. It is a method that is vaguely reminiscent of what happens when Dr. Watts's hymns are sung in the old familiar way.

With what I have just described I had in mind a beautiful song called "On Calvary" by undoubtedly the best group of this genre, The Spirit of Memphis Quartet.[28] If we listen to them more closely on their LP[29] that was released in 1958, it strikes us that we are far from having exhausted the subject. All a small choir (there are about seven vocalists) is capable of is utilized here to the full: polyphony, homophonic singing in unison or in chords, solo voice with rhythmic

28. **** Vogue LD073.
29. **** Parlophon PMD 1070.

accompaniment, and solo voice accompanied by the other voices singing a longer phrase slowly. The melodic given is always respected,
although it is varied by rubato passages (stretching the melodic line or
accelerating phrases), while everything is rendered on the fixed basis
of a rhythm, marked almost continuously by clapping hands or by a
low voice that may also be varied in all sorts of ways.

Just listen to one of their loveliest pieces, "Toll the Bells Easy."[30]
It is a familiar spiritual type of song with eight bars of verse and eight
bars of chorus. They start by singing the chorus three times:

Toll the bells easy, (x 3)
Jesus going to make up my dying bed.

Their ability is amply evident here. This simple theme is rendered
in very different ways, with syncopation, with apparent reductions
and accelerations of tempo—"apparent" because the joyful, steady
rhythm, made very quietly audible by the handclapping, binds all
together into one entity and is never abandoned. The words tell us:
just let the (funeral) bells ring cheerfully, for the Lord himself will
be at my deathbed. The verse that is sung after that with low voices
rendering a rhythmic accompaniment, goes on to tell us of the firmly
rooted belief that the Lord will take us to be with him in his future.

On the same record they sing "That Awful Day," a song that is
rendered in exactly the same way as the old Dr. Watts' hymns (it originated from his music no doubt), but it is sung here really artistically.
Another beautiful one is "Blessed Are the Dead," a song in which the
alternation of recitative voice and ensemble calls to mind the music
of Schütz (as we hear it in his *Musikalische Exequien;* the lyrics are
incidentally also related). This last relationship may be described as
strange, though less so if only we understand how similar attitudes to
life lead to related expressions of it. Incidentally, this development is
related in all sorts of ways to what is going on in the Protestant choral music of Distler and others in Germany in particular in the first

30. Ibid.

half of the twentieth century: the same shying away from solo performances, from continuing the Romantic concert tradition (which
otherwise still reigns supreme); a free singing-style; the use of logically
rounded off melodies and of a polyphony that is harmonically sound,
etc. One thing is certain—there can be absolutely no question of
contact or influence between the two movements.

Back to the African-American church-choir song. There are more
elements we can mention that typify this music. Something that the
Spirit of Memphis seldom used, but many other groups did, The
Christian Travellers[31] for instance, was to open with a long and slow
solo introduction, with structure and melodies strongly reminiscent
of those of a Dr. Watts song or a holler—a practice that certainly
stems from this tradition. We hear it too at the beginning of the Davis
Sisters'[32] rendition of the well-known spiritual "Go down Moses, tell
old Pharaoh to let my people go."

This music is not always straightforward. Those who think that
the Spirit of Memphis Quartet, which belongs to a Baptist church
in that city, sing light music that can be completely understood and
assessed the first time it is heard, are much mistaken. When hearing
it for the first time, there is the problem that the use of the voice
here takes some getting used to. Only then does it become clear
how peaceful and controlled this music is. There is no question at
all of trance, theatrics, of letting go or improvising. There is admittedly sometimes a trace of over-expressiveness, a sort of fervor that is
vaguely reminiscent of the style of swing, as in the case of the Davis
Sisters, for instance. It is possible that swing did have some effect here
or acted as a stimulus. The sense of over-emotionality is however very
different from that of swing, which was all about letting yourself go.
In this case it is more about expressing a certain mystical trait that
is characteristic of black American Protestants. There was a desire to
testify to the personal relationship with God, to a strong personal
experience of faith. Fortunately this is not the norm, but it makes

31. *** Vogue LDM 10008.
32. ***† Savoy MG 14014.

it harder to differentiate between the serious and the commercial spirituals of this genre. The latter are on occasion prone to excessive vehemence; more in the spirit of swing, true, but it does make it hard to tell the music apart from what the more church-oriented small choirs sometimes produced.

Black Folk Music after about 1940: "We Call 'em Reels"

We must not think that real black folk music disappeared around 1950 under pressure from later developments. Quite the opposite. Much of the music we discussed in the first few chapters was recorded only recently. That is quite simply due to the fact that the folk music of that ilk is only now being recorded for the first time. By way of illustration, real hollers can be heard on a recording of Lomax made in 1947.[33] That LP also features "Whoa Black," the holler we discussed earlier.

The Folkways releases must be commended. It is a label that specializes in folk music from all around the world, providing an invaluable service to jazz lovers and others who want to hear more of this music. Take the series of beautiful recordings made in Alabama by Harold Courlander and released on a double LP in 1950.[34] We would particularly like to draw your attention to the captivating spirituals sung by Doc Reed together with Vera Hall Ward, which were also released on a record[35] that is both interesting and especially lovely.

A set of nine LPs of beautiful and very important recordings by Frederic Ramsay Jr., made during a special expedition to the Southern States in 1954, was also released by Folkways. We hear what a farmer sings and what an old preacher sings; we hear the latest developments in rural church song, which did not escape the influences we mentioned in the previous chapter. We hear the song of a sect and a beautiful prayer by a female berry-seller in New Orleans, in the

33. *Murderer's Home*, *** Nixa NJL 11.
34. ** FoW EFL 1417-1418.
35. **** FoW FP38.

poetic language of the King James Version of the Bible. We hear evangelists, a string band, blues songs and guitar playing by a certain Scott Dunbar, of wonderfully good quality, and much more. An informative booklet is supplied with each record. Sometimes they are mainly interesting, other times they are movingly beautiful—but these records have become an essential source of information in the study of North American black music. This book would never have been possible without them.[36]

An interesting phenomenon is that one person almost never sings both blues and spirituals. No Christian is heard singing the blues, and no non-Christian is heard singing spirituals. The dividing line between Christian and non-Christian is very distinct in African-American society. I mentioned blues, but we should really call them hollers and other secular songs, because there is little evidence of the blues as such. That music is apparently the property of artists—the troubadours we talked about earlier.

Horace Sprott was a very poor farmhand who lived in rural Alabama. His mother was a Christian, his father a non-Christian. That is why he is familiar with both types of music. He is not particularly intelligent and he is slow, but he knows many folk songs and is able to tell us, lightheartedly, a bit about them in his own way. A few fragments of interviews with him have been included on the Ramsay LPs I have just mentioned. So, after he has sung one spiritual, he tells us that he learned it from a woman who was dying. He was the only one at the funeral who knew that song and for that reason would sing it:

> They wanted it sung over her body. Couldn't a one sing it? So I told 'em I'd sing it. Told 'em, yes I can, I can sing it like she sung. Say: 'If you sing it, I'm going to have the undertaker to call you.' So, at the moment before the sermon began they told me to stand up to sing that song for sister Sarah. I stood up . . . but when I was stood up I began to speak. I told them I wished they'd let me stay

36. FoW MS.

sitting. Because when I sit, my spirit goes high . . . but as soon as I stand up, my spirit [as it were] goes and sits down . . . And so they didn't let me sing that song. I couldn't sing it like I wanted, because they wouldn't let me do my own thing. They shouted and sang and spoke, and I couldn't do it while everyone was making such a racket. But they say that I did sing it. That I sung it and another one too, I was glad about that. The Lord gave me that talent. I didn't get it from myself, and it isn't from myself. It's from Him. That's why I don't sing many reels . . . naturally I sing them once in a while . . . about as often as church songs—By 'reels', do you mean blues, or . . . —That is correct. We call them reels.[37]

BLUES AND SPIRITUALS AMONG THE WORKING CLASS AFTER ABOUT 1940: "I CAN'T MAKE THIS JOURNEY BY MYSELF"

Make no mistake; the spiritual song in the old tradition is sung not only in the rural areas of Alabama. If you were walking around Harlem, the black neighborhood of New York, you might well bump into Blind Gary Davis, a singer just like Blind Willie Johnson. Blind Gary Davis is sixty and comes from South Carolina. While singing he accompanies himself on the guitar. Perhaps he would speak and sing like this:

This is the song, friends, I want you all to understand, is the song that I sing whenever I get to the place where I can't pray. I begin to let this song answer for prayer when it gets so that I can sing—you know the time comes when you can sing, but you can't pray—I begin to let this song answer for prayer:

Lord, I can't make this journey by myself, oh, Lord, (x 2)
On the land, on the sea,
I want Jesus to come and go with me;
Oh, Lord, I can't make this journey by myself.

37. FoW MS IV.

Then he continues with the next verses:

> I can't bear this heavy burden by myself
> I can't go in this dark valley by myself. Etc.[38]

In this personal way, he sings many other spirituals, both traditional and newly composed ones like "Say to the Devil, Say No." In Atlanta, Georgia, you may come across the Two Gospel Keys, Mother Jones and Emma Daniel singing in the street. They go around together, accompanying themselves on guitar and tambourine. They might sing a song like this:

> Oh, Lord, You know, I have no friend like You,
> If heaven's not my home, oh, Lord, what shall I do,
> No one to kick me from heaven's welcome door,
> I can't feel at home in this world anymore.[39]

We could tell of many more. As for boogie-woogie, it is still played as a living folk art. Ordinary folk playing for ordinary folk. In the same way the blues is around as well, sung by itinerant troubadours as of old. Lightnin' Hopkins,[40] for one, is a singer like that who started his career after the War. There are others—Muddy Waters Morganfield, Jesse Fuller and so on. Some of the older singers like Big Bill Broonzy, who died a short time ago, carried on playing also after the War.

It is not only in underdeveloped areas that we find black folk music—it can still be heard all over the USA. The traditions are not kept alive artificially by folklorists—they simply are alive, just as alive as spirituals are in the churches.

38. ***† Stinson SLP56 (recorded in 1954).
39. FoW FP53 (with several other recordings, also by Leadbelly).
40. † Score SLP 4022.

7

The 1950s and Beyond

JAZZ IN THE 1950S: "MARCH OF THE CHARCOAL GREYS"

Besides the music we dealt with in the last few chapters, all kinds of jazz music were being played in the mid-1950s. The Dixieland bands were there, of course, as was the music of Turk Murphy and co.—white New Orleans jazz. There were blacks in New Orleans who kept up the old traditions[1]—George Lewis being one of them. There were brass bands playing the music of old;[2] there were swing bands of various types and quality; there were groups of every category and grade of white Chicago-style, especially the ones led by Eddie Condon.[3] Then there was Ellington and his music which, on the one hand, was becoming increasingly ambitious and, on the other hand, sometimes dropped right down to the level of mood music.[4] There was Wilbur de Paris with his New New Orleans jazz and—we have by no means reached the end of our list—there was modern jazz of many kinds, ranks and stations. Sometimes it was music of high quality, alive and real, and at other times it was straightforward dance or entertainment music with modern influences (sometimes really quite enjoyable because the sharp modern spirit was absent and the

1. FoW FA 2463.
2. Eureka Brass Band. * FoW FA 2462; Young Tuxedo Brass Band, *** Atlantic 1297; Original Zenith Brass Band, * Riverside 283.
3. "Dazzling Jazz, Traditional," ** Philips B07226L.
4. "Solitude," Philips B 07302L.

expression toned down, more human. We are thinking here of the pianist Oscar Peterson, for instance). There was also rock-and-roll. In other words, even if we remain within the confines of the definition of jazz and forget all sorts of entertainment and dance music (for instance, Victor Sylvester's Metropole Orkest), there was such an abundance of trends and sorts, which clearly shows that we are not dealing with one single, straightforward development.

Fans of a particular musical preference, in general, and adherents of modern jazz, in particular, very often postulate that their music is the only really contemporary sort. They consider those who are still playing Chicago style, or worse, New Orleans or Dixieland style, as doing nothing more than imitate what has already been done—merely reproducing or imitating old music. But this assessment is fundamentally flawed because those who play Chicago jazz or New Orleans style are not concerned to establish a living museum in any shape or form. They are rather fighting in their own way for something they find more meaningful and useful than so-called modern jazz. They are not trying to evoke the past but are fighting for the future, and whichever side you are fighting on, you will not be able to predict the outcome.

The progress of history is at stake here—the formation of style and culture. Make no mistake; what the best connoisseurs of modern jazz say, and what the advocates of modern abstract art (from Miro and Klee to the Tachists, Experimentals etc.) say is true—namely that their new art form implies a new lifestyle and a new perspective on reality and that those who really want to appreciate this new music must be modern, namely people who are inspired, or who at least are moved, by the same spirit. Precisely for this reason they should not be allowed to force a dilemma on us: to have to choose to live either with the times or in the past. In fact, the Chicago tradition is alive and kicking, but so is the real blues, for each of these musical trends, though they may to a certain extent be determined by circumstances, is primarily the fruit of the spirit and attitude of the musicians who choose to play it, and of their audience.

The opinion that only one type of jazz can be real—"real" in the sense of being "with the times," artistically and culturally mean-ingful—is a grave fallacy. Rather, it appears that those who favor the latest movement as the only valid one are ascribing victory to themselves before the battle has even been fought. It is very easy to regard with suspicion those who behave differently, to label them as "conventional," not "with it," mere imitators, but that is not fair and neither is it right.

No, if musical expression is also a representation of a person's view of the world, and people have different worldviews, there will be many different trends. Folk music, as well as the marches from New Orleans or the blues, will live on in similar forms, as long as they satisfy a genuine demand. The different sorts of jazz will continue to exist as long as some remain unconvinced that the modern, more or less existentialist worldview, is the only possible and right one.

Wilbur de Paris's New New Orleans' Band[5] shows us that these problems are not as straightforward as the modernists think. The musicians who, one way or another, had kept a close track of devel-opments were Wilbur de Paris (trombone), who played with Ellington for a while, his brother Sidney (trumpet), who played swing and had already produced an updated version of the New Orleans style around 1942[6]—he was an advocate of this renaissance—and Omer Simeon (clarinet), who had made an early debut with Jelly Roll Morton but was hardly conspicuous since the 1930s. They came together in the 1950s to play New Orleans jazz, without imitating what had already been done and without compromising their knowledge of later developments, or their training and experience. Sometimes, as in the "March of the Charcoal Greys," it seems that they are telling us, with a smile, of the good old times. At other times they may play one of Morton's pieces or a slow rag, rhythmically and melodically first class. These are not people who continuously worked in a living New Orleans tradition; they are people with years of experience in the world of swing and the later type of jazz, who are attempting

5. *** London LTZ-K15024.
6. ITJ.

to win back something. The modern sound of the rhythm section, manifest in the drummer's continuous use of the cymbals in a swing-style steady beat, is interesting. We can also detect other elements redolent of swing—long solos, for example, though they do stick to the thematic given and vary rather than improvise.

Listening to this music conjures up associations with *The Family of Man* photographic exhibition, which used 500 photographs, chosen from many thousands, to illustrate the lives of people. The particular choice of photographs was guided by a vitalistic view of people and their lives: life goes on in its own biotic way, through birth, childhood, love, marriage, having children, getting old and dying. That is life. On this basis there is a place for culture, religion and so forth. This is the essence of human life. When we listen to the music of de Paris we sometimes get the same idea: the rhythm, continuous and unrelenting, is not an expression of great certainly and serenity as with Bach or Oliver but expresses the rhythm of life as the vital basis for everything. On the foundation of this rhythm, determined and as it were rocked by it, we hear the play of the melodies and variations as a representation of the cultural, the typically human aspects of human life which are limited and determined, but also driven, by the vital and biotic.

Thus there is a rich diversity of music, even if we remain within the confines of what we can call jazz, not to mention the many sorts of popular and dance music, some quite strongly influenced by jazz, others less so. Each sort of music has its limitations, its weak points and its peculiarities, and the good examples frequently show positive qualities, which make it worth listening to them. Not in order just to like everything. Those who like everything apparently are not moved by anything and cannot get past a clinical assessment of technique. Our generation will have to learn discernment, to recognize deceptive qualities, to gauge emptiness, to appreciate real beauty to reject effect for the sake of effect, to test principles as to their values and consequences, to reject and resist music that seems unhealthy, mechanical or boring, and to accept richness with gratitude. We must not deceive the next generation by keeping alive the myth that contemporary has to mean "modern"; rather, we should offer them an informed assessment of that which has been produced, giving real values the credit they deserve and pointing out the unartistic or unacceptable principles, after first having banished to the scrapyard all that is inferior, directed at money more than at beauty.

It is now time to look more closely at so-called modern jazz.

The Development of Modern Jazz: "Fontessa"

Ever since its birth and particularly since it became more popular during the War years, modern jazz has been evolving. New stars came, old stars went, bands and particularly smaller combinations got together and split up again. The importance of being "cool" increased, especially through the work of Miles Davis. There was experimentation with new types of rhythm, like the rhythms of Cuba. Improvisation remained the focus but here and there people were experimenting with arrangements. Stan Kenton ventured to have a large, strong, disciplined band perform this jazz, featuring some important jazz musicians. The result was music that resembled modern jazz in appearance only and not in spirit, except for the passages in which he allows one of his soloists a rare free hand. Perhaps Stan Kenton was the Paul Whiteman of modern jazz?

We could go into the progress of modern jazz in detail, but after the new developments of the 1940s there is nothing of much significance to mention. Modern jazz had made its mark and even if we account for all the individual differences there remains much unity in form and method. In other words, modern jazz has become a well-defined style. Incidentally, this remark is intended in support of modern jazz rather than against it. Trends and whims are, of course, present but these can be attributed to marketing hype rather than to essential changes.

Modern jazz became enormously popular in the 1950s, not in the sense that everyone appreciated it and that the schmaltz—the top hits of the day—were modernized, though a certain amount of modernism was present in strictly commercial jazz. Rather, modern jazz became popular in the sense that a great number of people—particularly young people—became interested in it and were taken with it. As a result gramophone record sales of modern jazz increased considerably at the expense of old jazz.

How did this popularity come about? I think it was because the music expressed not only something that appealed to young people but also something that was connected with their own self. It gave expression to familiar emotions, even if often they were unable to put these emotions into words. We will return to this later on.

Another proof that this music made a connection with young people was the extent to which they accepted and swallowed it, even though it was quite predictable, with little in the way of variation. That can be partly attributed to its method—a short theme, more or less in riff form, played ensemble, followed by long solos and then by a repeat of the short theme—but mainly it is to be attributed to the emphasis on a feeling of emptiness, meaninglessness, hyper-individualism, "playing God" and an aversion to reality. These things are expressed in a certain abstraction of tone and a strong irrationalism, whereas warm, caring humanness is all too often absent.

The last of these things is perhaps the most objectionable. Those who are down, going through an existential crisis, aware of their *nausée,* feeling rejected, uprooted, and regarding their life void of ideals, empty a sort of inevitable, unpleasant reality, need not pull others down with them. The highest and most fundamental norm—love—applies also to art and music. We have to love our neighbors by giving them joy and beauty, and not by confronting them with the epitome of hopeless human misery without pointing out the good things. The norm for art, which Philippians 4:8 formulates as "meditating on things true, noble, reputable, authentic, compelling, gracious—the best, not the worst; the beautiful, not the ugly; things to praise, not things to curse" is violated all too often. That does not mean that there are no very talented modern jazz musicians. It is not a question of being talented but of putting one's talents to good use. Our brief profile may have included too many generalizations, because there sometimes also is, almost contrary to its basic principles, a genial, warm sound to modern jazz, with some sense of rest and melodiousness.

Modern jazz, if at least it is really modern, emanates from inner tension, or rather, from acute inner tension. Some artists experience this to such an extent that they are in danger of falling apart and therefore may yield to the use of narcotics. In fact, this demonstrates the very existential, very heartrending reality of this music; it is anything but superficial entertainment. It is deeply rooted in a view of life and the world.

If we look around in the 1950s,[7] we discover all sorts of combos (a small band that plays modern jazz) each of which has its own type of music. There are the Jazz Messengers, who became the Horace Silver Quintet after their drummer was replaced, a combo that plays a consistent style of nervous jazz music. There is the J. J. Johnson Quintet, which is a bit mellower in its musical expression. There are various combinations which, even though they apply very modern influences, in fact perform a sort of music that is closely related to swing—Ruby Braff's band, for instance. As far as I am concerned, the Miles Davis Quintet is the best. They play consistently modern, highly tense, outwardly restrained but inwardly very emotional music with an irrational melody. This music is of a very high quality that makes the contestable elements all the clearer. In other words, this is the best music of its kind and therefore it should be the focus of our debate, because there is no point in quarrelling about third-rate music by musicians who are not capable of better.

We shall not be participating in the discussion jazz enthusiasts often engage in, as to whether "West Coast jazz" is a useful term to describe the sort of jazz that is associated with California. What is certainly true is that modern jazz there, possibly more than other types, attracted bigger and more serious audiences. Dave Brubeck and his band was the most successful, which is not surprising because while technically very clever, their music almost always lacked real depth and meaning, an easily digestible, uncomplicated product. When we

7. "Dazzlin Jazz, Modern," * Philips B07227L.

listen more closely, the constant evocation of an atmosphere that can almost be described as mild desperation, the inability to keep up a real atmosphere of tension, empty meaninglessness, *Geworfenheit* and *nausée*, becomes very, very tedious at a certain point. It is not only because the musicians do not quite manage to convince us that they *are* really struggling with deep issues of being human, but also because it becomes tedious when someone keeps making the same old negative claims.

We also find West Coast jazz[8] played by the group of musicians among whom Shorty Rogers and Jimmy Giuffre assumed an important and influential position. Musical arrangements played a bigger role here than elsewhere in modern jazz and musicians were more absorbed by music-technical problems, consciously focusing on contemporary, Western music by Bartok, Stravinsky, Milhaud, Honegger, Schoenberg and such. This should come as no great surprise to us. The spiritual background to modern jazz and to modern Western classical music is virtually the same; the difference lies in their historical backgrounds, either swing or Romantic music.

These developments may have strange consequences. It is not impossible that in the not too distant future a clever musician at home in both types of music will combine them. (John Lewis, whom we will be talking about shortly, went a long way towards achieving this.) That would mean that large audiences, who are now followers of jazz, would have to be moved to the large concert halls. In terms of cultural history it would mean that a larger group of people who had lost touch with the pursuit of Western music for all sorts of reasons would find their way back to the concert hall. This would heal the rift in our Western world between art and the public. It would also serve to give the number of admirers and lovers of modern art a strong boost. Strange visions. We will just have to wait and see if that happens, and only when it does will we be required to form an opinion about it. Even the question of whether it would be gain or loss, whether we should applaud it or not, is a question which cannot easily be answered.

8. Many recordings including RCA A130222.

We would like to mention one other ensemble, The Modern Jazz Quartet.[9] It is indeed modern jazz in the sense that it uses a combination of instruments of which the sounds and playing methods do not contrast but are closely related, like the piano and the vibraphone, the bass and the drums. Those who listen to the music carefully will understand why we group these instruments together like this. The band and its music are in many ways inspired by Western music: old forms like the fugue and Western harmony from Debussy onwards are implemented time and again. Although its music can certainly still be classified as jazz, of all the bands I have dealt with this one comes closest to playing contemporary Western music, not only in sound and timbre but also in its whole approach to art and music and the sort of musical problems they pose themselves. It will therefore come as no surprise that downright lovers and connoisseurs of Western music who have never had a good word to say about jazz show positive interest in this band.

Possibly their most characteristic piece is "Fontessa."[10] An interesting aspect is the assertion of their leader that the various parts might be typified by names of clowns. It is interesting in the sense that clowns have been prevalent in Western modern art since Picasso's blue period (around 1900). The appearance of a clown creates jollity and fun and though their behavior is extrovert they are inwardly melancholic—focused on the problem of their own existence. The clown reflects modern society where people don a mask to face the world, go along with it, while they are inwardly a long way off, like Gnostics, turning away in a sense from this wretched and, in principle, bad world. Listen to what Lewis writes about "Fontessa":

> 'Fontessa' is a small suite based on the *Commedia dell'arte* [a sort of (Italian) play in which the same character (Harlequin, Columbine, Pantalone, etc.) always performed in rather improvised roles] from the sixteenth and seventeenth centuries. I was particularly thinking

9. ** London LTZ-K 15022.
10. Ibid.

of their plays that consisted of a very sketchy intrigue whereby the details, the dialogues, etc., were improvised. This suite consists of a short prelude to open the curtains and to denote the subject. The first piece after this prelude has the character of older jazz (swing) and the vibraphone plays the improvised parts. You might well say that this part has the character of Harlequin. The second part has the nature of more recent jazz, and the improvised parts are for the piano. The character of Pierrot typifies it best. The third part has the character of even more recent jazz and reveals the principal motif. The rhythm section plays the improvised parts. Its character is possibly that of Pantalone [the old man, who is usually deceived in love]. The prelude is repeated at the end. 'Fontessa' is the principal motif of the suite consisting of three notes, and may be a description of the character of Columbine.

The drum solo mentioned is indeed the culmination of the piece which here, more than elsewhere, evokes a Debussy-like atmosphere that can best be described with the words "we are floating in an empty space."

SWING AD ABSURDUM: ROCK-AND-ROLL

You might be surprised that we have included rock-and-roll in our synopsis, but this type of music is too closely related to jazz to ignore it.

Technically speaking, this music is swing ad absurdum. Only a fierce and oversimplified rhythm remains. As far as melody is concerned, everything is kept as simple as possible and the harmonic schemes are of the least complicated sort. In other words, it is music that has been stripped of everything that makes it interesting. Only the heavily stamping beat is omnipresent. The idea is to strive for a fast release of emotion—very sensual, but without an iota of nuance, no sophistication; on the contrary, it is as crude and direct as possible. It is music exploited by clever and unscrupulous people. It is music that is consciously empty and hollow and simplistic—music created for the modern youth culture.

What is the sense of it? Is it proof that the Western public lacks any taste at all? Let us not jump to conclusions too quickly. For those who are said to lack the gift of discernment are also those whose fine intuition enables them to identify exactly what they want to hear and accept, therefore they definitely do have taste. No, the meaning of this music is its meaninglessness—its lack of content and eloquence. It is music that allows its audience to dance exuberantly on the edge of the abyss, driven by an intense longing to let go and live it up, all founded on the well-thought-out logic: "Let's eat and drink and be merry for tomorrow we die." Heidegger described it as "living to death"—*sein zum Tode*—but here there is no recognition of existential angst; there is no attempt to look for depth because that would mean looking into the abyss—the abyss that is illustrated to some extent by the drum solo in "Fontessa," the abyss the Surrealists paint, the modern poets describe, and modern jazz expresses in sound. It sometimes resembles a hell and at other times it is hell. You only have to take a sincere look at modern poetry or to check what kindred spirits have to say about the interpretation of modern art to understand how true this is.

It is on the edge of hell that people want to dance, live it up and let go. They find no real joy there, only a grim struggle to hold on to something, life itself, freedom, happiness, knowing that all of it constantly eludes them. Everything is meaningless, so dance, live it up and let go, but do not look into the abyss . . . because the abyss may open up.

Rock-and-roll is the flip side of the modernist record.

THE PROBLEM OF JAZZ IN OUR WORLD: "MAMMA DON'T ALLOW"

"Mamma don't allow no drummer man in here," is how one of the lines from a popular song from the 1930s goes. It is an American song. The problem turns out to be in no way representative of Europe, or the Netherlands, alone.

"No jazz in my house," the parents say. The children, teenagers, do not know why. They ask themselves why jazz should be inferior to Beethoven, and . . . continue listening in secret. That is often how it goes.

"Mamma don't allow no drummer man in here." Much of this trouble with jazz has more of a social than artistic character. Parents are not concerned about jazz as music. Perhaps they more than once forgot to switch off the radio in time when something jazzy was broadcast without prior warning. It is often a strange association of ideas that is the real reason behind the rejection of jazz. Jazz is associated with the jungle—primitive—uncultured—the pub—superficial—ugly—blacks—trance—sexuality—dancing—entertainment—low—bad. It is a strange sequence of ideas. They could of course be classified into all sorts of groups, but one thing is clear—jazz is wrong because it is music that belongs to a socially lower world, that of the "dirty blacks" who do not know how to behave and therefore live it up in a trance. It smacks of racism, snobbery, bourgeois mentality, fear of being shaken out of one's lethargy and of unfamiliar urges suspected there.

We say that the verdict is socially qualified because it is seldom based on the music itself, or on a real examination of the matter at hand. Beethoven is certainly held in esteem as the counterpart of jazz, but this implies nothing more than esteem of a time-honored Western concert tradition, and it can hardly be said of many of those who hold this esteem that they have a real love of Romantic or classical music.

There is also another argument: jazz is entertainment. That may certainly be true, because if we speak of jazz in this way, we are referring to jazz as an absolutely straightforward cocktail of any music that is based on a 4/4 beat, uses trumpets and possibly saxophones, and has lyrics in English. Since an awful lot of popular music (indeed, not without the influence of jazz) satisfies this definition, the verdict seems just. Nevertheless we must ask the question: Is the Romantic concert tradition and its music the highest standard? Should we demand that youngsters partake of this lofty fruit and look to it for their entertainment?

Please let us understand that popular music—a new Western substitute for folk music—also satisfies a need, in the same way that Beethoven, Bach and Mozart do. This music has a function, not so much as spiritual food or as something to be enjoyed, but much rather as a social binding agent—something that supports social contact.

That is why young people need it. Is it entertainment? Yes, certainly. At the same time we must remember that there is good popular music and bad popular music. You now know that I give rock-and-roll a place in the latter category, but I cannot and do not want to put all the different styles into neat little boxes.

Jazz too is the music of the youth. Certainly. Because young people are exposed to this music via popular music and also because it is burdened with a social taboo. The latter is one of the very strong attractions it has for teenagers. If we were to give jazz social status by donning evening dress to attend jazz concerts, it would stop being the music of teenagers before very long. But, do these arguments really relate to the jazz we have been talking about in this book? Sales of serious jazz records is proportionally negligible: for old jazz it is less than 1 percent, for modern jazz it is higher but by no means approaches the figures for classical music (i.e., Western classical) or any other socially accepted types of music, like French chansons, for example. Jazz is sometimes entertainment—as is a French chanson and a German song from a Lehar operetta—and we can distinguish between good and bad jazz, as well as all the intermediate stages. If, however, we want to use the word jazz to define black folk music and what evolved from it—well, then we have to distinguish carefully.

Do you not want your children to listen to modern jazz? Then withhold modern Western music from them too, and modern Western literature, and modern visual art, because the content in all these things is related.

Young people want Dixieland jazz. Certainly, because they can play it themselves. It gives them the opportunity to make music without having to lug the heavy burden of the Romantic music tradition around with them. Do you not want them to play jazz? Then turn to the direction that contemporary German church music is taking. There may be some good opportunities there. But maybe there is a lot to be said for playing collectively in the spirit of New Orleans and for exploring its art and life as well. There are many possibilities.

So what are the consequences for a young person who enjoys listening to modern jazz? We mean real, serious jazz and not the different forms of (possibly better) popular music in which there is only a slight influence of the new sounds and forms. There are in principle two possibilities: either he or she is just following the trend that appeals to his or her age group, without real interest in the essence, the content of the music, in which case it will be a phase that will pass without a trace; or she or he understands this music very well and can relate to the emotiveness of the music that expresses her or his own feelings (even if she or he cannot express that in words). In the latter case you will either have to submit to the idea that each new generation establishes its own attitude to life, or you will have to attempt to point the way to something you consider more positive. For Christians the Bible is there as a rich source of wisdom and joy, as a radical remedy for any negative attitude to life, but that means using it, reading it and studying it. Not just for the sake of doing so, but sustained by and aligned to the love of our Savior, Jesus Christ, and in the knowledge that God, the Creator of heaven and earth and our Father in heaven, if we believe in him, will sustain our lives, even now, so that a quiet, joyful, firm certainty may be ours, even in this world where sin has sometimes brought such misery. Faith in the God of Carmel means death to all nihilism, Gnosticism, existentialism and the hopelessness that ultimately regards death as the only absolute end and purpose.

What we want to say is that the problem of modern jazz has a spiritual and a social side, and that the most dangerous aspect of this is that people often do not get round to facing up to the spiritual problems, writing the music off as that of "blacks and brothels and people who are out for kicks." Whatever our attitude to these questions, one thing is clear to us: jazz in whatever form does not belong in church. That would only be expedient if almost everyone understood and accepted the music—and not even then. Bach's *Brandenburg Concertos* are not played during church services either, nor are quartets by Beethoven, irrespective of what we regard the music to be and even if we could defend the former as being Christian music. As for spirituals, they fall more into the category of hymns, but even then it is my opinion that these songs should first become generally accepted. That might happen if they were to be included in the repertoire of Christians—at home or in small choirs. These songs must first become familiar to us—become our own idiom. This, however, will take a long time. And should we even be looking in this direction? Why should we want to do that? Because of our own spiritual poverty perhaps?

Whatever our position, we have to watch out for the misleading associations: jazz and spirituals—black music—primitive—barbaric—wild—unchristian—ugly. Let us be fair in our judgment; black music, in its many varieties, is certainly worthwhile and sometimes is a clearer fruit of Christian civilization than a lot of Western music is. We should also consider that the later genres of jazz—swing and modern jazz—are fruits of white civilization rather than something blacks can be held responsible for.

We have to be honest and not allow ourselves to be distracted by unfounded prejudices. Black music is not by definition bad music. Holding this view is no better than the attitude that led to the recent refusal by a white school in Little Rock, to the great indignation of the general population, to allow a number of black children to attend.

We should also take the following song by an African American to heart. Would we be able to sing like this in similar circumstances, without a feeling of revolutionary defiance? The facts that are exposed in this song are, unfortunately, all too true. The same mentality is still found here in the Netherlands too, otherwise we would not have felt it necessary to write this chapter.

We are referring to Big Bill Broonzy's "Black, Brown and White":

This little song that I'm singing about,
People you know it's true,
If you're black and got to work for a living,
This is what they will say to you.

They say if you's white, you's all right,
If you's brown, stick around,
But as you're black,
Mmm, brother, get back, get back, get back.

213

I was in a place one night,
They was all having fun,
They was all buying beer and wine,
But they wouldn't sell me none. *Refrain.*

Me and a man were working side by side,
This is what it meant,
They was paying him a dollar an hour,
And they was paying me fifty cents. *Refrain*

I went to an employment office,
Got a number and I got in line,
They called everybody's number,
But they never did call mine. *Refrain.*

I helped to win sweet victory,
With my little plough and hoe,
Now I want you to tell me brother,
What you gonna do 'bout the old Jim Crow. *Refrain*[11]

Tragedy Threatens in the Development of Gospel Songs: "Didn't It Rain"

One of the greatest tragedies of African-American music is that it is a living folk art within a Western world where folk music has all but died out. Western civilization knows only a very refined, erudite art music, on the one hand, and entertainment music, which has been taken over completely by commercial managers and artists, on the other hand. The tragedy is that this living, black folk art might easily be exploited by shrewd business people who, in doing so, may also hope to breathe some new life into the otherwise soulless entertainment music. Dance music of our generation is very strongly rooted in black jazz. That is not bad in itself, but attempts are then

11. **** Vogue V134 (recorded in 1951).

made to have blacks sacrifice themselves to Mammon. It is easily done, because money and fame lead to social recognition, and blacks in their difficult position are understandably happy to acquire it. Only those of strongest character, people with the most deep-seated convictions, are capable of resisting it.

Alongside a great deal of black music, adapted and customized for the Western consumer of popular music, we still do find some real black folk music and serious jazz of all kinds. The Negro spiritual world has, however, managed best to steer clear of all this. The danger of commercialization is, after all, not so great if the songs are only sung in churches and by practicing Christians. We then have to exclude music of the well-established genre of "religious entertainment," by which we mean the small bands like the Five Blind Boys, the Golden Gate Quartet and others who made jazzed-up versions of westernized concert spirituals (in the vein of the Fisk Jubilee Singers or artists like Marion Anderson, Roland Hayes and Paul Robeson) fit for general consumption.

An important development in the area of Christian music has been taking place in churches during the last twenty years or so. This includes the emergence of females who sing gospel songs or spirituals, solo or accompanied by small choirs, during fellowship meetings or services. Most recently, however, the work of Mahalia Jackson and others has attracted attention from outside the circle of black churches, and that created a particular problem for these people. It was a blessing on one hand but, on the other hand, they were inclined, not as a result of commercial exploitation this time but with a view to confronting the audience with the gospel, to give in to the taste of the public in the hope of reaching a wider audience. This did not so much affect the lyrics as the performance of the music. Musically speaking this can have the same effect as commercialization.

An active faith, deep joy, a pure attitude keep things healthy and prevent excesses, but without them danger lurks. The reason we are taking up the subject here is that it helps explain some aspects of the performances of, for instance, Clara Ward at a gospel concert in New

York in 1958 or 1959.[12] A few of the numbers she sings, like "Didn't It Rain" and "The Old Landmark" (which did not just happen to be lyrics that are quite hollow when rendered this way) were definitely performed for effect and are actually pure swing music. Clara Ward hoped to use these pieces to attract her audience and to make the listeners receptive to her more serious numbers, some of which were good and pure, though we are not terribly impressed with the technique used on the Hammond organ.

The account on the sleeve testifies to the great success of this sort of music: people are fed up with modern jazz, with its tenseness, its super-individualistic mood, its refined effects, its monotony and emptiness; they are looking for something real, fresh and alive. This music has those qualities, sustained by an open attitude to reality, founded in a biblical faith in and love for the Father in heaven. It is music that has remained fresh, unspoiled and oblivious to alienation from reality. This essentially healthier sort of music is a breath of fresh air to adherents of contemporary jazz.

If we listen to Clara Ward, we find that her intentions are good, but here and there she makes concessions that are dangerous in that they affect the character of this church music. Fortunately a lot of her music is soundly rooted in the tradition and therefore remains beautiful and fascinating. It is certainly worth listening to. Nevertheless, we must keep our ears open and test the spirits, soberly and without contempt, with comprehension and prayers that it will not lead to this type of black music becoming denaturalized by Mammon, the greedy Moloch of our day.

We would like to point out that the sometimes dubious practices of the recording companies too may force some musicians along a road that is lucrative but hardly culturally responsible. Even some of the Spirit of Memphis Quartet records[13] are clearly commercially motivated. Hollow lyrics, soulless music with the emphasis on effect—rhythmic or sentimental—characterizes such renditions,

12. London LTZ-D15168.
13. Vogue EPL 7538 and on Vogue 30.056.

which are best forgotten and can open our eyes to the tragedy we have discussed.

SPIRITUAL SOLOS: MAHALIA JACKSON ("I'M GOING TO MOVE ON A LITTLE HIGHER")

We have already mentioned the fact that some spirituals and gospel songs were also sung solely by women. By 1940, Sister Rosetta Tharpe had already incorporated all manner of jazz and blues influences into this genre of spiritual, particularly in rendition and style of singing. There were many others besides Sister Rosetta: Lottie Peavey, Jessie Mae Renfro, Mary Knight, Georgia Peach (one of the first to pursue this genre, having given many concerts at Christian gatherings all over America as early as 1930), Clara Ward and so on. A refreshing aspect of this music is that alongside the 4/4 beat, we find 6/8 or 5/6. As for harmony it is the common chords that are played, not those which we would describe as "modern."

Alongside the development of the small choir, the significance of this genre on the Christian scene has increased greatly since the Second World War. In the larger black churches, at least, the liturgical emphasis is increasingly falling on solo singing and choir, and the song of the congregation has taken on a secondary role. The possible causes and consequences of this are not yet clear.

Over the last few years there have been some recordings made of parts of church services. Recordings made of smaller churches in Harlem show us that the congregation there still wholeheartedly joins in the singing.[14] On the other hand, recordings of Sister Ernestine B. Washington's rendition of all sorts of spirituals and hymns, solo or accompanied by the choir, conjures up pictures of a big church. The congregation is left merely to express their approval of what is sung.[15] Many churches have replaced their harmonium with a Hammond organ. While it certainly has its drawbacks, we must remember that it

14. ** Ducretet-Thomson 260 VB 069 (1955).
15. *** Westminster WP6089.

is relatively cheap and still very versatile, and is being used in almost all churches in the USA.

I will now conclude by telling you a bit about Mahalia Jackson, undoubtedly one of the most important female solo singers of spirituals. She was born in New Orleans in 1911 and is presently singing in Chicago. The song "I'm Going to Live the Life I Sing about in My Song"[16] is an artistic testimony of her faith. In it she makes clear that song and lifestyle have to correspond. It would be inconsistent to sing spirituals in the church on Sunday and then to give yourself over to rock-and-roll on Monday. It is a paradox to walk as a child of God in the daytime and to have the "devil on the cover" at night. "Make no mistake, don't underestimate me," she sings, "I want to follow the right path and walk in the light, even if people scoff at me for it." It is good to bear this in mind when listening to her music. She is not primarily an artist—someone who wants to serve art, someone who searches for beauty and focuses everything on it. Her priority is to serve the Lord and bring people into contact with the gospel or to strengthen them in their faith. As she sings in another song,

> Out of the depths of my soul I cry
> Jesus draw nigh, Jesus draw nigh.
> Lord lend an ear to my whole honest plea,
> Jesus draw nearer to me.
> Oh, Lord, I want to labour,
> Faithful each day, walking in your true way,
> Telling the world what a Saviour I found,
> Spreading the gospel all around.[17]

If we bear these words in mind, it helps us understand why she sometimes does things that are not entirely representative of good taste or pure artistic skill, like the songs of Western origin that she

16. **** Philips B 07077L.
17. Ibid.

sings, even though they do not really suit her style, partly because they do not belong to her own African-American tradition. She does it because she sees it as a way of reaching audiences that might otherwise not listen to her message. It is for the same reason that she allows herself to be accompanied by a band that is not really suited to her style.[18]

There is, incidentally, more to say about the accompaniment because even where these objections do not apply, we cannot say that the band that accompanies her is particularly proficient. It is not difficult to determine the reason for this. It would be ideal if she had a New Orleans ensemble. That this is not wholly inconceivable we can see by a few recordings made in that way. We refer to two beautiful little tracks sung by Lottie Peavey in San Francisco in 1944. She was accompanied by a New Orleans-style band, namely the Yerba Buena Band, with Bunk Johnson on trumpet. They sounded good together, forming a stylistic unity. "When I Move to the Sky" is particularly beautiful, a very solemn piece in which the bowed bass strongly adds to the character. They hum one of the choruses completely, while the trumpet plays a polyphonic countermelody. It is an extraordinary record if we consider that it features a very good and typically black rendition of a traditional Negro spiritual, accompanied by a largely white New Orleans band whose trumpet player is a black man from New Orleans. It can be described as a combination of the best aspects of the African-American tradition.[19] We know of one other exceptional example, namely the four tracks that Ernestine B. Washington recorded, accompanied by Bunk Johnson and George Lewis's band. Her voice is not as good as Lottie Peavey's, but *Does Jesus Care?* still turned out to be a very special record that is certainly worth listening to.[20]

However, these are rare exceptions, for there are not so many New Orleans bands around anymore. The black religious music that

18. Philips 429177 BE.
19. **** *Good Time Jazz* JS 845 and rereleases on EP.
20. **† Melodisc, 1102 Disc 7110 (of which there are also more recent releases).

we are hearing now has come into blossom after the era of New Orleans jazz which, for all sorts of reasons, started to die out. There is however a much more compelling argument which explains why solo gospel songs are seldom accompanied by New Orleans ensembles: the average black Christian feels roughly the same about jazz as the elder of a Reformed church in the Netherlands, partly because jazz musicians are often unbelievers—or non-churchgoing people—but mainly because it is not church music. Puritan tradition demands that only religious music be sung and approves of music only if it is explicitly Christian. New Orleans music would hardly fit into this category, the very nature of modern jazz would preclude it and a modern combo supporting a singer like Mahalia Jackson or Lottie Peavey would indeed be a curse.

There is little choice left than a more or less neutral ensemble that plays with a mere whiff of jazz—to put it very unkindly, a sort of cafe palm-court orchestra.

The band that accompanies Mahalia Jackson is fortunately so unobtrusive, and she is so good herself that it does not matter. The best recordings naturally are gospel songs—songs in her own tradition.[21]

The following song gives us a clear impression of Mahalia's faith and knowledge of the Bible. It is a song that tells of going to heaven, heaven being comprehensively illustrated for us using biblical terms. It is inevitable—and highly scriptural—that most of the words in fact refer to the new earth, after the Last Day, which is also referred to. Almost every line in the song refers to a biblical text. I have noted them at the end of the text and will thus conclude this book with a recent piece of work of pure African-American tradition, in a genre that is completely new within the tradition of solo per-formances. Mahalia does not sing as black people used to sing, in the manner of the westernized and romanticized performances of Marian Anderson and Roland Hayes and the well-worn style of the Fisk Jubilee Singers.

21. **** Philips B O7077L and other releases on Philips and on Vogue.

This song is an expression of a living, developing church art. It is a truly Christian song, one of the most beautiful products of twentieth-century Christian art:[22]

One day a morning, soon one morning,[23]
I'm going to lay down my cross, get me a crown.[24]
Soon one evening, right in the evening,[25]
Right in the evening, I'm going home[26] to live on high.

As soon as my feet strike Zion,[27] lay down my heavy burden
Put on my robe in glory,[28] going home one day and tell my story.
I have been coming over hills and mountains,
Gonna drink from the Christian fountain[29]
You know all, God shut the door that morning,[30]
We will drink from that all-healing water.
And we gonna live on the river[31]
We gonna live on forever,
We gonna live in glory, glory.
O, Lord, I am going out sightseeing Beulah,[32]
March all around by the altar,[33]
Gonna walk and never get tired,
No blight, Lord, never falter.
I'm going to move on a little higher, Gonna meet old man Daniel,[34]

22. **** Philips B O7077L.
23. Referring to the day she dies (or Judgment Day).
24. 2 Timothy 4:8; Revelation 2:10; 4:4.
25. See note 23.
26. John 14:2; 2 Corinthians 5:1.
27. The new, heavenly Jerusalem; Hebrews 12:22.
28. Zechariah 3:4; Revelation 1:13; 7:9–17.
29. Revelation 21:6; John 4:14; Isaiah 12:3.
30. Matthew 25:10; cf. Revelation 3:7.
31. Ezekiel 47.
32. A name for the land of Israel in Isaiah 62:4, referring here to heaven.
33. Revelation 9:13; 11:1.
34. In heaven or on the new earth she will meet Daniel.

I'm going to move on a little higher, Gonna meet the Hebrew
      children,[35]
I'm going to move on a little higher, Gonna meet Paul and Silas,
I'm going to move on a little higher, Gonna meet my friends and
      kindred,
I'm going to move on a little higher, Gonna meet my loving
      mother,
I'm going to move on a little higher, Gonna meet the Lily of the
      Valley.[36]

I am going to feast with the Rose of Sharon[37]
It will always be howdy howdy
And never goodbye.

O, will you be there early one morning,
Will you be there somewhere around the altar,
Will you be there when the angels shall call the roll?[38]
God knows I'll be waiting, yes I'll be watching somewhere at the
      altar,
I'll be waiting at the beautiful (yes) Golden Gate.[39]

Meet me there early one morning,
Meet me there somewhere around the altar,
Meet me there when the angels shall call all God's roll.

35. Referring to the three Hebrew youngsters in the furnace, Daniel 3.
36. Christ, cf. Song of Solomon 2:1.
37. Ibid.
38. "Roll" refers to the Book of Life, cf. Revelation 20:12; 21:27.
39. Revelation 21:12, 18–21; 22:14.

Selected Bibliography
to the First Edition

I would like to mention a number of books here. I have included a short summary of each:

J. Baldwin, *Go Tell It On The Mountain*. New York, 1954. [A novel which gives an excellent picture of the life of members of a sect in Harlem.]

J. E. Berendt, *Das Jazzbuch*. Frankfurt, 1953. [The history of jazz written from the standpoint of an adherent of modern jazz.]

Rudy Blesh, *Shining Trumpets, a History of Jazz*. New York, 1946. [This is one of the best surveys of the history of jazz (including a summary of spirituals and the blues), written by a devotee of Jelly Roll Morton, etc. There is also a later British edition.]

R. Bless and H. Janis, *They All Played Ragtime*. New York, 1950. [Ragtime and its impact. A new edition was published in 1959.]

W. L. Grossman and J. W. Farrell, *The Heart of Jazz*. New York, 1956. [A good book that concentrates particularly on the background and significance of New Orleans jazz as opposed to modern jazz. The second half is a detailed description of Dixieland and New Orleans bands that were playing in the USA at that time.]

Rex Harris, *Jazz*. Pelican, 1952. [A good introduction to the history of traditional jazz.]

Rex Harris and Brian Rust, *Recorded Jazz, A Critical Guide*. Pelican, 1958. [A good guide to the best records and a rundown on the musicians. Traditional jazz only.]

J. W. Johnson, *The Books of American Negro Spirituals.* New York, 1940. [Interesting introduction to the spirituals, which are primarily dealt with through the eyes of the black intellectual.]

R. W. Logan, *The Negro in the United States—A Brief History.* Princeton, 1957. [An excellent sketch.]

A. Lomax, *Mr. Jelly Roll.* London, 1952. [Jelly Roll Morton's biography. It provides some very important insight into the birth and development of jazz against a background of social problems.]

J. A. and A. Lomax, *Folk Songs: USA.* New York, 1947. [An interesting collection in which all genres are represented.]

J. W. Schulte Norholt, *Het Volk Dat In Duisternis Wandelt.* Arnhem, 1957. [A good book about the history and problems of black North Americans. The black intellectual viewpoint may be somewhat overemphasized.]

H. W. Odum and G. B. Johnson, *Negro Workaday Songs.* Chapel Hill, 1926. [Folk songs. Includes a lot of lyrics.]

F. Ramsay and C. E. Smith, *Jazzmen.* New York, 1939. [One of the first books about jazz that is devoted to historical research and knowledge of the facts. Still important.]

N. Shapiro and N. Hentoff, *Heah Me Talkin' to Ya.* London, 1955. [A collection of the reflections of jazz musicians. An important source of information and insight into what inspires these people.]

M. W. Stearns, *The Story of Jazz.* London 1957. [A rich source of information on the lead up to the birth of jazz, and a detailed study of the development of jazz. The author also focuses on problems "around" jazz. A very good bibliography.]

I also want to mention two gramophone records with recordings of lectures on jazz, with musical excerpts:

Leonard Bernstein, *What Is Jazz?* Col. (Am.) CL 919. [Excellent analysis of musical elements given by an educated musician, with well-chosen examples.]

Langston Hughes, *The Story of Jazz.* Folkways FP 712. [Pleasant, rather traditional introduction, with good excerpts.]

Updated Discography
and Resources

Most of the music discussed in this book has been rereleased on CD. It may however require a lot of research to track recordings down. In order to help you find CDs here follows a short list of guides, websites, compilation CDs and recommended CDs by particular artists.

GUIDES

Richard Cook and Brian Morton (eds.), *Penguin Guide to Jazz on CD*. London: Penguin, 2000, 5th edition. [The merit of recordings rated by stars.]

John Cowley and Paul Oliver, *The New Blackwell Guide to Recorded Blues*. Oxford: Blackwell, 1997.

Barry Kernfeld (ed.), *New Grove Dictionary of Jazz*. London: The Macmillan Press Limited, 1994, 2nd edition. [The most important reference work for jazz with an extensive selection of the most important releases.]

Colin Larkin (ed.), *The Virgin Encyclopedia of the Blues*. London: Virgin Books, 1998.

WEBSITES

On the site <www.allmusic.com> one can search for information about releases of particular artists.

Jazz: <www.allaboutjazz.com>
Gospel: <www.blackgospel.com>
Blues: <www.bluesworld.com>
Smithsonian Folkways: <www.folkways.si.edu> contains information about
    2300 LPs/CDs on the Smithsonian Folkways labels.

COMPILATIONS JAZZ

Ken Burns Jazz: The Story of America's Music (Sony/Columbia, 5-CD box).
    [Spans nearly a century of jazz styles.]
New Orleans Traditional Jazz Legends (Mardi Gras, 6-CD set).

JAZZ BANDS AND SOLOISTS

Louis Armstrong: *The Hot Fives and Hot Sevens* (CBS). [Armstrong before
    1940.]
Johnny Dodds: *The Chronical Johnny Dodds,* Volumes 1–3 (Classics). [The
    most creative moments of this leading clarinetist of the New Orleans
    jazz in small as well as big ensembles.]
Jelly Roll Morton: *The Complete Jelly Roll Morton 1926–1930* (RCA, 5-CD
    box).
King Oliver: *Volume 1, 1923–1929* (BBC). [Ten tracks of Oliver with the
    Creole Jazz band, and recordings of the Dixie Syncopaters, Oliver's
    second band.]

COMPILATIONS GOSPEL

All of My Appointed Time (Stash/Jass). [Forty years of a capella gospel by
    groups like the Golden Gate Jubilee Quartet and The Soul Stirrers,
    and female vocalists like Georgia Peach and Marion Williams.]
Jubilation Volume 1: Great Gospel Performances (Rhino). [Featuring tracks
    from Mahalia Jackson, The Soul Stirrers, Aretha Franklin, Shirley
    Caesar, and more.]
Oh Happy Day (New Cross, 4-CDs). [A compilation of 80 tracks from the
    golden age of gospel. Great recordings from the Chess and Veejay
    vaults, including the Five Blind Boys, the Staple Singers, and more.]

GOSPEL SINGERS AND GROUPS, RECOMMENDED CDs

Blind Gary Davis: *Blind Gary Davis Complete Recorded Works 1935–1949* (Document DC 5060).

Mahalia Jackson: *Gospels, Spirituals and Hymns* (CBS). [Beware of Mahalia reissues—many are of dubious quality. This, however, is the very best available, featuring Mahalia at her peak in the 1950s and 1960s.]

Blind Willie Johnson: *The Complete Blind Willie Johnson* (Columbia/Epic). [Double-CD of this great gospel blues artist.]

Negro Religious Field Recordings, Volume 1 (Document DC 5312).

Spirit of Memphis Quartet: *Travelling On* (Hightone).

The Staples Singers: *Great Day* (Milestone). [A fine selection of the Staples' early 1960s recordings.]

COMPILATIONS BLUES

Southern Journey, Volume 3 (Rounder). [Highway 61 Mississippi-Delta country blues, spirituals, work songs and dance music. Field recordings by Alan Lomax.]

The Best Blues Album in the World . . . Ever (Emd/Virgin). [A good mix of old school and new school blues.]

BLUES SOLOISTS

Big Bill Broonzy: *Trouble in Mind* (Smithsonian/Folkways 40131). [With topical songs, rural blues and spirituals.]

Ida Cox: *Ida Cox,* Volumes 1–5 (Document).

Blind Lemon Jefferson: *King of the Country Blues* (Yazoo); *The Best of Blind Lemon Jefferson* (Yazoo 2057).

Leadbelly: *Leadbelly, King of the 12-String Guitar* (Sony/Legacy 46776).

Bessie Smith: *Bessie Smith: Empress of the Blues,* Volumes 1–4 (Sony/Legacy).

Also from P&R Publishing

Like it or not, notice it or not, popular culture plays a huge role in our day-to-day lives, influencing the way we think and see the world. Some people respond by trying to pull away from it altogether, and some accept it without question as a blessing.

Here Ted Turnau reminds us that the issue is not so black and white. Popular culture, like any other facet of society, is a messy mixture of both grace *and* idolatry, and it deserves our serious attention and discernment. Learn how to approach popular culture wisely, separating its gems of grace from its temptations toward idolatry, and practice some *popologetics* to be an influence of your own.

"Ted Turnau does a great service toward helping Christians engage their culture with both conviction and open-mindedness . . . and offers excellent practical application for how to both appreciate pop culture and fairly critique it."

 —**Brian Godawa**, Hollywood screenwriter, author of *Hollywood Worldviews*